Theory and Practice of the Catechism

All rights reserved

The
Theory and Practice
of the Catechism

BY
DR. M. GATTERER, S.J.
AND DR. F. KRUS, S.J.
PROFESSORS AT THE UNIVERSITY OF INNSBRUCK

*TRANSLATED
FROM THE SECOND GERMAN EDITION*

BY
REV. J. B. CULEMANS

SECOND EDITION

Ad Clericatum

Frederick Pustet Co. (Inc.)
NEW YORK   CINCINNATI
1924

Nihil Obstat.

REMIGIUS LAFORT, D.D.,
Censor.

Imprimatur.

✠JOHN CARDINAL FARLEY,
Archbishop of New York

NEW YORK, April 6, 1914

COPYRIGHT, 1914
In the United States and Great Britain
FR. PUSTET & CO.
NEW YORK AND CINCINNATI

PRINTED IN THE UNITED STATES OF AMERICA

NOTE

THERE is no dearth of catechetical literature. Hence the present volume must be its own justification.

Its systematic treatment of the matter, by means of theses and proofs, may perhaps be found rather arid; it offers the great advantage of being clear and to the point. So much interest is taken in catechetical work at the present day, so many suggestions and personal opinions are offered on every side for our consideration, that a thorough review of the fundamental principles of the art and science of catechization seems timely.

In the very profusion of hints and helps to make our teaching of Christian Doctrine more efficient, "we meet with truths overstated or misdirected, matters of detail variously taken, facts incompletely proved or applied, and rules inconsistently urged or discordantly interpreted. . . . What we need at present . . . is not invention nor originality, nor sagacity nor even learning, — at least in the first place, though all gifts of God are in a measure needed and never can be unseasonable when used religiously; but we need particularly a sound judgment, patient thought, discrimination, a comprehensive mind, an abstinence from all private fancies and caprices and personal tastes, — in a word, divine wisdom." Under the *guise of returning to the method of Christ, to teach religion chiefly in parables and according to psychological methods (the two are held to be one and the same thing), there is a tendency, the authors notice, to do away with the catechism as no longer up to the requirements of present-day pedagogy. The treatment of this much-debated question in Nos. 57–83 and Nos. 112–135 is timely, while objective and exhaustive.*

While strong advocates of all sane modern theories in pedagogy by which catechetical teaching may benefit, the authors of the present work, however, with insight and discrimination, hold the balance evenly, and show from history, reason, and experience that the teaching methods of the Church, sanctioned by twenty centuries of practical results, are not to be lightly discarded; that the teachers, however, need to be frequently aroused to a full and clear realization of their duty to be self-sacrificing "Apostles of Jesus Christ."

The whole field of catechetical work is covered in detail in the present volume. It was written primarily for seminarians. Yet, a careful, thorough perusal of it by any one interested in catechization may set aright many a false notion, clarify many a hazy principle, show how to combine the old and the new in a harmonious manner, so as to be progressive without being subversive.

References to English sources have been substituted wherever practical for the copious bibliography in the German original.

TRANSLATOR

In festo Si. Vincentii a Paulo, 1913

INTRODUCTION

I. Definition and Object of Catechization and Catechetics

1.

THE Word "Catechesis" is derived from the Greek κατηχεῖν, a term but seldom used in profane literature, and meaning: to instruct orally, to teach by word of mouth. Etymologically, then, "catechization" means: oral instruction, oral teaching.

In ecclesiastical usage the word κατηχεῖν was made to designate *religious* instruction, and more especially that instruction given to tyros in the Christian faith. Although thus restricted, the word, however, took on a wider meaning in another direction: for in the life of the early Church catechization included not only instruction by word of mouth, but also various corelated practices, such as prayer, fasting, etc.

The expression κατηχεῖν is not found in the Old Testament. In the New Testament it is used only by St. Luke, 1, 3–4, and by St. Paul, Gal. 6, 6.[1]

During the first centuries those to be catechized were mostly adults. Since the beginning of the Middle Ages they are generally children. Hence the meaning

[1] See Cath. Encyclopedia, art. "Christian Doctrine," vol. V, p. 75.

of the word "catechization" underwent a still further evolution: at the present day it designates the religious instruction of school children, — and, it might be well to add, of all those besides who have not yet reached the adult age.

This latter clause is of the greatest importance. If catechists and all those who have the cure of souls were to rest satisfied with the instruction and training of school children only, their labor, despite all their exertions, would bear comparatively little fruit. For the average child, during his years of compulsory school attendance (until the age of fourteen), is never so firmly grounded in his religion that he stands in no further need of educational help and guidance amidst the bewildering array of present-day social and intellectual tendencies. Those who enter upon a secondary education are in so far favored that they enjoy full opportunity for further religious development; but the number of youths who go to work after completing the common-school course is much greater, while our modern school system makes so little provision for them that as a whole they are beyond the reach of regular educational influences. In order, therefore, that his work may bear fruit in later life, the catechist needs to put forth his best efforts, making use of all available means to keep the largest possible number of children on the road of virtue after they have left school.

Although the present volume lays special stress on school-catechization, catechists should beware lest they limit their activity to the schoolroom only. In short, school-catechization is but part of a thoroughgoing catechization. Catechization, therefore, must be defined: the religious instruction of youth from their tenderest years up, until the full maturity of their religious life has been attained. The catechist should always keep this in view as his ultimate end; getting the parents and the school to work hand in hand with him to realize it, he himself will cast about for means to make his school instructions bear abundant fruit, taking care besides that his pupils benefit by them through life.

In the expression "catechetical sermon" we have preserved to this very day a meaning of the word "catechetical," which carries us back to the early Christian ages: the catechetical sermon is intended not so much for children as for adults, i.e., the Christian people in general. And they should be instructed in the fundamental religious truths as laid down in the Roman Catechism.

Many manuals of homiletics designate all didactic preaching as catechetical preaching, since it has the same end in view as catechization, viz., thoroughly to instruct, while influencing the will to translate the teaching into practice. It were more appropriate to define catechetical sermons: coherent didactic discourses on Christian Doctrine as exposed in the Roman Catechism.

The meaning of the words "catechumen," "catechist," "catechism," is plain from their etymology as given above. A catechumen is a beginner in the faith, one still to be instructed in it. In the primitive Church catechumens were also called "rudes," i.e., ignorant, men with little knowledge of religion, no matter how proficient they might otherwise be in profane learning. Hence the title of St. Augustine's treatise: "De catechizandis rudibus," *On the Instruction of the Ignorant.*

A catechist is one who, as the representative of God and the Church, instructs the catechumens.

The word "catechism" was applied formerly to the act of instructing or catechization, e.g., in St. Thomas; now, however, it designates the manual used for religious instruction. Further on we shall have more to say about the nature of the catechism.

2. The Object of Catechization and the Means to be Used. — Catechization always has had a twofold end in view: (a) instruction in Christian Doctrine, and (b) training for Christian character and Christian life. Here it is important to avoid a misunderstanding, viz., that instruction and education, although distinguished for theoretical purposes, may be carried on independently of one another, that one may be pursued without reference to the other. This would be fatal. Therefore we insist from the outset that, during childhood, catechetical instruction should aim directly and wholly at the religious formation of the child; later on, when he grows in years, while it may be less direct, it must never be lost sight of altogether. The whole purpose of this volume is to show how this may be brought about.

Oral instruction is not the only means at our disposal to attain this twofold end of catechization. Already in the first centuries catechetical instruction went hand in hand with prayer, fasting, exorcisms, and other practices of piety. Their combined aim was, together with the instruction, to train the heart and to fashion the Christian character. Catechization designated, therefore, not only the oral instruction, but also all the other religious-educational practices. This is the wider meaning given by Christian usage to the word $\kappa\alpha\tau\eta\chi\epsilon\hat{\iota}\nu$, to instruct orally, to which we have already called attention. That this meaning of the word, and all it stood for, has been lost sight of later on, is greatly to be deplored; for hence have arisen many well-founded complaints about mere word-drills in religious instruction. It must be added, however, that this exaggerated insistence on the printed word is not of Catholic origin.

The twofold aim of catechization is analogous to that of the didactic sermon, as noted above. However, it has also called forth many objections, especially in recent years. In a laudable effort of reaction against an exclusively intellectualistic pedagogy, too much stress has been laid on the educational value of instruction; and especially since religious instruction and education were so intimately related, it seemed that a distinction between the two in catechization was not to be thought of.

We have treated this question at length in another volume.[1] One remark may suffice here. — It is all-important in modern times, that, when our youth leave school, they should have become so familiar with the fundamental doctrines of religion, that they are able to defend them against the more common objections. Such knowledge, however, cannot be acquired in a short time; hence the necessity of beginning early not merely with practical religious training, but with the formation of the mind. Both should go together, since all training that is not based on knowledge must fail. Therefore we may rightly assign a twofold object to catechization. For even when striving after the strictest unity in formulating this object, it does always remain necessary to lay down and prove some fundamental principles to govern the methodical teaching of Christian Doctrine. Consequently a certain distinction between instruction and education will always be necessary.

3. The Relation of Catechization to Education in General. — As consistent Christian teachers we cannot admit of any other than a religious education. Since

[1] Krus: Fundamental Questions of Pedagogy.

this is included in catechization as we understand it, it would seem that education and catechization are one and the same. However, a religious education may be considered from a twofold standpoint: first, it consists in teaching our youth to be guided by religious principles in their daily life, even in their material and temporal affairs; secondly, religious education in a more restricted sense should familiarize them with the knowledge and practice of directly religious actions such as prayer, the reception of the sacraments, etc. It is easily seen that school-catechization must mainly keep the latter end in view. Many factors enter into a religious education considered from the first viewpoint: the parents, the social environment of the youth, the associations he forms in life. Nay, school-catechization alone cannot successfully complete the child's direct religious education, even if we had not to contend with the deplorable neglect already spoken of, that falls to the lot of so many youths after they leave school.

From all this it does not follow, however, that the catechist should look upon his work in the school as of little consequence. For if he be well equipped for his task, his work will prove a valuable help in the child's general education. Only he should not neglect to take into account the various other educational influences at work on the child, and be ever on the alert to press them into service whenever they promise to be a good asset, or to counteract them when they prove harmful. Hence the catechist must: (*a*) Keep in constant touch with the parents and relatives of the child. Many parents at the present day are ignorant of their educational duties or fail in them, and the priest has a strict obligation to enlighten and help them by means of private conversations, sermons, instructions on the state of life, special "evenings for parents," the distribution of popular pamphlets on education, etc.

(b) He is in duty bound to familiarize himself with educational means and aims, to work in harmony with all the teachers of the school, and to be ready with a word of cheer and encouragement. Strict compliance with the school laws is essential; he should not forget, however, that the best laws, of themselves, offer not the slightest guarantee of a successful education if the instructions are not in harmony with the spirit that prompted their enactment. Facts innumerable confirm this view.

(c) All this supposes, moreover, that the catechist is sure of his bearings in the domain of general education. Catechization is a part of the general education and formation of youth, and it is doomed to failure unless it fit in harmoniously in the general educational scheme.

4. Catechetics is the theory of catechization, i.e., a complexus of systematically ordered truths and rules to be followed in the teaching of Christian Doctrine. How shall this theory be formulated? On one side the rules must be such as to be reduced to practice without inconvenience; yet on the other side a collection of practical norms only appears insufficient, for they should carry with them the scientific proofs of their validity. It is needless to show that catechization also, at the present day, stands in need of scientific treatment.

From the twofold object assigned to catechization it follows that catechetics also has a twofold end in view: it must furnish the minister of God and the Church with scientifically sound directions on the manner of instructing children in Christian Doctrine; and, in the second place, it must show him how to train their hearts in Christian virtue.

N.B. There are some good reasons in favor of the view that would make catechetics a part of homiletics. But in devoting a special treatise to the former we have ampler opportunity to bring out its importance to better advantage.

II. Importance and Obligation of Catechization

5. Let us beware lest we underestimate the importance of catechization because of the scant attention at times accorded to it in practice: some effort is made to prepare a good sermon, but no time is devoted to the preparation of catechetical instructions, convinced, as the catechist seemingly is, that anything is good enough for children. Unfortunately such a procedure is very much at variance with Christian ideals. The Catholic Church, from remote antiquity, has evinced great consideration for the training of youth, but particularly so in the matter of catechetical instruction, for it is concerned directly with the child's religious formation, which is the ultimate aim of all educational endeavor.

St. John Chrysostom's complaint about careless parents of his time sounds strangely modern: "When it becomes necessary to select a teacher for the child, they select one at random, although nothing is deserving of more careful thought." And he goes on to point out the importance of a religious education: "Can anything vie in importance with this art whose aim is to train the mind and fashion the heart and character of youth? He who is charged with this task must exhibit greater zeal than any painter or sculptor." In Math., 60th homily.

John Gerson (1363-1429) devoted his free time to the instruction of the Parisian youth. When blamed for his zealous endeavors, under pretext that it was ill-becoming a chancellor of the University to waste his time on children, he replied: "If I am blameworthy, it ought to be more on account of my presumption than of my too great condescension, since, in instructing sinful children, I dare to meddle with the work of deeply spiritual men. I am really in the position of a land turtle seeking the company of the feathered tribe. . . . And when it is further objected that I should devote my time to more important duties, I answer that I cannot conceive of any sublimer work that my insignificant personality could perform to some advantage."

Any disparagement of catechetical work for children is in open contradiction with innumerable exhortations on the part of all ecclesiastical authority. Its ceaseless warnings anent the necessity of religious instruction might almost seem exaggerated, were it not that the battles waged in the educational arena today show all too clearly that the importance of religious education cannot be overestimated. Every priest ought to make his own these words of Hirscher: "Cathechetical instruction takes first rank among all pastoral duties;" nor should this catechetical work be confined to the schoolroom and those of school age only.

What are, however, the deeper internal reasons why catechetical instruction was always held in such high esteem in the Church? The answer becomes clear from the following.

6. The Importance of Catechization Considered in the Light of Faith. — The light of faith shows the catechist:

1. That the child of man is also the child of God, made such in baptism, partaker of the divine nature, and destined to be forever happy with Him.

Long before modern pedagogs had begun to descant upon the "rights of the child," Catholic educators had given utterance to sublime considerations about the value of the child's soul. Sacchini (1570–1625) writes thus in one of his pedagogical works: "1. Every teacher should look upon the school as the small secret garden of the king, laid out with the greatest care, planted and beautified for his own delectation. 2. Let him also consider his school as a field of choice plants, not brought from India but descended from heaven. . . . 3. Let him also look upon his class as a school of young kings, seeing in all his boys the sons of princes, having kings for parents and brothers. They are called kings not merely because they have inherited this title from their ancestors, but because they are in reality reigning kings, each one possessing a kingdom and having to be trained to occupy a throne. Whether asleep or awake, they are surrounded by a princely retinue of wise teachers and great men, i.e., their guardian angels. Let this illustration enlighten him concerning the greatness of his task, and inspire him to treat his scholars with love and respect, after the example of the renowned Arsenius, who showed such honor to the young Arcadius and Honorius that, while they sat down, he taught them standing."

The catechist can contribute much towards the right training of a youth glorying in such noble descent; and it rests largely with him whether the child will attain the sublime end for which it is destined. His influence is great, because the child's heart is a receptive and fertile field. True, the consequences of original sin weigh heavily upon it; but the germs of virtue and good works have not been uprooted by personal sin, as is often the case with adults, and the Holy Ghost seconds the teacher's efforts.

Besides, the catechist's exertions tend to mold the *whole life* of the child as it shall be in the future.

Finally, the catechist has educational means at his command which are not within the reach even of parents: viz., the supernatural authority with which he is invested as a minister of Christ; the treasures of divine truth and grace, those paramount aids in educational work, are his to distribute; prayer, sacrifice, and good example are other helps at his command, and he disposes of them in larger measure than do other teachers.

2. A faithful catechist models his life upon that of the Saviour, the great friend of children, who pronounces His terrible woe against all who scandalize the little ones because their angels stand before God's throne.

3. Love for the Church bids the catechist be true to his vocation, for the future is in the hands of the youth of today. And should one fail to grasp the full strength of this reason, the ceaseless efforts of our enemies to gain possession of our children should drive it home very forcibly.

4. Finally, the reward is great. A good catechist finds it first of all in the schoolroom itself when he looks into those eager faces avidly drinking in every word falling from his lips; moreover, in years to come, they will hold his memory in grateful remembrance. The joys experienced in the discharge of pastoral duties are amongst the purest and holiest, and among these, the satisfactions that come to the catechist in the midst of his children easily take first rank. However, while contemplating the bright side of his work, the catechist

should not be carried away by an exaggerated idealism, he must not lose sight of the many obstacles confronting him. And these are bound to be especially numerous when children grow up without any religious home-training, or any reverence for the priest; or when he deals with children that are dull and slow. Being thus put on his mettle, he will find that an unlimited amount of patience and kindness is the prime requisite for success. In return he may look for an eternal reward.

. . . .

From all this it follows that the catechist should not rest content with drilling the children in a few catechism questions. Far from being a mere questioner, he ought to strive, as a loving shepherd of souls, to cultivate in his young charges an ardent love of Christ that prompts them to walk in His footsteps.

7. The Obligation of Catechization. — The importance of catechization is fully borne out by its obligatory character. The duty to catechize, i.e., to give religious instruction, constitutes one of the essential mandates given to His Church by Christ Himself: go ye therefore and teach all nations, baptizing them in the name of the Father and of the Son and of the Holy Ghost. This duty is incumbent in the first place upon the Pope and the bishops. Directly and by right divine they only have the obligation to instruct and train in the Christian truths all those confided to their care, hence also the young. But since it is physically impossible for them to perform this duty in person for all concerned, they appoint helpers, amongst whom must be reckoned in the first place pastors, assistants, etc. Whoever, besides the Pope and bishops, exercises the teaching office, which includes catechetical instruction, can do so only in so far as he has been explicitly or tacitly empowered by them; therefore he exercises his ministry *ex jure ecclesiastico*.

This, obviously, does not detract in any way from the dignity of the ordinary catechetical office; but it safeguards its divine origin and authority. It is and remains a responsible participation in the teaching office of the Church.

8. The Requisites for the Catechetical Office. — These may be deduced from the above. A juridical condition for the exercise of the catechetical ministry is "the canonical mission." When this is lacking there can be no question of authoritative teaching in the name of Christ, but at most of private, charitable help extended through good will.

The "canonical mission," however, supposes personal qualifications acquired by study, practice and experience, prayer and a virtuous life. The present volume on Catechetics is designed to facilitate the fundamental *study* of the subject. Various references in apposite places afford opportunity for further investigation.

Practical experience may be gained by intercourse with efficient catechists, assistance at catechetical conferences, and model lessons. When thus testing his ability and knowledge in a practical manner, the novice should beware lest he jump rashly to conclusions at variance with tried and true principles. Valuable experience can be gained only by exercising great circumspection.

The *virtue* the catechist stands most in need of is great love of children, a love that will fire him with enthusiasm and tireless zeal, and which possesses all those qualities which the Apostle extols in I Cor. 13, 3, ff.: "Charity is patient . . . beareth all things:" dulness, sloth, neglect on the part of the children, ingratitude and perhaps opposition, instead of appreciation of his zeal, none of these should discourage the catechist; "hopeth all things:" no lamb, however forsaken and seemingly beyond redemption, should be cast off by the good shepherd; failures or personal mistakes should never break his spirits. For true charity is known by this "that it seeketh not her own."

III. Division of the Treatise

9. The First Principle of Division and its Application. — From the twofold object of catechization and catechetics, as set forth in Nos. 3–4, naturally follows a twofold division of the subject-matter of this volume: (a) catechetical instruction, (b) catechetical training.

We repeat, however, that this division must be rightly understood. It means that the catechist must bring the children to the point where they have a thorough and accurate knowledge of their religion, and have acquired truly Christian habits of life. He must ever keep this twofold object in mind; should he neglect one in favor of the other, the spiritual life of the child will be stunted and one-sided. From a clear comprehension of this twofold object he will learn that they are so closely interrelated as never to admit of separation in practice. Instruction without education, training of the mind without training of the heart, would be fundamentally wrong; and to train the heart without regard to the development of the intellect would be attempting the impossible. The formation of a sound religious and moral character must be based on right religious knowledge.

Hence, the rules laid down in catechetics under the above double heading must not be envisaged altogether independently, as if exclusive treatment were reserved first for instruction, and separate treatment were afterwards to be accorded to education. Each head of our division receives full treatment in its place; yet while thus expounding catechetical instruction, we have to give many pertinent hints concerning religious education.

10. A Second Principle of Division. — For the sake of clarity and practical advantage we shall proceed to lay down, under each of the above divisions, the general principles, without going into too many details. The latter we reserve for fuller treatment under the heading "Special Catechetics"; there, dealing with practical concrete questions, the formal division between instruction and education need be no longer in the foreground.

Also with regard to this second principle of division we cannot follow hard and fast rules that would exclude matters of importance for the practical Christian life, such, e.g., as concern the liturgy of the Church.

The division of the subject into a general and a special part is in conformity with the now generally accepted division into theoretical and practical pedagogy. The former is occupied in scientific investigation; its object is to state general principles, to strive after systematic thoroughness, and to put forward the most approved theories in the realm of speculation. Practical pedagogy, however, is concerned with immediate results, and deals with actual conditions, and the means and helps close at hand.

11. About the Terminology. — Catechetical instruction and "religious instruction" are terms frequently used to designate catechization in general, although the latter, besides instruction, also includes education. In order to avoid all misunderstanding, we shall —

1. Use the word "catechization," or catechetical teaching, to designate the twofold object as stated above: to teach does not mean merely to impart knowledge, but also to point out practically the right way to follow by influencing the heart and will.

2. When we have but one of the two objects in view, we use the words "catechetical instruction," and "catechetical education," or formation of the heart and will.

12. Our Position with Regard to the History of Catechization. — Catechetics, perhaps more than any other branch of learning, must benefit by a historical survey of its object. And indeed catechization is not a product of mere human wisdom and invention, but of the unbroken stream of supernatural life-giving grace; going back to Christ, it courses steadily on through the Church, ever adding to her membership new generations of catechumens. The more we strive to know the catechetical methods of the Church in the past, back to its early days and to the First Catechist, Christ Himself, the more we shall familiarize ourselves with the best rules to govern our own catechetical work.

On the other side it must be acknowledged that

many a historical period is still awaiting a scientific exposition of its catechetical accomplishments; nor, in bringing these to light, can we overlook the need of setting aright the wilful ignorance, or persistent disparagement, of Catholic pedagogical achievements, exhibited by certain historians. And the results of historical research thus far verified can even be summarized only in this volume. This we attempt in the first part of the work.

The general divisions of the volume follow:

>   PART   I: HISTORICAL OUTLINE
>   PART II: CATECHETICAL INSTRUCTION
>   PART III: CATECHETICAL TRAINING
>   PART IV: SPECIAL CATECHETICS

PART I

HISTORICAL OUTLINE OF CATECHIZATION AND CATECHETICS

I. CATECHIZATION IN THE PRIMITIVE CHURCH

13. **FROM the Beginning till the Organization of the Catechumenate.** — We have already adverted to the fact that catechetical instruction in the early Church was given, not to baptized children, but to unbaptized adults. Hence, generally speaking, present-day catechization has but one thing in common with the older practice: both have the same end in view, i.e., to transform into thorough Christians those who are still novices in the life of faith.

1. Already Christ Himself had shown a special predilection for children. The Apostles also, in their epistles, frequently remind parents and others upon whom educational duties have devolved, of the importance of this obligation. But since this love for the little ones of the flock exhibited by Christ and His Apostles should be an object of frequent meditation for every priest, and since other branches of theology, especially Bible study, are more extensively concerned

with it, we give here but a mere outline of the pedagogical method of Christ.[1]

Christ Himself indicated the highest aim of all education, and the ultimate end of all catechetical instruction, when He commanded that the children should have free access to Him to listen to His words: for of such is the Kingdom of heaven. (Math. 19, 14.)

When the catechist has to deal with those sophisticated people who are heard to say at times: "My child is still too young to come to instruction, and unable to grasp religious truths," he must meet all such objections with the words of Christ: suffer little children and forbid them not to come to me, for the Kingdom of heaven is for such. And indeed, theirs is the Kingdom of heaven as established by God, and made known to us by Christ; not a vague ethereal dream, but the kingdom of God's love which is to be revealed in all its eternal splendor only to those who have grown in divine love here on earth with their whole heart and mind and soul, and whose faithfulness has stood the test of the commandments. Any catechesis, therefore, modeled upon that of Christ must aim at developing all the powers latent in the child-soul, and not merely its intellectual faculties. How can this be brought about? By having recourse to the means which Christ Himself has used: a thorough and yet plain, easily grasped exposition of the truths of God. These we should always clearly define, avoiding ambiguity or contradiction, as becomes verities ever new although uncreated. We should lead the young in

[1] Among works on this subject, Fr. Messchler's little book, The Humanity of Jesus, deserves special mention.

the way of the commandments, encouraging their halting steps in virtue by the promise of an eternal reward; we should inspire them with an aversion for sin by inculcating a great dread of the eternal punishment inflicted for its commission; we should dwell on God's inexhaustible love for the weak and the helpless, and teach them to rejoice in the conviction that the grace of our heavenly Father co-operates in our sanctification.

With the Divine Teacher constantly before him as his model, the catechist will readily realize the sublimeness of his task, towering high above all aims and means of secular pedagogy.

Let it be noted here that the above is anything but high-sounding rhetoric: it is a truth to be taken to heart literally and earnestly. Suffice it to recall to mind the vapid theories of modern pedagogy about the question whether individual or social education should be fostered most. Christian practice stands far above those aimless discussions! By an explicit command of God the child is already bound to show reverence for his parents and other superiors; he is also bound to respect every right of his neighbor. His participation in the activities of the Church introduces him to the corporate life of the parish, and makes him share in the work of the world-wide Church; nay, he is taught besides to include in his all-embracing charity those outside the pale, even if they be our enemies. And notwithstanding all this the child is sternly told: not if thou couldst gain the whole world, shalt thou suffer the loss of thy own soul! Here we have that peculiar combination of individual and social teaching that is found only in the Church of Christ.

2. With regard to adult unbelievers the Apostles carried out Christ's commandment: Go and teach all nations, baptizing them in the name of the Father and

of the Son and of the Holy Ghost. Formal reception into the Christian community was always preceded by instruction. What was taught these candidates for baptism?[1] The Jews were taught primarily that Christ was the Messias and the Son of God. Besides, the Apostles' preaching to the Jews included the following points of practical import: they were to do penance and break with all habits of sin, aspire after the new endless life, and humbly make use of the means of grace leading to the new birth, such as baptism and the other sacraments.

The heathens were first of all to be taught the doctrine of the One God, Creator of the world, judge of good and evil: Paul's discourse in Athens is a masterly model in this regard.

The "two ways" (of life and death) as we find them described in the six first chapters of the Didache,[2] composed in the first century (chs. 1–4, the way of life; chs. 5–6, the way of death), and the similar chapters (18–20) of the Epistle of Barnabas,[3] which is only slightly more recent, give us a clear summary of the ethical teaching, whilst the greater Apology of Justin Martyr[4] and other early Christian literature give us the doctrinal truths with which converts were to familiarize themselves before their baptism.

Up to the middle of the second century we have no record of an organized institution, or a catechumenate properly speaking, as a preparation for baptism.

14. The History of the Catechumenate. — In the second half of the second century there are many

[1] See, also, Cath. Encyclopedia, art. Catechumen, vol. III, p. 430; art. Christian Doctrine, vol. V, p. 75.
[2] See Cath. Encyclopedia, vol. IV, p. 779.
[3] See Cath. Encyclopedia, vol. II, p. 299.
[4] See Cath. Encyclopedia, vol. VIII, p. 580.

indications that the preparation for baptism was carried on in accordance with well-defined rules. As the number of converts increased, the Church was compelled to exercise greater care to assure herself of the worthiness of candidates, and to regulate in detail the preparation for baptism. No decrees are on record authoritatively prescribing any definite measures; but towards the end of the second century we gather from many sources that there existed an organized course of instruction for converts, and a code of ascetical and liturgical prescriptions to which they had to submit.

During protracted periods of peace these regulations were perfected. The sad experiences of the reign of Decius, when many Christians fell away from the faith, contributed not a little towards stricter regulation of the catechumenate. During the fourth and fifth centuries it reached its zenith.

The accession of whole nations to the Church, and the growing practice of infant baptism, slowly broke up the earlier organization. Only in the ritual of baptism have the elements of it been preserved in a condensed form even to the present day.

15. The Existence of Classes of Catechumens. — Until very recently historians admitted the existence of several sharply defined classes of catechumens: ἀκροώμενοι, γόνυ κλίνοντες, φωτιζόμενοι. Later investigations, however, have necessitated a modification of this view. The expression ἀκροώμενοι, *audientes*, or hearers, and γόνυ κλίνοντες, the *genuflectentes*, do not designate, as has been frequently maintained, two classes of catechumens, but two classes of penitents, who, moreover, were found only in the East. The terms point to the fact that those of the first class left the church immediately after the homily, whilst the second class of penitents stayed on to be present at the prayer and to receive, kneeling, the blessing of the bishop. If the catechumens also did the latter, then they could at most be included among the *genuflectentes*, but in opposition to them there was not another class of catechumens called the audientes or hearers. Moreover, the φωτιζόμενοι, (φωτισμός = *illuminatio*, baptism) in Rome; *electi* or elect in the West generally: *competentes* = *petentes baptismum*, or those asking for baptism, are not to be considered as a separate class of catechumens. Catechumens, properly speaking, were those who had entered upon the lengthy preparation for baptism. During the last forty days before its reception they were no longer catechumens, but constituted a special class entirely separated from the catechumenate, and they were called φωτιζόμενοι or competents. On the other side it is true that not only the reception of baptism set forth definite knowledge and qualifications in the candidate; but even those who applied for the first time as catechumens had to undergo a certain probation. We may therefore speak of different degrees among the candidates for baptism, as long as we do not understand thereby sharply defined classes.

16. Preliminary Preparation for Admission to the Catechumenate. — It was of prime importance for the Church to admit only such candidates as were determined to be earnest followers of the new life: curiosity or worldly advantages could not be accounted sufficient reason for reception into the Church. The conditions for admission are described at length in the eighth book of the "Apostolic Constitutions."

In a summary instruction the *accedentes*, or *rudes adhuc in fide* (those still untutored in the faith), were taught the futility of idolatrous worship; they were told about the One God, His divine Providence, the Redemption, the Resurrection, and the Last Judgment. The classical treatise of St. Augustine, De catechizandis rudibus, or *On the Instruction of the Ignorant*, gives the theory of this catechesis, and especially an outline of the preliminary religious instruction imparted to them. Besides theoretical principles, it also includes two model instructions.

St. Augustine was led to write this work at the demand of the deacon Deogratias, a catechist of Carthage. Although its primary end is to furnish the main points of preliminary catechetical instruction, it is replete with valuable information about catechetical work in general, and it may well be called the first treatise on catechetics. St. Augustine insists especially that the catechist should enter upon his task with a bright and cheerful disposition. He devotes several chapters to the causes that set at naught this important qualification, and also indicates the remedy.

17. Admission to the Catechumenate. — The preliminary instruction over, and the proselyte's qualifications being deemed satisfactory, he was enrolled amongst the catechumens with some show of solemnity. The accompanying ceremonies were not identical throughout the Christian communities. In Rome they consisted in breathing on the candidate while an exorcism was pronounced, signing the forehead with the sign of the Cross, imposing the hands on the head, and giving blessed salt. Augustine, Isidore, and Ildephonse also mention the custom obtaining in their respective dioceses, of anointing the candidate with oil. The latter ceremony corresponded to the practice of Rome and some other places, where, on Holy Saturday, at the end of the preparatory stage, and just before baptism, the breast and shoulders were anointed with oil. In the Greek Church salt and oil were not used.

The meaning of the sign of the Cross on the forehead is clear. The imposition of hands is the symbol of the communication of sanctifying powers; the salt signifies the divine wisdom imparted to the catechumen as an antidote against the corrupting influences of earthly desires.

John the Deacon writes in the sixth century to the noble Senarius: "The breathing over the candidate takes place to announce the driving out of the evil spirit, and to prepare the soul for the coming of Christ our God. . . . It also signifies the impotence of the evil one since he is so easily vanquished; and the ancient rebel against God does but deserve this contemptible treatment. . . . Salt, in the natural order of things, is used to spice and preserve flesh meat. We spice the soul of the baptized with the blessed salt of wisdom and the teaching of God's word, that the baptized may acquire health and strength to resist the allurements of a carnal mind."

18. The Instruction of Catechumens and their Rights. — The lessons from Scripture, and the homilies, which were part of the common worship, were designed for the religious instruction of the catechumens, who were permitted to assist with the faithful at this part of the service. The presence of the catechumens explains many peculiarities of the homilies. Doctrines which they were not yet prepared to receive were merely touched upon, and then only in symbolical language. But, besides, the catechumens also received special instruction from clerics or lay Christians. Their aim was, not merely to enlighten the mind, but to prepare the way for a change of moral life. With this end in view the lessons from Holy Writ were especially selected from the moral books: the Book of Wisdom, showing forth the emptiness of idolatry; the Book of Ecclesiasticus, which "serves to instruct and edify both those who strive after knowledge and those who already possess the same, that all may impress it deeply upon their hearts and order their lives according to the commandments" (In Eccl. Prologus); Tobias, Esther, Judith; the life of Christ and the Apostles, as recorded in the Gospels.

The Christians looked upon the catechumens no longer as outsiders; at times even they are designated as "Christians." They enjoyed the right already mentioned of being present, in a place assigned to them, at a part of the liturgical service. They listened to the sermon that followed the Scripture lesson; at its conclusion the deacon admonished all present to pray for the catechumens; the bishop prayed over them with extended hands, and then they left the assembly.

At times we find mention made of the dismissing of catechumens even before the reading from Scripture; this, however, was an exceptional case, traced back only to the fifth century.

19. Duration of the Catechumenate. — The catechumenate was not of equal duration everywhere. In the earliest times some months sufficed; later on a longer preparation was required for good reasons. In

Spain two years were prescribed, while three years was the rule in the East. The first Council of Nice condemns as an abuse a short catechumenal preparation.

The long probation was primarily necessitated by the austere requirements of a new moral life in which the novice was to be firmly grounded. The bishop, however, had the power to shorten the time, or also to lengthen it for good cause. Many of the Fathers deprecate an abuse introduced by the catechumens themselves of unduly extending the time of probation. This postponement of baptism was sometimes prompted by the stringent requirements of a Christian life, or at times by a desire to secure the full benefits of the sacrament of regeneration at the supreme moment of death.

20. The Competents. — At the beginning of Lent the bishop invited the catechumens to apply for baptism. Those who requested (*competere*) baptism, gave their names. The applicant had to undergo a new examination concerning his worthiness. As soon as his name was entered in the register he was no longer called a catechumen, but an *electus*, elect or competent, $\phi\omega\tau\iota\zeta\acute{o}\mu\epsilon\nu os$ one to be enlightened, or $\beta a\pi\tau\iota\zeta\acute{o}\mu\epsilon\nu os$, to be baptized. St. Cyril of Jerusalem makes use several times of the word $\pi\iota\sigma\tau\acute{o}s$, faithful. The complete separation of the competents from the catechumens was evidenced by the fact that the former were forbidden to impart to the latter anything of what they learned. This second probationary period lasted as a rule through the forty days of Lent. St. Augustine tells us what was done for them during that time:

1. Catechetical instruction now broadened out, and amplified the knowledge already gained concerning faith and the commandments. When we read that during Lent these instructions took place daily, we know too that they were not all intended exclusively for the competents. This appears clearly from the catechizations of St. Cyril of Jerusalem. During the lenten season of 347 or 348, when still a priest, he held but eighteen catechetical instructions (or nineteen including the preliminary one) for the competents exclusively. The five following ones (the mystagogical catecheses) were held during Easter week, for the newly baptized. From them we gain a clear idea of the instruction given to the competents: it was primarily concerned with an explanation of the articles of faith.

The formula of the profession of faith or the Symbol was communicated for the first time to the competents during Lent, and the ceremony was called the "tradition of the Symbol." In some places this was done in connection with the *aperitio aurium*, or the opening of the ears.

In Rome the tradition of the Symbol took place on the Wednesday following Laetare Sunday. Hence the characteristics of the Mass for that day: the allusion to baptism and the spiritual enlightenment are intended for the illuminandi. Generally a few days later took place the tradition of the Pater Noster. St. Augustine describes both ceremonies in these words: "You have first been taught what you should believe; today you are taught to invoke Him in Whom you have believed." The candidates for baptism were required to memorize the Creed and the Our Father, and then they were called upon to recite them: "reddition of the Creed and the Our Father," was the name given to this ceremony. St. Augustine required this to be done eight days after the tradition.

Both formulas, not their content only, constituted part of "the discipline of the secret" (*disciplina arcani*), since the institution of the catechumenate. The Symbol did duty as a password amongst the faithful. Hence these formulas were not written out, but handed down by word of mouth, even to the competents. The repeated exhortations found in the Fathers to the effect that the sacred words must not be written with ink on papyrus, but on the tables of the heart, are therefore to be understood partly in their literal meaning.

2. Reception into the catechumenate was preceded by an exorcism. When assisting at any liturgical function, the competents generally were subject to an imposition of hands and to exorcisms. The Church thereby gave them to understand that, as candidates for baptism, they were to sever all connection with sin and the author of sin. They were also enjoined to give themselves to prayer and penance. "Those about to receive baptism," writes Tertullian, "should prepare themselves by assiduous prayer, fasting and vigils, and by confession of all their past sins." The confession mentioned here by Tertullian, although not universally practised in the Church, was an important part of the ascetical preparation for baptism. It evidently was not a sacramental confession. The competents were aided in their prayers and penances by those of the whole community of the faithful.

3. The test of the candidates' faith and morals did not end with their reception amongst the catechumens, and later on amongst the competents. It was continued in the general assemblies, which therefore were called "scrutinies." The faithful were allowed a voice in the admission of the candidates to baptism. These scrutiny-assemblies, however, were not limited to probing the candidates, but there also took place all the other catechetical and liturgical functions already mentioned.

A complete description of these "scrutinies" is found in the seventh of the Ordines Romani,[1] dating back, in its main lines, to the sixth century, and also in that part of the Gelasian Sacramentary (fifth century)[2] which treats of baptism.

21. The Neophytes. — The solemn celebration that accompanied the conferring of baptism during Easter night,[3] and the administration of confirmation right after it, were in a certain sense continued until the following Sunday. It was the custom in Rome for the

[1] An "Ordo" is a book of rubrics describing in what manner and with what rites the liturgical functions are to be administered. From the beginning of the eleventh century "ordos" decrease in number, as their contents are divided up, and incorporated into various liturgical textbooks as "rubrics."

[2] A full description of these "scrutinies" and of the conferring of baptism is given in Grisar, S.J.: History of Rome and the Popes in the Middle Ages, vol. I.

[3] Besides Easter, Tertullian (see Cath. Encyclopedia, vol. XIV, p. 520) already mentions Pentecost as another solemn feast on which baptism was given. However, many dioceses held to the original custom of Easter; and where baptism was also given on Pentecost it seems to have been done principally for the benefit of those who on account of sickness or enforced absence were unable to receive it at Easter. For children and adults in danger of death these time limits were disregarded.

white-robed neo-baptized to gather on Easter Sunday afternoon, and daily thereafter during Easter week, at the place of baptism, and take part in solemn processions. The Missal to this day indicates the different churches or stations to which these wended their way: Monday, station ad S. Petrum; Tuesday, ad S. Paulum, etc. Moreover, the neophytes were instructed every day. The five mystagogical catecheses of St. Cyril of Jerusalem give us the most comprehensive idea of these complementary instructions: a thorough explanation of baptism (first and second catecheses), of confirmation (third catechesis), the Holy Eucharist (fourth and fifth catecheses). The fifth is more especially an explanation of the Mass, exclusive of the Missa catechumenorum, and takes occasion from the Pater Noster to branch off into an instruction on prayer.[1]

22. The Slow Disintegration of the Catechumenate as an Institution. — The principal causes of the decline of the catechumenate, a decline that became noticeable from the fifth century on, were : (a) The time of catechumenship was gradually shortened; (b) The days on which baptism was conferred, increased in number: besides Easter and Pentecost it was given on Epiphany, the feasts of the Apostles, and also sundry other feasts. Many papal documents, and also St. Augustine's work, *De fide et operibus*, inveigh against this growing custom, and show at the same time that the early conferring of baptism was made necessary by lukewarmness in faith and laxity of morals. (c) When the great missionary undertakings among the new nations began to bear fruit, it would

[1] Cath. Encyclopedia, vol. IV, p. 595.

also have been impossible for a few apostolic men, dealing with a prodigious number of converts, to adhere to the old catechumenal prescriptions. (*d*) The baptism of infants began to be conferred more frequently, and contributed in turn to the abolition of the catechumenate.

Many documents, such as for instance the following extract from a letter written by the deacon Ferrandus of Carthage to Bishop Fulgentius of Ruspe (sixth century), prove beyond doubt that, although the catechumenate was fast falling into disuse, traces of the former discipline were preserved in the liturgy.

"The Ethiopian about to be initiated into the ecclesiastical mysteries, thanks to the diligent help of faithful masters, is given in care of the Church. He becomes a catechumen, as is the custom. After a time, when the solemnity of Easter draws near, he is admitted among the competents; his name is inscribed in the register; he is instructed. After he has learned and mastered all the mysteries of the Catholic religion, and has undergone the solemn scrutiny, he is freed, by exorcism, from the dominion of Satan, whom he promises to renounce forever, and according to the custom he receives the Symbol of faith. Then he recites aloud the words of the Symbol from memory in presence of the assembly of the faithful; he receives the Lord's Prayer. Having thus learned what he should believe and how he should pray, he is prepared for baptism to be conferred afterwards."

It is an easy matter to follow, step by step, even in our present baptismal rite, the older catechumenal usages and prescriptions. The signing with the cross, the imposition of hands, and the giving of salt remind us of the rites in use for the catechumens proper. The exorcisms, the questions asked (scrutinies): dost thou renounce Satan and all his works, and all his pomps; dost thou believe in God; the recitation of the Creed and the Lord's Prayer, the *ephpheta*, were the rites proper to the competents. The remaining ceremonies, including the imposition of the white cloth, recall very vividly to mind the old baptismal custom of wearing the white tunic until the Sunday of the deposition of the white garments: Dominica in Albis.

23. Retrospect on the Catechesis of Christian Antiquity. — That catechetical instruction in the primitive Church was thorough, is abundantly shown by the magnificent results attained. The aim was to imbue the converts with a deep knowledge of Christian doctrines in order to offset the manifold errors prevalent in the pagan world that surrounded them on all sides. Even greater stress was laid on strengthening their moral life. Hence it was that even the pagans praised the blameless conduct of the Christians. The magnificent results are the legitimate boast of the Church to this day: the Church of the martyrs, for 300 years, was the Church at the zenith of her beauty and strength and glory.

Whence these results? Most certainly they are due first of all to the grace of God vouchsafed more abundantly during those early periods of severe trial. But they were brought about also by the ceaseless efforts of priests and catechists. The two catechists whom we know best of all, St. Cyril of Jerusalem and St. Augustine, are conspicuous examples of this tireless zeal.

What can we learn from this period? To exert ourselves zealously, after the example of the deacon

Deogratias, who, being himself a capable catechist, nevertheless had a humble opinion of his ability, and asked St. Augustine to direct him in his task. Moreover, we may learn to lay special stress on the educational side of catechization, and to make the training of the heart our paramount concern. If we cannot make use of all the means employed in the primitive Church, still some of them are freely at our disposal: personal prayer, seconded by the prayers of the whole parish; practice of the theological and other virtues, fasting and other mortifications, blessings, exorcisms in the form prescribed by Leo XIII,[1] — many of these means can be used in connection with catechetical instruction, and will surely make it a power for good, fruitful in spiritual benefits.

II. Catechesis in the Middle Ages

24. The Parental Home. — While catechetical instruction in the primitive Church was chiefly concerned with unbaptized adults, it was intended, in later periods, for children already baptized. These naturally received the rudiments of doctrine in the parental home. Hence the Church explicitly demanded of the newly married that they know the cardinal points of faith, in order that they may instruct their children. In the absence of the parents this duty devolved upon the godparents, who were also called *patrini catechesis*. The children, according to the desire of the Church, were to be familiarized as early as possible with the

---

[1] Roman Ritual, Appendix, *Exorcismus in Satanam et angelos apostaticos, jussu Leonis XIII editus.*

Our Father and the Creed, and accustomed to the practice of the Christian virtues.

25. The Clergy. — It was the duty of the clergy to see to it that parents and godparents lived up to their obligations. But besides they were themselves to instruct the children, and especially to prepare them for the reception of the sacraments of Penance, Holy Eucharist, and Confirmation. This was the primary duty imposed upon all priests having cure of souls. However, clerics of inferior rank also assisted in this work. In some places it was prescribed that the pastor alone should give this instruction, to the exclusion of any other clerics whom he might be obliged to keep in order to help him in the work of church and school. Sometimes also laymen took the place of priests and clerics.

Religious instruction was given on Sundays and feast-days. Thus the synod of Albi (1254) explicitly enacted that on these days all children seven years old should be brought to church, there to be instructed in the Christian religion, and to learn the Our Father, the Hail Mary, and the Creed. Of course, religious instruction was also given in the schools, which prospered under the fostering care of Charlemagne, and developed into cathedral, collegiate, monastic, and parochial schools.

In order to convey an idea of the importance the school had acquired in early medieval times, we quote the decree of the synod of Aachen held in 989: "To every monastery and cathedral foundation a school must be attached, in which the boys shall be taught the Psalms, the alphabet, singing, calculation of the feasts of the Church, and grammar." This decree was especially designed for the education of clerics; but Charlemagne did all in his power to extend its benefits to schools for the people.

All the efforts of Charlemagne were directed towards one goal: to establish on a solid basis a comprehensive system for the religious education of youth, and the people in general. Even that seemingly essentially modern element in popular education, compulsory school attendance, was already known to Charlemagne; but because circumstances militated against a complete carrying out of his plans, he was forced to mitigate the punishments meted out to delinquents. The emperor's aim to provide a general religious education for his people becomes of still more far-reaching significance when we take into account the especially strong influence exercised by Alcuin on the legislation of Charlemagne. For ecclesiastical decrees binding the clergy to instruct not only youths at school, but also all other children, were in vogue in Alcuin's home already since the time of St. Boniface. The general catechetical instruction made obligatory by Charlemagne's laws was not limited to preaching only: it consisted in the methodical study and explanation of the Athanasian and Apostolic Creeds and the Lord's Prayer. Soon there were added, at least in the schools, explanations of the capital sins and the works of mercy; finally all efforts of the teaching corps were centered on imparting a thorough knowledge of Scripture and a familiar acquaintance with the life of the Church.[1]

---

[1] For a more detailed account, see Catholic Educational Review, Nov., 1911, p. 805 ff.; Jan., 1912, p. 13 ff.; Feb., 1912, p. 114 ff.; May, 1912, p. 385 ff.; also: J. Bass Mullinger, Schools of Charles the Great, New York, 1911.

The many manuscript explanations of the Creed and the Lord's Prayer still extant from this period prove conclusively that the decrees concerning general catechetical instruction were carried out in practice. "These laws remained in effect all through the Middle Ages. A fresh impetus was constantly being given to them, even if at times they were not strictly lived up to, especially when compulsory measures were no longer used by the civil authorities, and confession became the only means of exercising control over the religious knowledge of the laity."

It may be readily seen, therefore, how much truth there is in that hoary calumny still cropping out at times, that Luther was the first to provide general catechetical instruction for the young.

26. The Instruction for Confession deserves special attention, since much labor and care were spent on it during the Middle Ages. "It is worthy of note that, as we gradually acquire a better knowledge of the vigorous Christianity that flourished among the tribes of the great Frankish kingdom who entered the Church during the course of the eighth century, we come upon irrefragable proofs of tireless priestly activity in connection with the administration of the Sacrament of Penance, and the practice of self-accusation among the faithful. . . . In agreement with it we find this other noteworthy fact, that many of the oldest monuments of our German language, dating from the eighth to the twelfth century, relate to the Sacrament of Penance."

"Because great stress was laid on a worthy preparation for the reception of the Sacraments of Penance and Holy Communion, the greater number of catechetical works, at the end of the Middle Ages, appeared almost year after year in the form of confession books, confession mirrors, treatises on the Ten Commandments, the different kinds of sin, the preparation for Holy Communion. In the many German prayer books and manuals of piety also, the greater part of the contents was devoted to instructions on Confession and Holy Communion."[1] The spirit animating this rich literature is indeed the opposite of that "decadence, ignorance and unnaturalness" that even now is frequently and opprobriously fastened upon medieval Catholic asceticism. That these works were especially intended for the instruction of youth appears from the following quotation from Geiler of Keisersberg, in his translation of Gerson's tripartite work on The Ten Commandments, Confession, and The Art of Dying: "Priests, parents, teachers, should all take care that the contents of this book be written on tablets to be hung, all or in part, in public places, such as parochial churches, schools, hospitals, religious institutions." The book is also intended "for children and young people who from their earliest years should above all things be instructed in the general contents and the principal parts of our faith. . . . Parents, fathers and mothers, should demand this from the schoolmaster in behalf of their children."

For the years 1450–1520 we can trace about fifty such "Confession books." The oldest printed one has been republished by Falk in the Zeitschrift f. kath. Theologie, xxxii, 1908, pp. 754–

[1] See Janssen, History of the German People from the Close of the Middle Ages, vol. I.

775. The Katechetischen Blätter, 1903 p. 141 ff., have re-edited several specimens of this interesting literature. In the early Middle Ages the so-called "Confession formulas" served the same purpose as the later "Confession books." At first they were based principally on the scheme of the seven (or eight) Capital Sins; afterwards the Decalog constituted their framework.

27. Means of Instruction. — For all those who were able to read, the important truths of Christian Doctrine were made available not only in print, but as we know from the above testimony of Geiler of Keisersberg, they were also written on wooden tablets hung up in churches, schools, or hospitals. Especially was this the case with whatever related to Confession, and such information was made freely accessible in the churches. However, the other rudiments of faith were also added to these "Confession tables."

For the benefit of those unable to read it was provided that the most necessary points (Creed, Lord's Prayer, Decalog) should be read in church before the sermon on Sundays and holidays. Pictorial representations, however, were more especially pressed into use for the "poor in spirit": the children and those unable to read. An anonymous preacher of the Upper Rhine speaks thus towards the end of the thirteenth century: "As the sun illuminates the darkness, so does Holy Writ illuminate the whole Christian world. . . . The Lord has also given us another writing, a writing for the laity. For there are many unacquainted with the written words of books. Therefore God has given them another writing to teach them how to attain the heavenly kingdom. And this writing is found in the pictures adorning our churches and representing the

Saints, their lives and what they have done for God." The Picture Bibles,[1] which only at a later period were called the "Bibles of the Poor," were above all intended to be a means of instruction, and go back probably to the middle of the thirteenth century. In the center of each picture was found the chief scene, taken from the New Testament (the Annunciation, the Nativity, the Presentation in the Temple); around it were grouped prototypes from the Old Testament (Eve and the Serpent, Gideon's Fleece), while appropriate inscriptions were added at the top. These catechisms in pictures strove to represent in a realistic and vivid manner the catechetical formulas. The third commandment of God, e.g., was illustrated in this manner by two pictures: a preacher in the pulpit surrounded by attentive listeners, and its counterpart, two men seated at a gaming table where devils bring them wine-flask and dice.

As a further aid in religious teaching, recourse was had to dramatic representations to instruct the people. The whole history of divine revelation was spread before them in these plays, in pictures on the altar and the church walls, in cemeteries, and in the Stations of the Cross, and their meaning was easily grasped by all.

28. Catechetical Instruction was Held in High Esteem During the Middle Ages. — This is apparent from the fact that men of great learning, like Alcuin, Thomas Aquinas, Bonaventure, wrote catechetical manuals for the use of priests.

---

[1] For a fuller account of medieval "Picture Bibles" and "Bibles of the Poor" see Cath. Encycl., vol. II, p. 546 ff.

It was probably Alcuin (735–804) who originated the Latin explanation of the Lord's Prayer and the Creed, upon which all catechetical instruction during the Middle Ages was patterned. His treatise is made up of questions and answers, and may therefore be regarded as the prototype of our modern catechisms. Until recently this book had been attributed by mistake to the celebrated catechist and saintly bishop Bruno of Würzburg (died 1045). It is found in the 11th and 12th chapters of the *Disputatio puerorum per Interrogationes et Responsiones*. A disciple of Alcuin, Hrabanus Maurus, gives us, in his *De Disciplina Ecclesiastica*, many methodical helps for catechization. By the catechism of St. Thomas Aquinas is generally understood his explanation of the Apostles' Creed, the Lord's Prayer, the Hail Mary, and the Decalog. Of Gerson's *Opus Tripartitum* we have already spoken. His work On Leading the Little Ones to Christ, deserves special mention for its excellence.

Until close to the end of the Middle Ages there is scarcely any theologian of importance who does not call attention in his writings, when opportunity offers, to the importance of religious instruction. The number of commentaries on the cardinal doctrines of faith is very large, as is also the number of catechismal helps for the reception or the administration of the Sacraments, and more particularly for Confession.

With the close of the Middle Ages, however, there is frequently noticeable a tendency to neglect or underestimate catechization.

An episode full of significance in this regard is thus reported by Possevinus,[1] a later pedagog: "When the storm of schism had rent the Church in twain, Gerson saw no better means of pacifying the spirits than to re-establish primary schools for the youth. Hence he took upon himself the pious instruction and training of children. Where love impels to sacrifice, says St. Bernard, no

[1] Cath. Encyc., vol. XII, p. 317.

effort is painful or too great. But scarcely had Gerson entered upon his zealous task, when a tempest of disapprobation broke loose. Many thought it undignified that a theologian and preacher of such repute, and a chancellor of the Paris University, should lower his dignity by such seemingly humble and useless work. With the only end in view of defending those whose cause Christ Himself had so lovingly championed, Gerson then wrote his book On Leading the Little Ones to Christ. Illuminated by the Holy Ghost, and intimately convinced that knowledge puffeth up unless held in check by humility and love, he sets down on the first page of his golden booklet the words of Christ: Suffer the children to come unto Me. And then he goes on to give various reasons why a theologian should not despise this holy task."

29. Retrospect on Catechization During the Middle Ages. — Some characteristics of medieval catechization worthy of imitation are the following:

1. The great care taken to make religious instruction perspicuous. At that time recourse was had to visual teaching spontaneously — and necessarily, since many people were unacquainted with reading and writing, and printing was not invented.

2. The truths of the catechism were put before the people in a practical manner, in the form of rhymes and songs. This feature also might be copied to a certain extent. Mere abstract book-knowledge is fraught with many disadvantages, and cannot claim Catholic tradition in its favor. The fight waged by modern pedagogy against overestimation of the book and of word drills is but another vindication of old Catholic teaching methods.

3. Great stress was laid on the old "formulas" of the Church: the Creed, the Lord's Prayer, the Hail Mary, the Seven Sacraments, the Ten Command-

ments, the Seven Capital Sins, the Works of Mercy. But these formulas were not hollow sounds committed to memory and repeated by rote; they were "prayed." And herein lies a lesson: prayer is an integral part of catechization. And the method to be followed in teaching it is simple, e.g.: we pray Thee, O Lord, that we may avoid the Seven Capital Sins: Pride, etc.

III. The Sixteenth Century

30. The Reformers. — Up to this very day we hear it said that Luther was the founder of our modern school system, or at least that he was the first to call attention prominently to the need of schools for the people, and of religious instruction for the young. What the Reformation did in reality for education in general, we have set forth in another volume.[1] Its influence can be summed up in a few words: it was a violent repression of a newly born and promising intellectual life, which owed its inception to the older German humanists.

Luther is said to be especially deserving of praise for his efforts in behalf of the religious training of the rising generation, because of his catechism. He is credited with being the very first to publish a book of this kind. But the recent investigations of von Brück, Falk, Hasak, Janssen, Münzenberger, have shown the falsity of this assertion, which is based on a misleading confusion of several things, all included under the same name variously understood. Sundry catechismal writings are met with even before the art of printing was

[1] Krus, Zur Gesch. des Unterrichtes u. der Erziehung.

invented. Such were: Alcuin's explanation of the Creed and the Lord's Prayer; a catechism of the year 1368 for the use of those having the care of souls and prescribed by the synod of Lavour, France; a Spanish catechism of 1429. Catechisms multiplied apace with the printing presses. And even if they differ in form from our present books, they are catechisms nevertheless. Hence some better-informed Protestants have ceased to claim that Luther was the first to compose a catechism. What remains true is, that since Luther's time the word "catechism" has been used to designate the book itself, while formerly it was applied to catechetical instruction taken in conjunction with all the liturgical functions preparatory to baptism. The fact also remains that the Reformers displayed great zeal in using the catechism for the spread of their doctrines: they were close enough to Catholic times to be fully aware of the strong influence exercised by short popular religious tracts.

In K. A. Schmid's Encyklopädie des ges. Erziehungs u. Unterrichtswesens, Weidemann writes in a fairly objective manner thus: "Luther did not arbitrarily determine the content or the form of the catechism, but followed the practice in vogue in the Church for several centuries. . . . In composing his catechism Luther adhered to the customs consecrated by long usage; he unified the materials at hand and generally accepted, and put the same at the service of the Church under a time-honored name. . . . Not only did he leave the chapters on Faith, the Lord's Prayer, the Sacraments, the Decalog, in their accustomed places, but he preserved the old formulas used in the administration of Baptism and Penance; in his answers to questions Luther did not scruple to transcribe literally the words of the 'Catechesis theotisca,' a German catechism of the ninth century composed by the monk Otfried von Weissenburg; his explanation of the Lord's Prayer is familiar to Kero, a monk of St. Gall in the eighth century, and is found even in the Sacramentarium Gelasianum."

31. Revival of Catholic Catechization. — Already in the first half of the sixteenth century we witness a revival of zeal for the catechization of the people and the young, which was partly a continuation of the true reform of the religious life already inaugurated in the fifteenth century, while it received a new impetus from the very violence of the religious revolution.

This regeneration of Catholic life, and especially the revival of catechization, was brought about not only by a few men of mark, but sprang from a concerted effort of the universal Church, due to the energetic stimulus given by the Council of Trent. The latter dwelt with anxious insistence upon the need of preaching and catechization. Already in the fifth and again in the twenty-fourth session pastors were most emphatically reminded of their duty to provide religious instruction for the people and the young. Bishops were enjoined to carry out these recommendations in a vigorous manner, and were given ample powers to that effect. These measures were soon followed by results. The ceaseless vigilance of the Popes, such as St. Pius V; the organization of Confraternities of Christian Doctrine; the frequent convocation of synods solicitous above all for the education of youth; and very especially the foundation of new religious orders whose primary object was in many cases the training of children, brought about very consoling results, even in places that seemed irremediably lost to the faith.

The results of historical research about pedagogy and catechization published thus far give but an imperfect idea of this Catholic revival. The danger of forming a biased opinion in this matter is all the greater because non-Catholics claim undue credit for nearly every worthy pedagogical achievement. Catholic historical investigators will find here a wide and largely untilled field for the exercise of their zeal.

32. The Most Important Catechisms. — As was inevitable since the invention of printing, printed books and catechisms designed as helps in the work of instruction are from now on met with in great numbers.

The Augsburg Catholic catechism appeared immediately after the Diet of 1530.[1] . . . From this time on catechisms in German, in Latin, or in both languages follow one another in quick succession. Some were written by bishops, such as John Maltiz of Meissen and Michael Helding of Merseburg; others were written by University professors or by religious. Amongst them we may mention: Mathias Kremers, Francis Titelman, Peter de Soto. The catechism of John Dietenberger, the translator of the Bible, had passed through eight editions before 1550. In Cologne alone six catechisms were printed in the first half of the sixteenth century.[2]

Earlier catechismal writings obviously could not have the wide circulation of the printed books. The former were mostly intended for the use of the teacher; but when the period of printing set in, every child could enjoy the use of a catechism. It is impossible to give here a complete list of all the catechisms that came

---

[1] It was at this Diet that the "Augsburg Confession" was first presented by the Reformers as their authoritative creed. See Cath. Encycl., V, p. 760.

[2] English catechisms before and after the Reformation are summarily described in Cath. Encycl., vol. V, p. 78.

from the press; suffice it to mention those of Blessed Canisius, Bellarmine, Edmund Auger, and to add a few words about the Roman Catechism.

1. Peter Canisius wrote several catechisms. His large Latin catechism appeared in 1555, and contained 202 pages small octavo. It was entitled: "Summa doctrinae christianae. Per questiones tradita, et in usum christianae pueritiae nunc primum edita." The name of the author is not given. "I desired," Canisius tells us later on, "to please God more than man in the composition of this work." The use of Latin is explained by the purpose the author had in view: his book was intended for students, and it must be remembered that in this humanistic period Latin was taught even in village schools.

Canisius published a revised edition in 1566, and this time his name is found on the title page. This second edition has been often republished later on, and was in great demand amongst students. In 1569–70 Peter Busaeus published a commentary in four volumes on this catechism, and he took special pains to give in full the texts from Holy Writ and the Fathers which Canisius had merely indicated. This work was soon called *Opus catechisticum*, or, The Large Christian Doctrine.

In 1556 appeared the "Summa doctrinae christianae per quaestiones tradita et ad captum rudiorum accommodata." A German translation of this work appeared in 1558; this is the smallest of the catechisms published by Canisius, and it became so popular that "catechism" and "Canisius" were for a long time synonymous expressions.

A third catechism, which from its size comes midway between the two others, appeared in 1559: *Parvus catechismus catholicorum.* A German translation was published in 1563.

This was considered to be the best catechism of the three. "It held to a golden mean. It may be compared to a basketful of ripe fruit, gathered from the tree of the larger catechism."

The division of the subject-matter in the Canisian catechisms is as follows:

1. Faith (Apostles' Creed); 2. Hope and Prayer (Lord's Prayer, Hail Mary); 3. Charity and Commandments of God and the Church; 4. The Sacraments; 5. Christian Justice, i.e., the shunning of evil (sin and its kinds), and the doing of good (prayer, fasting, almsgiving, virtue, evangelical counsels, the last things).

It is worthy of note that Canisius touches but lightly on those fundamental doctrines that were not jeopardized by false teaching; but he develops at length those doctrines attacked by heretics: the Sacraments, the Church, Holy Orders, Mass, the obligation of fasting, the veneration of the Saints, Communion under one kind. He even takes up the question: What is to be thought of bad priests? His is indeed a catechism adapted to the times. His exposition is ever dispassionate, to the point, dignified; the very antithesis of that controversial bitterness characterizing his antagonists, whom he does not even name. "This book," writes Canisius in his Confessions, "strives, in a charitable manner, to raise up those that have fallen, and to bring back, with the help of divine grace, those who have gone astray." This irenic attitude was maintained throughout the large catechism, which forms the basis of the others, and is largely due to its being but a close-knit exposition of passages from Holy Writ and the Fathers: in the first edition are found 1100 quotations from Scripture, and 400 from the Fathers.

Concluding his study on the catechisms of Canisius, Braunsberger sketches briefly the new springtide of Catholic life at the death of the great catechist. We need not picture the latter as the fountainhead of all the blessings of this stirring epoch; but "it is no exaggeration to say that in this glorious battle the catechism of Bl. Canisius acted as an inspiring banner ever carried on the firing line, and leading to numerous victories." The Canisian catechisms held a dominant place in Germany until the eighteenth century, and became the basis of many others. One of the best of these is the "Small Catechism of P. Canisius, by Priests of the Society of Jesus, with Scriptural Proofs of the Doctrines therein contained. Erffurt, 1714." This recension was incorporated into the catechism of Mainz of 1760, a later revision of which came into the hands of Father Deharbe, serving as the nucleus of his own catechismal works. In this way there has been an uninterrupted tradition from Canisius to our own day.[1]

2. Bellarmine published in 1598, by order of Pope Clement VIII, his catechism entitled: *Dottrina cristiana breve da impararsi a mente*, or Compendium of Christian Doctrine to be Learned by Heart. For the benefit of catechists he published: *Dichiarazione più copiosa della dottrina cristiana*, or, A More Thorough Explanation of Christian Doctrine. In Rome these books were used exclusively in the instruction of youth: in other dioceses their adoption was ordered by the Pope. Translations in various languages followed soon; although officially approved by the Pope, they never

[1] See exhaustive article on Canisius and his work by Otto Braunsberger in Cath. Encyclopedia, vol. XI, p. 756 ff.

enjoyed the widespread popularity of the Canisian catechisms. In the schema, *De parvo catechismo*, of the Vatican Council, Bellarmine's catechism was made the norm for the universal uniform catechism contemplated at that time.

As a clue to the value of his modest catechism we have Bellarmine's own admission that his small *Dottrina cristiana* had required far greater exertion on his part than his large work, *De controversiis fidei*. And in the following remark Bellarmine has unconsciously given the highest testimony of himself: "If the small catechism of the revered, — and this is my firm conviction — nay saintly Peter Canisius had been known to me at the time when by order of my superiors I composed the Italian catechism, I most surely should not have gone to the trouble of writing it, but I should have merely translated Canisius' Latin work into Italian." [1]

3. Edmund Auger, the son of a workingman, was received into the Society by St. Ignatius himself. Auger has been called, and rightly so, the Canisius of France. His French catechism appeared in 1563, and enjoyed a wide circulation. The charitable disposition of the author was not unlike that of Canisius: the heretics pursued him with a deadly hatred; at one time even the rope had been fastened around his neck, but he remained ever faithful to his fundamental principle, that kindness and charity constitute the best weapon against error.[2]

33. The Roman Catechism. — The Vatican Council's schema, *De parvo catechismo*, gives briefly the origin of this important manual:

[1] A good account of Bellarmine's personality and activity is found in Cath. Encyclopedia, vol. II, p. 411 ff.
[2] See Cath. Encyclopedia, vol. II, p. 72.

Our Holy Mother the Church, guided by the teachings of her spouse, Our Saviour Jesus Christ, has always manifested great care and solicitude for the education of the young, so that they might be fortified with the milk of celestial doctrine, and thoroughly imbued with piety. Hence the Holy Tridentine Synod has not only ordered all bishops to provide for the instruction of children in the rudiments of faith, and their training in diligent obedience to God and their parents (Session XXIV, cap. IV, *de Reformatione*); but it has moreover declared it to be its intention to edit a Compendium of Christian Doctrine for the people which should be followed in all churches by all those in duty bound to the office of pastors and doctors. But since the Holy Synod could not bring this work to completion, the Apostolic See, in compliance with the Council's express desire (Session XXV, *Decret. de Indice librorum, Catechismo*, etc.), has done so by publishing the Catechism for Pastors.[1]

The Roman Catechism, therefore, is not a school manual, or a book for the people such as our other catechisms are; but it is a handbook for catechists and teachers. St. Chas. Borromeo deserves the largest share of credit for the composition of this work. Pope Pius IV in 1565 appointed the four theologians who under the direction of Charles Borromeo planned the outline of the work. Cardinal Serlet undertook a complete revision of it, while the renowned humanists Giulio Poggiano and Paolo Manuzio cast the work into classical Latin. During the pontificate of Pius V it appeared both in Italian and in Latin under the title: "Catechismus ex decreto Concilii Tridentini ad parochos Pii V jussu editus, Romae, 1566." Reimpressions and translations followed quickly. The first German edition was due to Paulus Hoffaeus (Dillingen,

[1] See Cath. Encycl., vol. XIII, p. 120: Roman Catechism.

1568). The last Latin-German edition was published in Regensburg, 1905.[1]

The division of the subject-matter follows the four formulas: The Creed, the Sacraments, the Decalog, the Lord's Prayer. The introduction states the reasons that have prompted this division.

> ". . . The truths vouchsafed to us by divine revelation are so numerous and so varied that it is no easy task either to acquire a knowledge of them, or having acquired that knowledge, to retain them in memory, so that when occasion may require, a ready and prompt explanation may be at hand. Our predecessors have very wisely arranged this whole force and scheme of the salutary doctrines under four heads . . . Hence it follows that when these four points have been fully explained, there can scarcely be wanting anything to be learned by a Christian man. . . . In his teaching and his explanations (the pastor) shall never lose sight of these four heads."

Catholics welcomed the Roman Catechism with great joy, while Protestants were taken aback by it. The Lutheran polemist Hesshus expressed the opinion that it was the craftiest book written by the Papists during the last hundred years: when it extols the merits of Christ and the power of the Holy Ghost, when it exhorts all to shun evil and to do good, it does it in a manner so cunning that it could not be improved upon. But all this is so far from being done with an honest intention that it is calculated merely to deceive the people. It is not without reason that later Popes such as Clement XIII, and more recently Pius X in his

---

[1] A very good English translation is the one made at Maynooth College in 1829 and recently reissued by James Duffy & Co., Dublin: Catechism of the Council of Trent, translated into English, with notes, etc., by Very Rev. J. Donovan, D.D.

Encyclical on the teaching of Christian Doctrine, have strongly recommended to the clergy the study and practical use of the Roman Catechism.

34. Catechetics. — It was inevitable that with the renewed interest taken in catechization and the rapid spread of catechisms there should appear theoretical helps for religious instruction, i.e., attempts at catechetics.

Canisius himself was probably the author of the catechetical manual, *Practica catechismi*. It requires of the catechist, "first, that in his prayers he should recommend this meritorious work to God the Lord and implore His assistance." Besides, the catechist "should be endowed with those eminent virtues of humility, patience, charity, etc." It also recommends "objective teaching by means of stories, especially from the lives of the Saints; use also should be made of parables. . . . At Christmas time there should be erected a crib with Mary and Joseph, the angels, the ox and the ass, and before it should be sung the *Puer Natus*, or, *In dulci jubilo*, in German and Latin. . . . The Jews know their Talmud better, and the Turks their Coran, than many Christians know their catechism."

Several catechetical handbooks written by non-German Jesuits were introduced into Germany through the close intercourse existing between the various provinces of the Order, e.g., the small work of Jacobus de Ledesma, *De modo catechizandi* (1573), and the "Antonii Possevini Epistola ad Ivonem Tarterium de necessitate, utilitate ac ratione docendi catholici catechismi." This letter appeared in 1576 and was printed for the first time in Ingolstadt in 1583. It does not yet give a systematic method, but "it is stimulating throughout and rouses the true catechetical spirit, something that a hundred skilful rules cannot supply."

Bishops and synods also provided the clergy sometimes with short, sometimes with more extended, catechetical manuals. Thus a pastoral letter of the Archbishop of Treves, in 1588, descants upon "the utility and necessity of catechetical instruction," and describes "a method of teaching Christian Doctrine to the uneducated." In 1590 these instructions were presented to all the catechists of the diocese together with the *Piae ac solidae catecheses*.

Only a few more names can be quoted from among the many distinguished leaders of later periods. Francis de Sales (died 1622) wrote *Instructio catechetica*. Barth. Holzhauser (died 1658), the originator of the community life for secular priests, was a zealous catechist, and in the statutes of his society he laid particular stress upon catechization. He wrote *De tradenda doctrina christiana parvulis in catechismo*. Claude Fleury,[1] in his "Discours du dessein et de l'usage du catéchisme historique," inveighs against mechanical memorizing; but he makes the mistake of underrating the importance of definite and clear catechismal teaching. In 1679 appeared in Dillingen, in the seventh part of the *Institutiones practicae* of Tobias Lohner, S.J., a valuable manual on method, *De catechizandi munere*. In 1688 was printed in Landshut a German translation of a French catechetical work by Boudon, entitled, Salutary Science of the Catechism. In this

[1] Cath. Encycl., vol. VI, p. 103.

work memorizing is strongly deprecated: "We do not condemn learning the catechism by heart but we do condemn the practice of being satisfied with that." [1]

IV. DECLINE OF CATECHIZATION DURING THE RATIONALISTIC PERIOD

35. New Catechisms. — The eighteenth century at first throve on the heritage of the past; the second half, however, is marked by a decidedly superficial and enervated view of supernatural revelation. The rationalistic tendency, so apparent in theology, was carried into the domain of catechization. The catechisms in use, mostly revisions of the Canisian Manuals, gave rise to widespread dissatisfaction. Canisius himself was represented as dry, unpractical, scholastic, and not even sufficiently Christian. Very instructive in this regard is the declaration of the Vicar General of Mainz in his circular letter of November 13, 1788: "For several years past we have heard loud complaints that our diocesan catechism is no longer up-to-date. Scholastic notions unintelligible to the mass of the people; general dryness; lack of vigorous instruction on virtue, and endless polemics are some of the regrettable and evident shortcomings of this catechism."

Were these complaints well founded? No doubt the older catechisms were not perfect. Progressive

---

[1] Valuable information with regard to catechisms and catechization in England after the Reformation may be found in the Cath. Encyclopedia, vol. V, pp. 79–80. Exhaustive data on the same subject for the United States may be found *ibid.*, p. 80 ff. Also in Archbishop Messmer's: Spirago's Method of Christian Doctrine, p. 532 ff.

improvements and gradual adaptation to the needs of the times would not have been in any wise contrary to tradition, since Canisius himself had set an example in this regard. But who was ultimately responsible for the general decline of religious instruction, and education in general, which had now become so apparent? Only a few years after the religious upheaval of the sixteenth century had begun, Melanchthon, speaking of the new theologians, exclaimed: "Good God, are those men theologians! Shall not their teaching give rise to a new and still more atheistic sophistry?" His fears were realized all too soon: instead of the simple older teaching always submissive to authority, there came a period of fruitless and scandalous wrangling. It is easy to understand that this restless spirit found access into Catholic books and schools. But improvement could come only through steadfast adherence to the spirit of the Church. Instead, Illuminism, consciously and unconsciously, made a return to the old traditions all the more difficult. Only then did a change come about when the real worth of the latter came to be fully appreciated once more.

The consequence of this dissatisfaction with existing catechisms was that numerous attempts were made to compose new and better manuals of study. But while Canisius's works had held the upper hand for two centuries, these modern books did not live for as many decades. Most of the new catechisms were stamped with the hallmark of rationalism. Some examples may suffice: original sin consists in this, that it has become increasingly difficult for man to practise virtue; in many of these manuals with rationalistic tendencies no mention is made of the *reatus culpae,* or the fall from the supernatural state of sanctifying grace. Grace "makes virtue easy"; but the supernatural character of the life of grace is overlooked. Vitus A. Winter, Domherr of Eichstätt, a disciple of Kant, writes that he who in his catechetical instructions "should seek to gratify our desire for eternal happiness, should be poisoning the hearts." His work, Religiös-sittliche Katechetik, presents a strange mixture of sound ideas together with dangerous superficialities and exaggerations.

We give a few quotations, characteristic of the spirit of the book. "Catechization, in the proper and better meaning of the word, consists in helping the child to unfold gradually the moral and religious concepts deposited in his mind, and to awaken kindred feelings in his heart, so that he may mount to the highest plane of moral perfection. The art of the teacher consists above all in setting in motion the child's latent powers, and although this does not exclude all positive teaching, it none the less constitutes the very essence of catechetical work." Intr., 3.

The author is fond of calling all faith grounded on authority "a crutch," still sorely needed by the great mass of believers. "For intent on providing for their bodily needs, they move in an atmosphere of material preoccupations, and cannot rise to a study of the philosophy of religion." The catechist, when treating of the Sacraments, should avoid all useless controversies, e.g., about the real presence of Christ's Body and Blood, and confine himself to explaining the end for which they were instituted and the right manner of receiving them. He should barely touch on the *opus operatum,* but insist at length on the *opus operantis,* since so large a number of people have a presumptuous confidence in the former, and are concerned all the less about the latter." While Winter strives to reduce all "positive (in opposition to philosophical) religious teaching" to a minimum, he advocates at length the necessity of a "pedagogical or catechetical law course," which he explains thus: "We should select (*a*) from the natural law the easiest principles of most common application, presenting them to the child-mind preferably in stories; and (*b*) from the body of positive laws some that affect the conditions of the catechumens more immediately, and also others that show forth plainly the wisdom and the sympathetic heart of the legislator. . . . This practice would, moreover, acquaint the child with the expressions so often recurring in positive legislation. . . ." In recommending familiarization with juridical language, he contrasts it with "the language of the Church," and by this he understands not the Latin language as a whole, but certain technical terms, derived, however, mostly from ancient languages, such as person, consubstantial: "We attach even less importance to the language of the Church (than to that of the learned), for it was invented mostly in order to refute heretics. As we have made it clear already that polemics ought to be excluded from the catechism class, it follows that we must do away with polemical language."

36. The Theory of Catechization was infected also by the poison of Illuminism. The Lectures on the Art of Catechization, written by the otherwise reliable pedagog, Ign. von Felbiger, show this plainly, as do also many other catechetical works whose authors were mostly animated by the best intentions. But, perhaps unconsciously, they had imbibed the spirit of rationalism, and were swayed by it in their catechetical work.

The underlying principle of Illuminism is rationalism: "We must view all truth with our own eyes only, independently of all authority, since to pass judgment even on religious verities is only a matter of sane human reason." Hence the fundamental dogma of its catechetical method: "The task of the catechist consists in evoking and developing the religious and moral conceptions latent in the child's mind. For, whatever the child does not draw from its deep inner self is alien to him, unnatural, untrue. The catechist should not force any truth upon the child's understanding, but should call forth all truth from the child's own soul." This method of catechization was termed the "socratic method," and its protagonists were called "the socratists."

What benefits accrued from the use of this method? One of its champions, the above-named Winter, declares that "the expository, positive or authoritative method used by unskilled teachers indiscriminately and under all circumstances, has produced mere automatons; the socratic method, however, gives us independent thinkers who originate new scientific truths. . . ." If this latter assertion be applied literally to catechization, the socratic method stands self-condemned, for an "originator" in matters of faith is no longer a Christian.

Winter himself, theoretically at least, was on the whole in favor of a combination of both methods. But the exaggerated praise bestowed upon the socratic method and the constant belittling of authoritative teaching necessarily gave rise to onesidedness in practice. Many of the so-called "socratics" did scant honor to the master by calling their rationalistic method after him. Indeed, by propounding questions Socrates strove to make his pupils frame correct answers, and to lead them gradually to see new truths, but only such truths as could be deduced by assiduous mental application from the fund of knowledge already acquired. It never occurred to him to draw from his pupils, through questions only, truths that could not possibly be discovered by logical deduction, e.g., historical facts. He would never have applied his method to a positive religion grounded on historical data and the testimony of reliable witnesses. Even in the profane sciences the socratic method failed to produce the desired results, as the unbiased testimony of Pestalozzi proves:

"In the days when the socratic method was held in high esteem, men imagined that they could evoke truths from the mind to such an extent as almost to produce something out of nothing. I am convinced, however, that those dreamers are waking up sadly disillusioned." And forsooth, "one cannot help noticing that the hawk and the eagle do not rob the nests of birds that have not yet laid their eggs."

It is the deliberately expressed conviction of Auxiliary Bishop Knecht that the catechetical works of Graser, Schwarzel, Winter, "exhibit Catholic catechetics at its lowest ebb."

We should not forget, however, that in the midst of these errors are found indications of a sane reform of methods and echoes of the sound old tradition. In an epoch characterized by general pedagogical enthusiasm it seems almost inevitable that false ideas should come to the fore, together with well-grounded theories. And the reaction against the false ideas of a given period must necessarily call forth forgotten truths.

V. The Restoration of Catechization in the Nineteenth Century

37. Overberg, Hirscher, Gruber, played a leading rôle in the restoration of catechization in the nineteenth century.

1. Bernard Henry Overberg [1] (1754–1826) may be called the reformer of the common school system, and remains a model both for educators and priests.

Born in Höckel, Osnabrück, he became a priest in 1780, despite many handicaps. He chose a place of curate in preference to

[1] A good sketch of his life and activity is found in the Cath. Encyclopedia, vol. XI, p. 362.

several better positions. His successful catechetical work at once drew attention to him. He was almost forcibly brought to Münster by Vicar General Fürstenberg, there to be placed at the head of the "Normal School," to reform the teaching corps. During 43 years he labored with the greatest success for the betterment of the school system. His clear and heart-winning instructions in the convent church were largely attended even by adults. His coming in contact with the cultured company that gathered around Princess Galitzin broadened his views. In 1809 he was appointed director of the theological seminary; from then on his great aim was to give the candidates for the priesthood a thorough ascetical training and to inflame them with a love for schools. It was with great joy that he saw the foundation of a "Teachers' Seminary" to take the place of the Normal School.

Lorenz Kellner, a competent critic, writes of him: "Overberg far outranks Felbiger in pedagogical ability. If the latter displayed perhaps greater talent for organization, Overberg surpasses him in efficiency, in his grasp of the intellectual and emotional side of the teacher's office. . . . He it was who knew so well how to conciliate and combine faith and science, intellectual and moral training; in this respect he ranks much higher than Rochow and Pestalozzi, while in his deep love for the people he is in no way second to them. Peace dwelt in his noble soul, and working thus, a stranger to all bitter contentions, he died as he had lived, and his memory has not suffered from the attacks of partisan passion." "No one can succeed in making others love and appreciate the Christian religion who has not succeeded himself in finding in it true peace, love of his fellowmen and spiritual joy." These words were the guiding principle of Overberg's life, and show that he was ever mindful of St. Augustine's advice to cultivate "cheerfulness" in the exercise of the catechetical office.

The principal work of Overberg is entitled, "Guide to Successful Schoolwork" (1793). His teaching on observation and mental development is valuable to this day. In 1799 he published his "Bible History of the Old and New Testament for the Instruction and Edification of Teachers, Advanced Students and Parents." In 1804 appeared his "Manual of the Catholic Religion for Personal and Mutual Instruction," to which were appended a smaller and a larger catechism.

2. John B. Hirscher (born in 1788 in Altergarten near Ravensburg, died in 1865 in Freiburg i. B.) [1] became a priest in 1810, professor of Moral and Pastoral Theology in Tübingen in 1817, professor of Moral Theology in Freiburg in 1837. As dean of the cathedral since 1850 he became the mainstay of his archbishop during the troublous times through which the Church passed in Baden. Standing at the turn of two periods, he combines in his person the characteristics of both. He was a man of deep-rooted piety, and contributed greatly by word and example to the revival of Catholic life. But unconsciously he was still dominated by many prejudices inherited from a superficial Illuminism, which caused one of his works to be put on the Index.

In 1831 he published his "Catechetics," which enjoyed a great popularity. The work he published in 1863, "Hints for Successful Religious Instruction," contains many sane and sound principles. His "Catechism of the Catholic Religion," of 1842, was less

[1] His somewhat checkered career is described in Cath. Encycl., vol. VII, p. 363.

successful; his "Smaller Catechism," of 1845, showed a slight change in his one-sided views.

3. Augustin Gruber was born in Vienna in 1763. He became Bishop of Laibach and was Archbishop of Salzburg from 1823 until 1835. The catechetical conferences and exercises, which as archbishop he held for his clergy, were published under the title, "Catechetical Conferences on St. Augustine's work: On the Instruction of the Ignorant." The first volume contains St. Augustine's theory of catechization translated and explained with a view to present-day needs. The second volume is entitled, Practical Manual of Catechetics, and contains valuable sketches for practical instructions.

Gruber breaks off completely with rationalism. For him the catechist is no longer a Socrates, but a messenger of God and the Church, coming in God's name to teach the children revealed truths and to demand of them faith in his teaching. Thus he educates believing Catholics, not rationalistic philosophers. The spirit of faith pervades Gruber's entire catechetical work. A second characteristic of his catechization is his unction: he knows how to win the heart of the child, and his instructions are aglow with warm religious feeling. In this respect Gruber is to this day a perfect model, and it is no easy task to imitate him.

38. Catechisms. — Overberg and Hirscher wrote catechisms. Hirscher especially was not fortunate in this regard. His historico-synthetical catechism appeared in 1842. Although Alban Stolz wrote a commentary in two volumes on it, a book that even to this day is a rich mine of instructive matter, the catechism did not succeed: true Catholic tradition did not come into its own. The old and venerated formulas on which the Roman Catechism bases its doctrines and their subdivisions, and in which the rudiments of faith are so plainly stated that the ignorant may grasp them while the learned can never fully exhaust their contents, these formulas Hirscher designates as "commonplaces" that should make way for a scientific and systematic exposition.

The catechisms of Deharbe enjoyed the widest diffusion of all. The first appeared in 1847 in Lucerne. Since 1848 the various recensions have been published in Regensburg, whence the designation: Catechism of Regensburg.

This catechism was introduced in Limburg in 1848; the dioceses of Bavaria adopted it in 1853; Cologne in 1854; and in the following years, Mainz, Paderborn, Fulda, Ermland, Kulm, Gnesen-Posen. It came into general use in the Swiss dioceses about 1850, while it also found its way into North America.[1] The translations of this catechism are very numerous.

Even in Freiburg it took the place of Hirscher's catechism; in Münster and Osnabrück it displaced Overberg's catechism. The catechism of Schuster was in use in Rottenburg until 1887, but the new catechism of this diocese in many ways resembles Deharbe's. Thus Deharbe's catechism has brought about a certain uniformity, which however is not complete, as different contexts were used in different places. Since the last few years a movement has been under way in Southern Germany to bring about this much-desired uniformity. In the diocesan papers one may find reports of the progress made in this direction.

The preference for Deharbe's catechism is founded on good grounds. The author preserves religiously the

[1] Compare: Cath. Encyclopedia, vol. V, p. 82.

good points of the older catechismal tradition, especially the simple divisions based on the cardinal truths. He himself possessed the requisite theological knowledge, and, in consequence of his long familiarity with this work, also the practical experience indispensable for the writing of a catechism.

39. A Schema for the Composition of a Small Catechism was presented to the Fathers of the Vatican Council, the salient points of which were: a uniform catechism should be composed with Bellarmine's as a model; it should be translated into various languages, every bishop being left free to add an appendix written with a view to the needs and conditions of his diocese; the text proper of the catechism, however, must remain unaltered. The Roman Catechism, moreover, is strongly recommended to priests.

Forty-one speakers expressed their views on the schema. Some brought forward reasons against a uniform catechism: the differences among children, the difference in nationalities and educational facilities were insisted upon; it was also pointed out that the liberty of bishops would be curtailed.

The reasons adduced in favor of a uniform catechism were weightier: unity of doctrine would be more easily preserved; uniformity in teaching is more needed now than it ever was, since many children spend even their earliest years in different dioceses; certain shortcomings that might easily creep into diocesan catechisms are forestalled by a uniform catechism; the prestige of the catechism would be enhanced if it were introduced in the name of the whole episcopate.

After these debates the schema was once more thoroughly worked over and slightly changed: other catechetical models besides Bellarmine's were to be consulted; the bishops should be allowed to make additions to the text, provided these were conspicuously indicated by a change of type; translations need not be verbal as long as they render the meaning of the original faithfully.

The Council never took final action in the matter.

VI. THE LATEST CATECHETICAL MOVEMENT [1]

40. Leaders of the Movement. — During the last ten years a strong movement has been set on foot by practical catechists, — and it has also gained adherents among theoretical exponents of this science — with a view to improving, and as far as possible perfecting, catechisms and catechetical instruction. Southern Germany and Austria are more especially to the front in this work. It was launched by the Society of Catechists of Munich, and their official organ, Katechetischen Blätter, — a paper in the field for a long time, — was pressed into service for the discussion and diffusion of its plan of reform. Their efforts were ably seconded by the Christlich-pädagogischen Blätter of Vienna, the organ of the Society of Catechists of that city.

41. Negative Factors. — The causes to which the movement owes its growth are partly negative, and partly positive. Among the former we may quote:

[1] In this connection Bishop Bellord's Religious Education and its Failures, Ave Maria Press, 1901, is very valuable. See also for full account of the Munich Method: Cath. Encyclopedia, vol. V, pp. 85–86; American Eccl. Review, January and May, 1908. For a succinct report of the first Catechetical Congress for German-speaking Countries, see: Cath. Educat. Review, Sept., 1913, p. 133 ff. The ideas here developed were exhaustively discussed at this congress.

1. The shortcomings of existing catechisms and present-day catechetical methods, and the resultant dissatisfaction. Among such defects were enumerated: an overabundance of material, which prevents in most cases, where but a short period of time is available, a thorough exposition of the truths of faith; the use of abstract language, ill-suited to the child-mind; the treatment of the matter after the manner of scientific theology, setting out from abstract general concepts. This method was called the "analytical" method, although in the phraseology of Aristotelian philosophy it should be called the "synthetic" method.

As is often the case with movements born from practical needs, some went too far at first in counteracting the defects complained of. Thus, e.g., in the search for childlike expressions all definitions were rejected. But gradually the points at issue became clearer, and at present all are fully agreed on this: the ideal catechism — if it ever come into existence — should not be written exclusively from a theoretical viewpoint; neither should it be based entirely on practical requirements. Both sides ought to be taken into consideration: the catechism should be composed under the supervision of able theologians so that no statement of doctrine shall creep in that is not absolutely safe; and it should enlist the co-operation of capable and experienced teachers, so that its expressions shall be adapted to youthful minds.

The method thus far quite generally followed in catechization, i.e., the "analytical" or exegetical method, came in for a large share of adverse criticism. The adherents of the Munich school oppose to it their own method, which they called at first the psychological, then, after one of its best-known exponents, the Stieglitz method. It is now generally known as the Munich method. The many objections urged against the "analytical" method have to do not so much with the method itself, as with the one-sided use made of it; and on this point untrained catechists have much to answer for.

2. Another negative factor in the reform movement: the shortcomings in the preparatory training for the catechetical office. The reason for this deplorable lack of theoretical training is that the theory of catechetics in many places is imparted mechanically: rules, perhaps singly valuable and practical, are inculcated in great abundance, but without reference to underlying fundamental principles. This came about because the above-mentioned great catechists, such as Gruber, had once more been lost sight of. Jungmann's Catechetics is entirely free from this defect. It has not enjoyed, however, the success it deserves, partly because of its being included in the author's larger work on Sacred Eloquence.

It must be granted also that until the present day, catechists, when entering upon their work, have had little practical experience. This could be gained by assisting at instructions under the direction of capable catechists, and by experimental lessons given under the supervision of a practical teacher. This lack of previous experience is largely attributable to the unfavorable school conditions obtaining in many districts.

42. The Positive Factors. — The positive factors at

work in this new movement have been partly mentioned. They are the catechetical societies with regularly recurring meetings, at which papers are read and stimulating discussions take place; also the catechetical magazines. To the above-quoted organs of the Munich and Vienna catechetical societies may be added the Katechetische Monatschrift of Münster. Besides, there are pedagogical courses on catechetical methods, which are held with great success in Salzburg, Munich, Vienna, and Lucerne. Over and above all these there is the laudable desire to vie with the progressive pedagogy of the day. If this rivalry proves to be stimulating in many respects, it also gives rise to one-sided and incorrect views. Catechetical science encounters here the same difficulties that would beset the science of homiletics if it were to take over bodily the rules of profane oratory. It should never be overlooked that the end we have in view in our catechetical work is entirely supernatural, and that religious instruction is not to be put on the same level with ordinary school lessons; but in common with the sermon it conveys spiritual truths. Profane learning aims at the natural development of the soul's faculties, and the acquisition of natural virtues; religious training strives to build up in us supernatural virtues.

43. Conclusion: The Conditions of Success in Catechization. — This historical retrospect has enabled us to gain a deeper insight into the qualifications of an efficient catechist. A good catechism no doubt is of some importance, but in the last analysis the success of all catechetical work depends on the catechist himself, in so far at least that a capable catechist can do more with a poor catechism than an untrained catechist can do with the best of books.

What then is required for the thorough training of catechists? First of all, a good theoretical foundation. As regards the fundamental principles, Jungmann's theory is thorough and reliable, and we shall not deviate from it in any important point. His directions, however, need to be methodically arranged and completed as to details. This we shall endeavor to do as far as possible in the present volume.

In the second place, practical preparation is necessary; but this would still be insufficient.

Thirdly, a thorough theological and especially dogmatical training is as important for this work as it is for the office of preaching. The Roman Catechism affords valuable help in this regard.

Lastly, the priestly spirit. It fills the catechist with love for his work; it spurs him on to zealous endeavors that seek an outlet in a thousand different ways unknown to the indifferent; it makes light the sacrifices that efficient catechization necessarily entails. Whoever is filled with true priestly zeal brings to his task that cheerfulness and equanimity of mind without which one cannot gain the children for Jesus. Such an one values highly the supernatural character of his office; he endeavors to impart, not mere knowledge, but the spirit of faith, and to awaken the life of faith; he builds on the grace of God and uses all means requisite to obtain the help and assistance of the Holy Ghost.

Herewith we have also laid bare the fundamental cause of the manifold shortcomings in catechization: no doubt, there has been and there still is a painful lack of theoretical and practical preparation for the work in our seminaries and universities; but the ultimate cause of all failures in the religious education of our youth is traceable to a lack of theological and ascetical progress. The whole history of catechization confirms this view.

For a short notice on the life and works of Joseph Jungmann, S. J. (1830–1885), whose treatise is largely followed in this volume, see: Cath. Encycl. vol. VIII, p. 566.

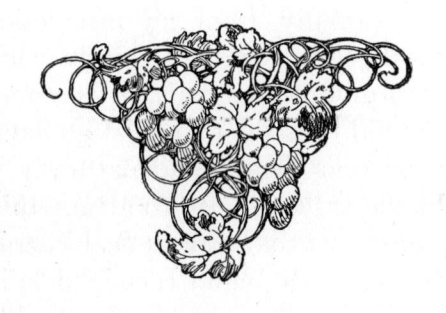

PART II

CATECHETICAL INSTRUCTION

44.

SUMMARY. — This subject is treated under three heads, answering the following three questions:

1. What is the direct aim of catechetical instruction? For, the end the catechist has in view must determine the means he shall use. We refer here to the "direct" aim of catechetical instruction, because in this second part we have to consider the theory of catechization especially from an instructional viewpoint. We shall, however, realize right along that it is impossible to divorce religious instruction from religious training, and that the two must go hand in hand. The second question then would naturally be: What means should the catechist use to attain this end? It is clear from the outset that catechetical instruction consists in imparting to the child certain definite notions in such a manner that they may be thoroughly grasped, and lead to the end we have set before us. Hence the second question resolves itself into the following two:

2. What should the children be taught? What constitutes the subject-matter of catechetical instruction?

3. In what manner shall the matter be presented to the mind, so that the end may be attained, i.e., what is the right method to be followed in catechetical instruction?

CHAPTER I

THE END OF CATECHETICAL INSTRUCTION

I. The End in Itself

First Principle. — *The direct aim of catechetical instruction is not the training of the natural faculty of cognition, but the development of the supernatural virtue of faith* .

45.

EXPLANATION. — As in every Christian, we must distinguish in the baptized child two orders of cognition: the natural and the supernatural. The natural faculty of cognition belongs to every rational creature, and is called understanding, reason, thought, or, sometimes, from its manifold activities, introspection, discrimination, self-consciousness.

In baptism man receives a supernatural power of cognition: the infused virtue of faith.[1] The latter is not a special faculty after the manner of the intellect, but must be conceived as an habitual, permanent property of the intellect itself, elevating it to a perfection which it could not attain of its own nature; viz. a perfection consisting in this, that "through the inspiration and co-operation of divine grace the mind is enabled to hold as true whatever God has revealed,

[1] Con. Vat., *De fide catholica*, cap. IV.

not because of the internal evidence of the mysteries grasped by the natural light of reason, but because of the authority of God who reveals them, who can neither deceive nor be deceived." [1]

Man's natural faculty of cognition, as well as the virtue of faith, is capable of perfection. This is proved:

1. By our own natural desire of knowledge, which is an inclination and an impulse to exercise and enlarge our knowledge. Experience proves that this desire stimulates man in the natural order, while, together with the habitual virtue of faith, God also infuses into the soul the desire for more complete supernatural knowledge; and this accounts for the avidity with which the child, not prematurely and forcibly corrupted, imbibes the Christian verities. Reason and Revelation, however, both warn us to direct this desire for knowledge into right channels, thus to fructify the most precious talents the Lord has given us.

2. The following analysis, based entirely on daily experience, affords a further proof, and at the same time an explanation, of the perfectibility of reason and faith. The development of the mind is continually taking place in three directions: in extent, for new objects and truths are constantly brought within our range of knowledge, which thus grows in volume, and develops into erudition; in intensity: when the mind does not rest satisfied with knowing what is, but seeks the how and why, tries to penetrate to the ultimate causes; this is knowledge or science, properly speaking, viz., the knowing of things in their causes; it is true and thorough culture; in time: for the maturely devel-

[1] *Ibid.*, cap. III.

oped mind retains habitual possession of the extensive knowledge acquired through intensive study.

The growth of supernatural knowledge may be analyzed in a similar manner.

As more truths are learned by faith, it grows in extent, develops in volume: the advanced scholar in this respect outranks the beginner. Intensive progress in faith depends upon various factors: first of all upon a deepening insight into the motives of faith, into the how and why of each revealed truth in so far as the human mind may search for comprehension and demonstration in these matters. Hence, considered in itself, the faith of the theologian must be more intensive, for he is able to prove why he should believe in the Real Presence, how the same must be understood, why Christ desires to remain with us. In the second place, the intensity of faith increases with the steadfastness and completeness of our own free submission to God included in faith; and in this respect the simple Christian may surpass the most learned theologian. In the third place, a vivid operative faith is more intensive than an indifferent, slumbering faith, just as in profane sciences greater proficiency is gained when theoretical knowledge goes hand in hand with practical applications.

Finally, faith is perfected when, through the assimilation of as large a body of truths as possible, and their permanent retention based on deep insight and constant practice, it becomes habitual, lasting, and even under adverse circumstances continues to be a guiding beacon light throughout a Christian's whole life.

It is easily seen that, among all the factors making for a perfect faith, the steadfastness of our own free submission, the active exercise of faith and staunch perseverance in it, are the most important. One might acquire a wide and thorough knowledge of religious matters, and yet not have true supernatural faith. From this fact we shall soon draw important conclusions (No. 51, No. 56).

46. Proof of Our Principle. — Since natural and supernatural knowledge can and must be perfected, it is easily seen that the proper and paramount object of catechetical instruction is the training and development of faith. For the development of the children's natural faculty of cognition by all the profane branches of learning is directly provided for in our schools, and outside of the schoolroom many influences contribute their share towards it, such as intercourse between members of the family and friends, reading, meetings, lectures, etc. Some school branches promote more especially the development of the memory, on which even today too much stress is laid sometimes, e.g., literature, history, natural history. The intellect is developed by the study of mathematics, philosophy, and to some extent, although indirectly, by language studies. School exercises and reviews are intended to secure the permanent retention of the knowledge thus acquired.

But by whom and how shall faith be built up? Numerous are the influences which, in good Christian families and communities, contribute to fostering, in its various aspects as above described, the life of faith in the child. But the school should take up this work systematically and thoroughly; and even profane studies, in the hands of good teachers, can be made valuable adjuncts, at least indirectly. But the building up of the life of faith is directly and pre-eminently the work of the catechist. This special task is assigned to him by episcopal authority, which, in turn, is derived from Christ Himself: Go and teach all nations. To impart to the children a knowledge of the true faith as the source of all true supernatural life: that is the proper object of catechetical instruction. Expressed in our first thesis, it marks the pivotal point around which center all subsequent rules concerning the aim of catechetical instruction, so that we may designate these rules as mere "conclusions." The more important of these, however, we shall state as separate principles.

II. Conclusions

47. First Conclusion. — *Catechetical instruction indirectly also develops the mind; nay it helps to bring the child's natural reason to the highest degree of perfection.*

It might seem out of place to deduce this conclusion from our first thesis, which was not concerned with the perfection of natural reason as an object of catechization. And yet this conclusion is legitimate. For faith is subjectively and objectively a true and even the highest perfection also of natural reason. Subjectively it is a virtue infused into the intellect. As the virtues, directly rooted in the will and heart, perfect these faculties, so does faith elevate and perfect reason.

This perfection of course directly relates to supernatural knowledge; but the latter is exercised by the one human reason, and the power communicated to it by faith must also indirectly benefit its natural activities. Objectively considered, faith imparts the highest truths. Now the acquisition of every new truth constitutes a perfecting of the spiritual cognitional faculty, and thus faith leads reason to the highest level of perfection. And again, the influence of faith is not limited to supernatural truths; for these in turn diffuse an abundant light on every province of natural science. Widening the field of knowledge into the infinite, making secure the very foundations of natural knowledge, warning against errors, fostering the feeling of responsibility: these and other benefits faith procures to natural reason. And since, notwithstanding the legitimate distinction between the natural and the supernatural order, the ultimate and highest aim of all life is supernatural, faith is a sure pledge of the highest perfection to which natural reason may attain in the present order.

The same conclusion is reached when we analyze faith with regard to its end (*finaliter*) or its origin (*causaliter*). Faith in every way furthers all human knowledge; it is a participation of the divine knowledge, the source of all natural and supernatural wisdom. Hence our first conclusion is well founded in every respect.

48. Second Conclusion. — *Catechization viewed as instruction is not a branch co-ordinated with other school branches, and only partly or accidentally distinct from* *them: but it is superior to all other instruction, and essentially distinct from it.*

Many educationists — non-Catholics among them — grant that religious instruction is entitled to first place in the school curriculum. It would be erroneous, however, to conclude therefrom that it ranks above other branches in the same manner as, e.g., reading and writing rank above geography. There is no question here of an accidental, but of an essential difference, something easily overlooked when "Religion" as a branch of study is put alongside the other branches. The difference between the two is as fundamental as that between a school study and life, between the natural and the supernatural order, between the useful and the needful.

And this differentiation should be outwardly marked; hence prayer before, after, and during catechism lessons should never be omitted. In former times the catechism was taught in church by the priest vested in surplice; in many places this custom has survived. It were at least desirable that the priest always appear in his cassock, unless very grave reasons militate against it. However, let him never forget that he is engaged upon a religious task, which becomes insipid when losing its supernatural unction. Also the examinations in religion must be carefully differentiated from all other examinations, and it would be a deplorable mistake to turn them into an exhibition of feats of memory. In chapter 3 we shall return to this subject. It is also desirable to bring out clearly in the school reports this difference between religion and other branches, e.g., by devoting to it a special place in the list of subjects. The children should be constantly reminded of the distinction between the hour devoted to religious instruction, and the other branches.

SECOND PRINCIPLE. — *In catechetical instruction the priest should appear before the children as the messenger of God and the Church, and he should endeavor to base their faith in God's word which he teaches, on God's authority, and the testimony of the Church.*

This statement also formulates a conclusion from the first thesis; for as we shall proceed to show, it follows from the nature and the properties of supernatural faith, the training and development of which is the main object of catechization.

49. The First Part of the Thesis, i.e., that the catechist is the messenger of God and the Church, follows from the manner in which God intended supernatural faith to be spread among men, viz., not by means of human speculation, as is the case with philosophical truths; not by means of teachers in the ordinary sense, who establish their doctrines by arguments from reason or human authority; not by means of private illumination vouchsafed to individuals; but by means of messengers, witnesses, delegates, empowered by God and testifying to objective facts.

St. Augustine expresses our thesis in one word when, in speaking of catechetical instruction, he designates it constantly by the word "narration." For "narration" is but an objective statement of facts, which statement is accepted on faith by the hearers because of the credibility of the witness.

"Faith," the Apostle tells us, "cometh by hearing, and hearing by the word of Christ." Rom. 10, 17. And the whole history of revelation shows that this is and must be the case. To teach mankind supernatural truths, divine wisdom always had recourse to credible witnesses. In the plenitude of time the Son of God Himself appeared as "the faithful witness" (Apoc. 1, 5) "to declare" to man the knowledge of God which He alone possessed in the bosom of the Father; "what He speaks He knows, and testifies what He has seen," and the sin of unbelief consists in this, that "His testimony has not been received." I John, 3, 11.

Hence the task of those whom the Lord has deputed as the messengers of truth on earth consists in giving testimony of Him and His doctrine before the world: "You shall receive the power of the Holy Ghost coming upon you and you shall be WITNESSES unto me in Jerusalem and in all Judea and Samaria, and even unto the uttermost parts of the earth." Acts, 1, 8. Therefore "hath God raised Him up the third day, and gave Him to be made manifest not to all the people but to WITNESSES preordained by God."

It was therefore the will of the supreme Founder and Lord of the Church that the truths of revelation should be preserved and spread by witnesses whose testimony should be believed because they had seen and heard what they preached, and to whom He had promised the never-failing assistance of the Holy Ghost to preserve them from all error.

When seeking to determine how to proceed in teaching the doctrines of faith, we must have regard above all to the will of Him who is their "beginning and end." Hence the truths declared by God and testified to as such by the Church, must be presented to the children as based on this infallible testimony; they must receive them and assent to them on the authority of God Himself.

In the catechisms of the Middle Ages the question is assigned to the child, and the answer to the teacher; this is also the case in the larger catechism of Bellarmine. A Protestant scholar claims to discover in this arrangement the true spirit of the Catholic Middle Ages, according to which the teaching Church alone is the organ of all truth, which is to be kept inviolate by her and taught to the human race. This conception is undoubtedly the true one; only it denotes the Catholic spirit not only of the Middle Ages, but of Christian antiquity and of modern times as well.

The Church always knew but one way by which men could come into possession of supernatural truth: to receive it from her, and to acknowledge and believe it on her authority.

We have already indicated (No. 7) in what way the ministers of the Church share the power to teach in the name of Christ. The Apostles and their successors, the Pope and the bishops, exercise the teaching office as the direct representatives of God in matters of faith; through their word faith comes, is nourished and spread; and for the children also the Pope and the bishops are the immediate representatives of Christ. By virtue of an old custom, and for reasons readily understood, the Pope and bishops may appoint representatives and helpers: catechists belong to this class.

The catechist's place in the magisterium of the Church is therefore evident: he is directly the delegate of the Church, indirectly the delegate of Christ, whilst the bishop, exercising the catechetical office, is not the messenger of the Church, but in the literal meaning of the word, the messenger of God. Every catechist may say: I am an ambassador of Christ, but in the case of the bishop, the expression is to be understood literally.

> Our theory, so openly advocating authoritative teaching, is not likely to meet with favor from those many moderns who are averse to the claim of authority. This, however, need not disconcert us. Förster discourses thus on the authoritative character of even profane teaching: "Many young teachers imagine that they must set out to gain their pupils by putting themselves on a familiar footing with them. . . . They are mistaken. The teacher should not put himself on the same level with his charges, but should appear before them clad with authority. He owes this to the representative character of his position. He has no right what-

ever to be primarily a companion. He himself represents that higher learning to which the young are to be introduced through the school. When he has succeeded in bringing home to the pupils this fundamental characteristic of his profession, by his outward earnest bearing, then he can afford, without danger, to become their friend: his condescension will be doubly appreciated, and work no harm."

50. The Representative of God Before the Children. — How should the catechist proceed in order that the children may indeed come to look upon him as the messenger of God and the Church?

(*a*) He must instruct them to that effect; he must tell the children so plainly, not only the younger ones who begin catechism, but for the others also the explanation should be explicitly repeated from time to time. He must tell them again and again what his position is with regard to them, and make sure that they understand it thoroughly. They are not looking for scientific proofs of his mission, but for a simple correct explanation of it: parents need not prove to their children who they are, but must nevertheless make clear their position to them.

It may be done in this manner: I come to you, dear children, as the messenger of God and the bishop. Do you know what a messenger is? (One may recall here, or explain if necessary, Gen. 37: Jacob sent Joseph to his brethren in the field. Joseph was to tell them many things from his father; Joseph was therefore the messenger of his father.) Thus also God has sent His Only-Begotten Son to us as His Messenger. And the Saviour Himself sent His Apostles: go through the whole world, and tell all people what you have heard me teach. Thus the Apostles were the messengers of Christ to men. Now, the Saviour can do all things; He is almighty, and He has taken care that the Apostles were good messengers: they have told nothing but what they had heard the Saviour teach. But the Apostles had to die, and therefore Christ has willed that there should always be new messengers from Him until the end of the world: they are the bishops and the Popes of Rome. What is the name of the present Holy Father, and of our bishop? (Show their pictures.) The messenger whom Jesus Christ has sent to you is the bishop; but he himself cannot come to all churches or schools; therefore he orders priests to speak in his name, and to teach what Jesus Christ has taught. You see then that the bishop has sent me to you so that I might tell you what the Divine Saviour has said and done and prescribed.

In this way you bring before the children (1) Christ Himself, the Son of God and Founder of the Church; (2) the teaching Church in its concrete embodiment: the Pope and bishops. In this manner it becomes easy to instil in them reverence for God, the Church, and their messenger: the catechist.

(b) The second means towards the above-indicated end is to appear before them in a manner worthy of the high position of a divine messenger. In the chapter on Discipline we shall have more to say on this subject.

51. The Second Part of the Second Thesis follows directly from the notion of faith. Faith, the Catholic Faith, is a supernatural assent to what God has revealed because He has revealed it, and because it is attested as such by the Church, i.e., the messengers sent by God Himself.[1] And this holds also for those truths which may be discovered by natural reason alone: e.g., when we believe God's wisdom, omnipotence, justice, or when we believe the immortality of the soul, our belief is founded not on any natural grounds which may also lead to a knowledge of these

---

[1] Con. Vat., *De fide catholica*, cap. III.

truths, but on the infallible word of the Lord. Hence catechization must be conducted in such a manner that the children admit the truths proposed to them on God's authority.

How is this end to be attained? A distinct help is found (a) in the conviction imparted to the children that the catechist is the representative of God. Yet since it remains true that (b) only a divinely ordained messenger can claim faith in his teaching, the catechist must take care to lay down the doctrine of the infallible magisterium of the Church, merely explaining it at first (No. 50), but corroborating it with proofs later on, proofs of course that are suited to the age of the pupils. (c) The catechist should propound all doctrines, even those attainable by natural reason, as objectively the word of God. "Thus speaketh the Lord": this was the way the prophets taught.

The many objections urged against such a thoroughly authoritative catechismal teaching may be readily answered by pointing to the manner of proceeding in other branches of the school curriculum: does the child always see the underlying reasons for every one of the teacher's statements? E.g., why the customary multiplication method is right? And not only the child, but even the scholar admits many truths on the authority of others, and not because he has demonstrated them to his own satisfaction.

Bishop Theodoret of Cyrus wrote thus in the fifth century: "Are we not constantly leaning on faith, even in human concerns? Can any one, without faith in another, learn an art, undertake an ocean trip, be a farmer; will he, without it, submit to medical treatment when sick? Knowledge is not the property of every one, but only of those who through assiduous application and long experience have acquired a mastery of the subject in question. . . . It is therefore a contradictory and altogether inadmissible theory that, while in every other science the teacher dispenses knowledge which the pupil takes for granted, in matters of religion the opposite should be the case, and understanding should precede faith."

And Origen long before had answered the attacks of Celsus on "undemonstrated faith": "Our opponents cannot reconcile themselves to the fact that we demand faith in God's and the Church's testimony; yet they themselves do likewise. For when one turns to philosophy and subscribes to the tenets of a given school because the theories of one of its teachers please him, is he influenced in his action by anything else save by the belief that that school is the better one? . . . If therefore it is reasonable to believe in the founder of a Greek or barbarian school, why should it not be even more reasonable to believe in God the Lord, in Him who teaches He must be adored, while all other beings must be held of no account since they are nothing; or if they are something, can claim only respect, but not adoration or reverence?"[1]

THIRD PRINCIPLE. — *The catechist, therefore, must endeavor to awaken and cultivate and bring to its highest perfection in the child's soul a feeling of unconditional and absolute dependence upon God and of complete submission to the authority of the Church.*

52. Explanation. — This is also a conclusion from our first thesis. (1) The assent of faith is indeed an act of reason; yet, it is not necessitated, but is completed by a free act of the will. The act of faith is an act of the intellect, but also at the same time an act of obedience (compare the quotation from the Vatican Council's Dogmatic Constitution on Catholic Faith given below) of free submission by the created mind to the absolute authority of its Creator. Essentially, then, faith de-

[1] *Contra Celsum*, I, cc. 10, 11.

pends upon an inclination of the will to subject reason also to God. (2) But how is the word of God presented to man's mind? Not in any miraculous manner, as was done to Moses in the Burning Bush; not by direct inspiration from God; but through the intermediary of the Church. She, and she only, is the legitimate organ of God's revelation, and this she proves to every man according to his intellectual capacity. To the scholar she demonstrates it with scientific precision; to the unlearned she proves it first by her own wonderful existence, which suffices to ground her authoritative teaching. But gradually she adduces further testimony, pointing to her sanctity, supernatural permanence, and credibility founded on miracles, as irrefragable proofs of her divine mission. Besides the willingness to submit completely to God's word, faith also presupposes the unconditional admission of the authority of the Church.

"The more a Christian is imbued with the feeling of complete dependence upon God, the humbler he is in spirit, or to use the words of Christ, 'the poorer he is in spirit,' the more completely his soul opens to the light from above, the more closely he clings to the Church, the deeper faith takes root in his heart, actively governing and directing his life. To foster this poverty of spirit was no doubt the aim of Divine Wisdom when making the knowledge of supernatural truth dependent upon submission to the witnesses appointed by Him. And it also must be the chief aim of every priest to foster and develop in the child this poverty of spirit, this humility and simplicity of heart, this feeling of unconditional surrender of all finite knowledge to Infinite Wisdom."

Only when the catechist has thoroughly imbued the child with these feelings will the latter's faith be firm enough to withstand future assaults of doubt, and to submit to the living magisterium of the Church in all things, convinced that, while our own reason often falls short, a divine institution cannot err or deceive.

Besides authoritative, and at times explanatory, teaching when circumstances demand it, there are other means of cultivating successfully this attitude of mind, viz., frequently praying the act of faith, instilling into the children great reverence for God, the Saviour and His Church, often repeating, explaining, and inculcating the following words of the Vatican Council: "Since man is entirely dependent upon God as his Creator and Supreme Lord, and since created reason is entirely subject to uncreated Truth, we are bound entirely to submit our intelligence and will, by faith, to God's Revelation." Const. dogm. de fide catholica, cap. III.

53. That Catechist Offends against the second and third principles who sets out by adducing in the first place proofs from reason for the truths of faith, and only afterwards brings forth proofs from Revelation, as if the latter were secondary. In this way children are trained to accept the doctrines of faith because they understand or believe they understand them. Even our preaching for adults should not lay too much stress on proofs from reason to the detriment of those from Revelation: the latter are the essential and primary proofs of sacred eloquence. And this applies with even greater force to catechization. In the lower school grades arguments from reason are altogether superfluous. In the higher grades, however, they should be given, so that the children may not go out into a godless world unequipped for the battle which faces them. But these arguments from reason should never usurp the place of the proofs from revelation, and in familiarizing the pupils with them the teacher must avoid whatever might weaken faith, or leave the impression that they are essential and all-sufficient foundations of faith. When treating of the catechetical method, we shall have more to say on this point.

Gruber touches upon and criticizes the above-mentioned faulty method, which, in the rationalistic period in which he lived, as well as at all other times, led to deplorable consequences. "This mistake is almost universally made in catechetical instruction. The teacher dwells on the notions of omnipotence, wisdom, goodness, justice, sanctity, spirituality, eternity, all the important attributes of God, and treats of them from a natural standpoint, as deduced from our knowledge of the soul's properties. When the children have been sufficiently tortured in the endeavor to make them comprehend these properties of the soul, — and besides the questions are often asked in such a manner that they answer yes or no as fancy dictates because they have failed to grasp the truths explained — and the teacher at last believes he has given them a clear notion of God's attributes, he then brings forward the authority of revelation thus: God has revealed all this about Himself in Holy Writ. He quotes one or more texts at random, and is convinced he has done all that is required of him after he has made the children repeat the text and explained it to them to show that what God has revealed agrees perfectly with what our reason tells us. Is it not abundantly plain that in the child's mind the authority of God is relegated in this way to second place, that the children are trained to look upon religion as a product of their own mind, while they do it a great honor indeed in establishing to their own satisfaction that God teaches the selfsame truths they have discovered without His aid? Is it not evident that the young Christian, with all his knowledge of religion, is misled since he learns to look upon himself as the originator of his religion, and returns no thanks to God Who has vouchsafed to him a knowledge of the same? And how much more serious are the consequences when besides, all unconsciously, the conviction grows upon him that he needs to hold fast to these self-discovered truths only as long as they please his fancy, and can let go of them, as of mere man-made theories, as soon as they begin to pall him. At this juncture, the authority of God relegated to the background in the first place, and used merely to buttress what he had already discovered by personal exertion, will no longer avail to stay the assaults of sensuality upon the self-originated convictions of his mind. And even if the outcome should not be so deplorable, is it not the height of pride for a man tossed to and fro by the storms of passion, to hold fast to his religious principles only because he has personally discovered them?"

It is almost superfluous to add that Gruber does not intend to condemn all proofs from reason and to reject all explanation of divine doctrines based on analogies from the natural order. He merely inveighs against excesses in this regard.

54. A Second Mistake: excessive and inappropriate questioning. The positive character of the doctrines of faith stands in direct opposition to that tendency which favors the child drawing upon his own mind as the source of all knowledge. Ill-advised socratizing, as far as it means excessive questioning, has been fully criticized above, No. 36.

Gruber has the following with regard to inappropriate questioning: "Sometimes catechists ask questions which make the religious doctrine under consideration appear as doubtful or erroneous; e.g., how is it possible that God is everywhere: I do not see Him? — Or: Perhaps the world came into existence of itself? Or: Our bodies return to dust; how can they rise again? Sometimes, in order, as they think, to make themselves better understood, they use expressions which are unbecoming in connection with God's word. Thus a catechist in order to make clear the expression, 'a virtue infused into the soul by God,' asked the question: Does God pour virtue into the soul by means of a funnel? Such language is calculated to destroy completely the authority of God, often already sufficiently thrown into the background. Religion is made to appear as the product of human reason; unarticulated doubts rise up in the child's mind: is the teacher really sure of the doctrine he proposes? Religion as faith ceases to exist, and the human knowledge acquired is not only sterile, but it becomes subject to those ceaseless changes of opinion which are the fate of all human science."

In extenuation of these shortcomings it might be argued: questions like the above, while seemingly casting doubt upon doctrines of faith, are but analogous to the methodical doubt so useful in science and cannot really unsettle the mind. But the point is not well taken. In scientific work the methodical doubt serves a useful purpose, and St. Thomas himself introduces his disquisitions on the most uncontrovertible dogmas by such a doubt: it would appear that God does not exist. Children, however, are unable to distinguish between various kinds of doubt and are therefore easily led into error. If objections against faith are to be met, — and they should undoubtedly be met towards the end of the school curriculum, — it must be done without injury to the impressionable soul of the child.

One might proceed in this manner: you have learned that the resurrection of the body is absolutely certain, for Christ Himself said so, who cannot deceive us. Yet there are people who deny what Christ has taught. They say: our bodies crumble into dust, and how can they come to life again? How can you answer these unbelievers? You can answer briefly thus: God has made man out of the dust of the earth; therefore He can also call back to life the body that has returned to dust. Yet often it may happen, children, that you are unable to answer such people correctly, and therefore I advise you not to argue with them overmuch, or to converse with them only on other topics.

55. A Third Failing often met with during the rationalistic period consisted herein, that in religious instruction the doctrines of "natural religion" and of "revealed religion" were too sharply marked off, in an endeavor to educate the children first as "sensible men" and only then as "Christians."

Although it is obvious that many religious truths may be apprehended by reason alone, and that the act of faith presupposes a certain knowledge of God (preambles of faith), this sharp differentiation between natural and supernatural truths is fraught with great danger.

For, 1. The effort to have the child master the preambles of faith is superfluous, as he is long since in possession of them. Moreover, that teacher labors under a delusion who imagines that the child can grasp metaphysical proofs: the road to faith best adapted to the child is the authority of his parents and teachers, not philosophical argumentation. 2. It easily leads one to think that man belongs to two different orders: the natural and the supernatural; yet the Christian's life is wholly centered in the supernatural order. 3. This distinction may give rise to pride and arrogance, leading man to believe that, unaided, he can discover natural religion. He can indeed, and should discover it, but in reality the majority of men fail to do so.

Jungmann's teaching with regard to the preambles of faith is as follows: "It is certain that all supernatural knowledge presupposes the natural knowledge of God, together with some of His attributes. But any priest who thinks it is his duty to impart this knowledge first is mistaken. The ground has been prepared for him: when the children come to catechism the first time, they are already in possession of this preliminary knowledge, viz., the existence of God and the other requisite notions that go naturally with it. For this preliminary knowledge need not be, in every Christian, the result of personal investigation and dialectic argumentation: by far the majority of people have no other means of attaining to this knowledge than instruction from others in whom they believe. And their conviction of the truth of what they learn rests exclusively or almost entirely on the testimony of credible persons. Now the children who start catechism have not led a vegetative or animal life: they have not come from the desert, but from the parental home with its Christian atmosphere. The speech and the life of those with whom they dwelt, more especially the training given them by a pious mother who taught them to fold their tiny hands in prayer and to invoke the infinitely Holy, Omniscient, and Omnipresent God, has long ago bred in them the conviction that the Lord of Heaven is their Creator, Father, and God; that to His invisible majesty they owe adoration and submission. The grace of the Holy Ghost which they have received in baptism, has strengthened this conviction and made it the firm basis on which to build religious knowledge and Christian character. Under those circumstances the catechist cannot consider the child's mind as a *tabula rasa*, and it is a waste of time to set forth learned metaphysical proofs to establish that which the mind is unable to grasp. The inevitable result of such a proceeding is to mar the openness and simplicity of the child's soul, and to upset the firm convictions thus far acquired: for since the children hear the catechist treat of God's existence as of an unknown fact that needs to be demonstrated, and are unable to grasp the proofs adduced, the outcome is: doubt and uncertainty."[1]

FOURTH PRINCIPLE. — *The children must be thoroughly imbued with the conviction that the only true, perfect, and divinely ordained faith is the one which manifests itself in works, effectually influences one's life, becomes a living faith.*

56. Explanation of the Principle.

— We do not intend here to contrast the Catholic doctrine of faith with the many false views concerning it, and to prove that (1) a faith limited to the admission of revealed truths, without any accompanying works (a dead faith), is not the one ordained by God; nor do we intend to prove (2) the truth of the Tridentine Council's decree: Any one saying that when sanctifying grace has been lost by sin, faith also is lost at the same time, or that the faith which remains is not a true, although not a living faith, let him be anathema.

[1] "The first religious instruction which we children received was given by our mother. There being quite a difference in our ages, she took one child every morning and taught us to pray the Our Father, the Hail Mary, the Creed, morning, evening, and meal prayers, the Angelus, etc. The older children had to lead in prayer. We also went to Mass daily. God's omnipresence and His knowledge of even our most secret thoughts were vividly held up to us, and as a consequence the oft-repeated injunction: Remember God's presence, left a particularly strong impress upon our minds. Our Guardian Angels and the Saints were also represented as the constant witnesses of all our thoughts and actions. Great modesty was enjoined, together with this fundamental doctrine of the omnipresence of the All Pure and All Holy, as well as strict veracity." Ringseis, in Hist. Pol. Blätter, LXXV, 401. Not all children, alas, are brought up in this manner, but fortunately mothers and families of this stamp are still met with in great numbers. Do children educated in this way need any metaphysical proofs of the existence of God or the immortality of the soul?

Presently we are concerned with the didactic-pedagogical reasons that compel us to lay stress on this self-evident truth.

1. The aim of catechetical instruction is to build up faith in the soul. But what is faith? What does it embrace? The doctrines of faith are not mere theoretical statements, but most of them are at the same time practical norms for the conduct of life. According to the teaching of Holy Writ and the Fathers, according to the deep conviction of the Church as manifested in the baptismal rite, faith in its fulness demands also the complete submission of the heart to the rules recognized by the light of revelation. It is that faith operating through charity which the catechumens, according to Apostolic tradition, demand of the Church before baptism, when they ask faith that gives life everlasting; and this faith cannot give without hope and charity. (Con. Trid., sessio VI, cap. VII.) Hence religious instruction must not stop at the theoretical exposition of truth; it must go farther, and translate those doctrines into practice, as far as circumstances will allow. In this regard religious instruction is on a level with the other practical branches of the school curriculum: no teacher may rest content with theoretical instruction only, e.g., how to hold the pen; but he must give the child practical exercises in holding the pen right. Our subsequent exposé of the catechetical method shall make this clearer.

2. Another reason why the self-evident truth expressed in the above thesis is insisted upon is this: in many diocesan catechisms faith, hope, and charity are so sharply differentiated, that the children might infer

these various expressions of the religious life to be really distinct from one another, and especially that faith has nothing in common with the commandments and with the practical life as a whole. Incoherence, formalism, and superficiality in the religious life might result. Catechists of deeper insight favor a division of the catechism in accordance with the Roman Catechism: the Symbol, the Sacraments, the Decalog, the Lord's Prayer. This at first sight "external" and therefore often criticized division is nevertheless one that makes for a well-rounded and strong religious life in the children. No matter, however, on what pattern the diocesan catechism may be gotten up, the catechist, in presence of the dangerous tendencies of intellectualistic modern pedagogy, must take particular care to foster a living faith in the hearts of children.

CHAPTER II

OBJECT OR CONTENT OF CATECHETICAL INSTRUCTION

57. SYNOPSIS. — We shall first consider what kind of catechetical instruction is to be given in the common school considered as a whole. Historically, catechetical instruction has come to be subdivided into three branches: Catechism, Bible History, and complementary instruction in Church History and Liturgy.

Accordingly we divide the chapter into three paragraphs. The question of the further subdivision of the matter according to the age of the children is reserved for treatment in the third chapter, dealing with the catechetical method.

§ I. THE CATECHISM

58. The "Catechism Question" is one of the much mooted questions of the day. Already at the Vatican Council it gave rise to lively debates. Discussions generally center about the following problems: shall we keep the catechism as it is, or shall we teach it by means of Bible History? What place shall the catechism occupy in catechization? How should a good catechism be planned?

For the final solution of all these questions we must look, not to the catechist, but to those in authority in the Church. However, every catechist should have clear views on those topics, and he needs to grasp aright the place of the catechism in catechetical work. A few preliminary remarks on (*a*) the history of the catechism (as far as it was not treated in the first part of this volume); (*b*) on the scope of a diocesan catechism; and (*c*) on the qualities of a good catechism, may therefore prove useful.

PRELIMINARY REMARKS

A. THE HISTORY OF THE CATECHISM

59. Did the Primitive Church Possess a Catechism? — The answer depends on what we understand by a catechism. The essence of a catechism is found herein that it sums up Christian Doctrine in a few short, abstract didactic formulas. "Didactic," i.e., in order that Christian Doctrine may be grasped correctly and clearly, and easily committed to memory; "abstract formulas," as contrasted with "concrete facts" such as we find described, often to their minutest details, in the Bible.

Keeping this in mind, we may say that the catechism is as old as Christianity. For all documents of primitive Christianity point to the fact that from the earliest times definite abstract formulas were offered to the faithful and inculcated to them.

It is unnecessary here to dilate further on the purely methodical question whether these formulas in the primitive Church constituted the starting-point of the instruction, or came only at the end, to sum up the results of previous teaching. We are only considering the fact that already the ancient Church condensed her teaching into short formulas and used them in catechetical work.

60. A General Proof. — That no other course was possible appears clearly from the positive character of Christian faith and morals. Christian Doctrine is not an empty mold which the individual is free to fill with whatever pleases his fancy: clearly defined facts and doctrines about God and His Only-begotten, crucified, and glorified Son make up the rich and life-giving content of Christian teaching. It is obviously impossible to speak of it, much less to comprehend it, unless it be clothed in clear language. If special circumstances demand that the true meaning of the doctrines of faith be stated concisely either for the benefit of the faithful or in order to confute error, then the formulas and terse statements of our present-day catechisms will result. Undoubtedly, the verbal formulation of the doctrines may come to vary in consequence of their widespread diffusion, but the meaning remains unchanged. And it is thus we must understand the words of St. Paul: "But though we or an angel from heaven preach a gospel to you besides that which we have preached to you, let him be anathema." Gal. 1, 8. The more sacred the doctrine, the quicker it comes to be summed up in formulas unalterable even in their wording.

Father Suitbert Baeumer, O.S.B., in his excellent monograph: Das apostolische Glaubensbekenntniss. Seine Geschichte und sein Inhalt (Mainz, 1893), develops this proof thus, with especial reference to the Creed: "As soon as the Apostles, instructed by the Lord Himself and endowed individually and collectively with infallibility in teaching, left the scene of their earthly labors, it became absolutely necessary that the *basis* of Christianity should be firmly secured, and set down in an easily intelligible form. For preaching and catechization, for personal meditation and as a guide for science and life, it was indispensable that the doctrines contained in the Gospel as well as in the writings of the Old and New Testament and the Apostolic Traditions should be stated in clear propositions, that they might serve as a shibboleth for the Christians dispersed over the face of the earth. It also seemed useful to have at hand such a concise formula or rule, to be used as a norm for the preaching and exposition of the truth, for the explanation of Holy Writ, for the testing of old and new revelations and human theories. The need of such a profession of faith or Symbol, of such a concise statement of the truths of faith which every Christian had to accept, in short, a baptismal vow, must have been more pressing than that of a common formula of prayer. For how could the Church admit to baptism in the name of the triune God, to the Holy Eucharist and all the other mysteries, how could she incorporate into her closely guarded membership the candidates who presented themselves, without requiring from them definite guarantees in the form of a profession and promise?"

The baptismal vow mentioned here by Baeumer embraced a twofold duty: to believe, and to live in accordance with the law of Christ. The oldest baptismal rites also require the recitation of the Lord's Prayer, as has been explained at length above, No. 20. The reception of baptism was preceded by instruction on that most necessary of all Sacraments, and a more thorough instruction was given afterwards (No. 21). Hence we have the four divisions usual in catechetical teaching: the Creed, the Commandments, the Lord's Prayer, the Sacraments.

61. Closer Investigation Confirms the General Proof. — New investigations and literary discoveries all tend to confirm, day by day, the general proof just given and generally accepted. Already Baeumer could say, in his above-mentioned book: "The Christian writings and fragments from post-Apostolic times, from A.D. 90 to A.D. 120, have unexpectedly furnished irrefragable proofs that at an earlier date than many were willing to admit, the Catholic Church used and handed down clearly outlined liturgical formulas for public prayer and teaching. This is abundantly shown in the Didache and the explanations appended to the Epistle of St. Clement of Rome to the Corinthians."

It is obviously beyond the scope of the present work to follow in detail the historical development of every Christian doctrine in particular. One example, from recent research, may be adduced in confirmation of our contention.

For some years past Prof. Alfred Seeberg of the Protestant theological faculty of Rostock has been endeavoring to prove that "shortly after Christ's death there came into existence a catechism made up of His sayings. The contents of this catechism were preached by the missionaries during the time of the Apostles, and taught to those who applied for baptism. Catholic critics in general did not take kindly to Seeberg's view; for although his conclusions contain nothing new, his arguments were not always convincing. It is noteworthy, however, what a reviewer in the Theologische Literaturzeitung published by A. Harnack and E. Schurer has to say about Seeberg's book: "I need not point out," he writes, "how far-reaching Seeberg's conclusions are — if he be right in his contention. In that catechism of primitive Christianity we would have not only the starting-point for the whole processus of doctrinal development and formula-building in post-Apostolic times; but Apostolic times themselves appear in an entirely new light. For with the Apostles themselves there began a dogmatical evolution in a restricted sense but of far-reaching import. During the Apostolic period itself the schema, the formula, tradition, played a more important rôle than we have hitherto been willing to grant, and which we were more inclined to point out as a characteristic of an already nascent Catholicism(!)." Although this reviewer himself does not consider Seeberg's arguments as conclusive, he nevertheless admits: "There is no doubt, and no one denies, that, in Apostolic times, including St. Paul, stereotyped Christian expressions and formulas were in vogue."

In another work: "The Gospel of Christ" (1905), Seeberg comes to the conclusion that recent Protestant theologians who try to point out a contradiction between the pure Gospel and man-made dogmas attempt the impossible; "for the Gospel of Christ is, — according to the oldest meaning of this word, — the dogma of the Church in its original form."

62. Evolution of the Fundamental Formulas of the Catechism. — To the fundamental formulas of the catechism others were added in the course of time: the corporal and spiritual Works of Mercy, the Capital Sins and Virtues, the Precepts of the Church, etc. The slow development of these doctrinal formulas remains largely to be investigated by historians. For a long time only six corporal Works of Mercy were recognized in accordance with Christ's description of the Last Judgment. Math. 25, 35–36. Later on the seventh was taken from Tobias, 1, 20; 12, 12: to bury the dead; and even to the present day the Precepts of the Church are not the same in number all over.

We have already described to some extent the catechism explanations of the Middle Ages for the use of catechists; also the confession books and didactic pictures, and how the word "catechism" came to be applied to the book itself, together with the evolution of the Canisian catechisms. We have also adverted to the more recent discussions started around the little book. From the following summary of the points common to all catechisms, a better idea of their nature may be gained.

63. Characteristics Common to All Catechisms. — The catechisms that came into existence since the sixteenth century, have the following points in common:

(*a*) Christian Doctrine is given not in the form of a connected exposition, but in questions and answers. Methodically this way of proceeding is correct; it lightens the task of the catechist and the child, and affords the parents a good opportunity to test the knowledge of their children at home. Repeated attempts to do away with questions and answers have not in the long run given the hoped-for results. The new Augsburg catechism offers a happy combination of the two methods: connected exposition together with questions and answers.

(*b*) All catechisms, even the oldest ones, present also this common feature, that they are built up around the four formulas constituting the skeleton of Christian Doctrine: the Creed, the Sacraments, the Commandments, the Lord's Prayer, even if at times the order of their presentation undergoes a change, or modifications are introduced in the grouping of the formulas.

Canisius' division is as follows: Faith, Prayer, Commandments, Sacraments, and he adds a fifth chapter on Christian Justice: sin and virtue, good works, the four last things. Bellarmine also adhered to this fourfold division. Deharbe groups together Prayer and the Sacraments under the heading: Means of Grace, and thus obtains but three main divisions. Even

Fleury and Bossuet (1679 and 1686) preserve the fourfold division: Faith, Prayer, Commandments, Sacraments. At the head of each lesson is found an appropriate narrative from Bible History, and from this story the doctrine in question is evolved.

(c) A custom of long standing favors the publication of diocesan catechisms in two or three editions: small, medium, and large catechism. They are concentric, so that the second contains the questions of the first, and the third the questions of the two preceding ones. This arrangement proved very practical whenever the formulation of the questions common to all remained the same throughout.

It was also customary, in the large or even the medium catechism, to mark with an asterisk some questions considered as less important. The questions not thus marked were given to all the children indiscriminately; the others were reserved for the abler or older ones. Regard must be had in this connection to the program prescribed by episcopal authority.

64. Conclusion. — The four formulas mentioned above have ever been considered as the essential foundation of the catechism, and their explanation was always given in short abstract sentences. No one ever attempted to substitute a compendium of Bible History for the catechism, not even Fleury and Bossuet, who laid such great stress on the historical setting in the teaching of Christian Truth. Herein lies food for thought: to let Bible History take the place of the catechism is to court failure. We shall have more to say on this subject when developing our fifth principle.

We are also in a position now to solve the question concerning the division of the catechism: the division sanctioned by long tradition is the one based on the four old and venerable formulas. Recently a demand has arisen again for a scientific and systematically ordered catechism. Militating against such an arrangement is the antiquity of the division according to the formulas. And there is, besides, this decisive objection: we have no scientific system of Christian Doctrine sanctioned by the Church. Any such system that may be in existence expresses the private opinion of learned men, who do not agree on any one in particular. Scientific systematization is naturally unstable and subject to such changes as should under no conditions invade the doctrinal manual of the children and the faithful. An able catechist never finds it difficult to combine the advantages of a systematic instruction,— in so far as systematization does not detract from the vividness of educational work, — with the use of the present catechism.

B. What is the Purpose of a Diocesan Catechism?

(From the answer to this question it becomes easy to derive the qualities which a good catechism should possess)

65. The Diocesan Catechism is Primarily the Official Manual of the Christian Religion, in the first place for the children, but, moreover, also for adults and the people in general.

In the catechism the deposit of faith is presented to the children and the people by its divinely appointed exponent. It is a textbook; yet it is not on a level with other secular textbooks used in the school. For not only does it differ from them in its content and its aim; but the essential difference lies in the AUTHORITY with which it is invested. Other textbooks are based on human authority; in the catechism, however, we have the written word of a divinely commissioned teacher who is God's direct representative in the diocese. It is not the work of a learned theologian, be he a Deharbe or a Canisius; but from the moment its use has been prescribed by the bishop, it becomes the teaching of a "representative of God," of whom it has been said: "He who heareth you heareth Me." That the bishops themselves regard the catechism in this light, shall appear presently (No. 66). Hence the catechism should be received by the children, the adults, and the catechist alike with loyal and obedient reverence.

66. Proof. — That in the view of the bishops the catechism is indeed invested with the above-mentioned authority, can be proved in this wise:

(*a*) Catechisms always appear in the name of the ecclesiastical magisterium's official representatives, i.e., bishop, or the bishops of a whole province. The jurisdiction of the teaching Church extends to whatever appertains to the catechism.

(*b*) One of the objections urged against a uniform catechism at the Vatican Council was: the right of the bishop to instruct his flock by means of the diocesan catechism would be curtailed. While the objection was answered by pointing out that the bishop's right would not be curtailed by adopting such a catechism, the existence of the right was not contested.

(*c*) Several recent provincial councils speak in the same strain. The bishops assembled in Graz in 1858 declared: "The catechism is not only a school manual, but it is a compendium of what we must believe and do. . . . The catechism must constitute the foundation of all religious instruction; a more thorough explantion of the faith, such as is given in sermons, must be based and built upon the catechism, which should be the companion not only of children, but also of adults."

The provincial council of Prague in 1860 declared: "The book on which we must by all means base our teaching of Christian Doctrine is the catechism to be revised and published by this synod for our whole province. No one shall be allowed to deviate from it, or to alter it in any manner, so that the teaching be identical for all, and that a change in diction may not seem to imply a change in doctrine. This is all the more necessary as the catechism is the foundation of all religious instruction." What follows is identical with the decree of the council of Graz.

Thus also the council of Vienna (1858): "The diocesan catechism should form a synopsis, for the benefit of our Catholic people, of the mysteries and commandments of God: and although those are to be greatly commended who afterwards seek richer sources of Christian Doctrine, it is all-important that a firm and stable foundation be laid."

(d) From the declarations of individual bishops as many testimonies in favor of the official character of the catechism could be adduced as there are pastoral letters on the catechization of the young and the people.

Bishop W. Emanuel von Ketteler, in one of his most beautiful pastoral letters (Lent of 1858), treating of religious instruction in the common schools, writes: "Every Catholic catechism always contains but the doctrine of Christ." The whole letter is concerned with the one paramount issue of giving to priests, teachers, parents, useful directions for the right use of the catechism, "in the exceedingly important affair of the religious instruction of the children." From the nature of the divine magisterium von Ketteler draws the conclusion that "no one should dare to exercise the office of religious teacher unless he be delegated by his bishop, who is the divinely appointed dispenser of the mysteries of Christ in the diocese." Hence every authorized religious teacher must "subject himself to the general regulations made by the bishop as regards religious instruction, and use the catechism prescribed by him. I declare therefore on this occasion that, in virtue of the power with which the Lord has invested me, I bind in conscience and before God all those who in this diocese are engaged in the religious instruction of youth, to use only the catechism which I have prescribed, both for public and private instruction, in the lower and intermediate schools. . . . To all those who do not heed this admonition, apply the words of the Saviour: He that entereth not by the door into the sheepfold, but climbeth up another way, the same is a thief and robber."

The Bishop of Eichstätt, Fr. Leopold von Leonrod (died 1905), devoted four pastoral letters to the treatment of the catechetical question, which he calls "a very important part of our diocesan charge." He declares: "The catechism is not a profane schoolbook, but the textbook of the Church; and only the bishop as a member of the teaching Church has the right, nay the inalienable right, to determine on a diocesan catechism, and to prescribe its use." And "the catechism is the Church's manual, in which the deposit of faith is presented to the lay-people."

67. The Diocesan Catechism must besides Serve this Double Purpose:

1. It must do duty as a book from which the Christian religion may be learned by heart, i.e., as a manual the chief points of which should be committed to mem-

ory. This is not the case with all manuals, not even theological ones.

Hence it is easy to see the practical conclusions following from the above: questions and answers, conciseness, vividness, etc. More is to be said about this further on.

2. The catechism, moreover, should be a book of edification, i.e., it should stimulate to a life in accordance with faith, a Christian life and a Christian character. Consequently the catechism should not rest content with stating theoretically the rules of Christian conduct; it should strive at the same time to appeal to the child's heart, and to inspire him with a wholehearted enthusiasm for a life of virtue.

The first-mentioned requirement (No. 65) is essential to a catechism; the second is necessary; the third is at least very desirable.

68. The Diocesan Catechism as a Book for the People. — The catechism should serve the purposes already mentioned, at least the first and third, not only for children, but also for adults. The highest authorities of the Church have so declared, as have also various councils: witness the councils of Graz, Vienna, Prague (No. 66). Many catechists view the subject with a certain amount of skepticism, and despair of making the catechism a thoroughly popular book. We answer: the catechism was admittedly a popular manual during long periods of history; is there any *a priori* reason why we cannot once more make it an up-to-date book full of interest for the masses? All the more so since in a certain sense the catechism has remained the people's manual in so far that pulpit instruction of adults ultimately always falls back on it?

Bishop von Ketteler, in his pastoral letter already quoted, reminds Christian parents of the duty incumbent upon them to assist their children in acquiring religious instruction by enabling them to attend school regularly, by testing their knowledge personally, etc. "Only then can the parents fulfil this duty when the catechism becomes once more the familiar and well-beloved book of the whole household. . . . The catechism is the textbook from which all, not the children only, should draw that knowledge of which the Saviour says: 'This is eternal life, that they may know thee, the only true God, and Jesus Christ whom thou hast sent.' Oh indeed, that is a sight pleasing to God when all the members of the family gather often for the study of the catechism; when, sitting at the same table where they provide for the needs of the body, they also partake together of the heavenly bread, each according to his capacity."

C. Qualities of the Catechism

69. The Two Most Necessary Qualities. — Theological accuracy is absolutely required in every catechism. The Christian doctrines must be stated correctly. For the catechism is primarily intended to familiarize the young and the people with the deposit of faith (No. 65).

Hence follows another necessary quality: precision, definiteness of expression. When the tenets of faith are not expressed in very limpid and definite language, the result will be: vague, and not unfrequently false notions concerning points of faith. Even although the catechist, in his explanations, may endeavor to clear up the vagueness of the book, it is to be feared that the oral explanations will be easily forgotten, whilst the obscure text remains fixed in the memory.

These two qualities: correctness and precision, the catechism must possess by all means, even at the cost of easy understanding of the text. "Rather a text difficult of understanding than one lacking in precision," writes the able catechist, Bishop von Leonrod, in his pastoral letter already mentioned. The complete understanding of many doctrines and expressions comes only in the course of time. For did not the Lord Himself tell his Apostles many things the full meaning of which they came to grasp only later? It is a far more difficult task to set aright errors that have become rooted in the mind.

70. Completeness. — The catechism should contain the whole Christian Doctrine, in so far as it bears upon the Christian life. Hence it is that, according to the diversity of time and place, many additions or omissions have to be made in the catechism.

In his pastoral letter of 1858 Bishop von Ketteler writes: "We can but recognize the Providence of God herein that the Blessed Canisius has succeeded in writing a catechism used so long with loving devotion by our Catholic people, and given up at last only with regret. But no catechism can retain its usefulness for all time. If a change is detrimental, it may yet be imperative. The doctrine of the Church never alters, and she preserves Christ's every word until the end of time. But the enemies of the Church adopt new tactics; the assaults directed against the doctrines of Christ assume new forms, and the defense must constantly provide for these changes of front. . . . Since Catholic children should be trained as good soldiers of Christ Jesus (II Tim. 2, 3), the catechism must undergo alterations and adapt itself to the vicissitudes of the gigantic struggle between the kingdom of God and that of Satan. It must aim at treating the immutable doctrines of Christ in such a fashion as to answer the needs of the children, and lay particular stress on these truths which contain the divine remedy for the errors of a given period."

In our own day the catechism should give the Catholic doctrine on cremation in connection with the commandments of the Church; on duelling in connection with the Fifth Commandment; on elections and our duty of participating in them in connection with the Fourth; on newspapers, in connection with scandal; on Socialism, in connection with the Seventh Commandment.

71. **Other Qualities that should Distinguish a Good Catechism are:**

1. Brevity. Since it should contain what is to be committed to memory, it should be as concise as possible. Many catechisms fail in this regard. Short explanations of the essential truths, e.g., quotations, examples, etc., may be incorporated provided they be differentiated from the main text by a change in type.

2. Easy style, i.e., expressions easily grasped, clear connection between parts, perspicuous and concrete language. This quality may easily conflict with the two prime requisites of accuracy and brevity. The language of the catechism should never be that of the nursery. With due regard for the intellectual capacity of the child, the language of the Church must yet so far be taken into consideration that, aided by the explanation of the catechist, he be prepared to understand the Church's prayers, sermons, and devotional books. Although marked by great simplicity, the language must ever be reverent and noble; it must be characterized by a certain dignity and solemnity that shall appeal even to the educated man, all the more so

since the catechism is equally intended for adults (No. 68).

3. Edification. Catechization should above all be edifying. The result must be attained chiefly through the oral exhortations and the personal influence of the catechist himself; effective use of Bible History contributes greatly to attain this result. The brevity required in the catechism does not allow room for many pious considerations; additions in small print may, however, be of great benefit. Passages from Holy Writ, biblical examples, brief practical hints at the end of the lesson, promote the cultivation of piety.

4. Dignified external appearance. The catechism, as the most important of all manuals for the people, should profit by the progress made in typography and bookbinding. Recent attempts at illustrating the catechism deserve great commendation in view of the long-standing predilection of the Church for such catechetical helps (Nos. 27–29). However, the price of the catechism should not be raised overmuch in consequence. In this connection Spirago remarks very appropriately that pearls and gems are mounted in gold.

THE PLACE OF THE CATECHISM IN CATECHIZATION

FIFTH PRINCIPLE. — 1. *The diocesan catechism constitutes the chief object and the center of all catechetical instruction.* 2. *It also offers the groundwork and must serve as a guide for the catechist's more detailed oral explanations.*

72. Explanation. — The first part of the thesis states the relation between the catechism and the other objects of catechetical instruction; the second part, the relation between the catechism and the catechist.

The catechism is the "chief object," i.e., catechetical instruction must endeavor to impart a correct comprehension of the catechism's contents, and rigidly adhere to the same. This does not mean, however, that already in the first school year a beginning must be made with the explanation and memorizing of the catechism: we still refer here to catechetical instruction in general, as extending over the whole primary school period.

Nor should it be concluded that, from a methodical standpoint, i.e., in order to facilitate the understanding of the catechism, the text should occupy first place.

It is also far from our mind to assert that the catechism is the all-important thing in catechization as a whole; for from an educational standpoint Bible History is of equal if not greater moment. Hence the principle states plainly that the catechism is the "chief object" of catechetical *instruction*.

The catechism is also "the center" of catechetical instruction in this sense that all other catechetical teaching, by means of Bible History, Liturgy, Church History, should be grouped around it, and arranged in such a manner as to be of real assistance to the children for a better understanding of the truths of the catechism, and a thorough, vivid, practically operative realization of them.

The second part of the thesis should not convey the false impression that the catechist must confine himself to reading the printed book. For the catechism comes into its own only through the vivid explanatory presentation of the catechist; "the catechist, therefore, is the instructor, not the catechism." The meaning of the second part of our thesis then is: the catechist may not teach Christian Doctrine from private sources, for this would lead to most deplorable consequences. He must strive above all to impress the contents of the catechism upon the children's mind, and to make its truths operative in their hearts. Should he then rest content with being a mere commentator of the catechism, limiting himself to a lifeless philological analysis of the catechismal text? Such a catechist stands self-condemned. But there is an exegesis of the catechism which lays stress primarily on the truths contained therein, and this is what the catechist should offer the children.

What we have said thus far applies obviously only to the diocesan catechism prescribed by the bishop, and not to catechisms published by private individuals.

73. Opponents of Our Theory. — The position which we have assigned to the catechism is often lost sight of in practice, i.e., in actual catechetical work. But of late various attempts have also been made, more or less openly, to prove theoretically that Bible History and not the catechism, should constitute the chief object of catechetical instruction. It is insisted more particularly that the catechism should not be the guide of the catechist, making the latter a mere commentator of the former; but it should be at most a didactic help for the teacher.

We may distinguish two kinds of opponents. Some would preserve our catechism as an abstract compendium of Christian truths, divided according to the ancient formulas; in their mind it would be very useful for memorizing purposes, but of secondary importance in the hands of the catechist and his pupils.

Others are averse even to a catechism of this kind, and would do away with it altogether. They clamor for a return to the ways of primitive Christianity, and insist that a manual of religion should be based solely on Bible History, the historical periods in the development of Revelation offering the ready-made divisions.

In considering these questions, let us bear in mind that even our most determined antagonists are not actuated by any desire of revolt against ecclesiastical authority. They mostly endeavor to promote their reforms subject to the approval of the Church.

74. Proofs of Our Principle. — To demonstrate the validity of our principle, we shall point out first that the catechism rightfully occupies the position which we have assigned to it in accordance with the existing prescriptions of competent authority; then we shall investigate whether it would be wise and useful to try new ways and attempt to give catechetical instruction in a historical manner, and whether the catechism, cast in the usual form, is indeed no longer adapted to our times.

The catechist is the messenger of God and the Church, i.e., of his bishop; he teaches by virtue of a delegated authority (No. 49). Hence he must submit in everything to the authoritative regulations, emanating from the bishop. It has been pointed out already (No. 66) that the bishop intends the catechism, and not any other book, to be the official textbook of religion, i.e., the book in which the Church presents the doctrines to be believed by the child. If this in the mind of the bishop is the function of the catechism, catechetical instruction must necessarily be based upon it and center in it; it must at the same time be the guide for the catechist in all his work.

This latter conclusion is self-evident; the catechism being the episcopal teaching addressed to the children, all other means of instruction, as well as the catechist himself, must become the organs of the living episcopal magisterium.

Against our contention that the bishops themselves assign to the catechism the position we claim for it, it cannot be urged that for over a thousand years the catechism in its present form was not known, and consequently was not the basis of catechetical instruction. For the objection would at most go to show that formerly the catechist was not bound to follow a catechism. Yet, for present circumstances, the present will of the bishops is to be considered. The argument does not carry any further weight, since we have insisted right along that the essence of the catechism is not found in the fact of its being a printed volume (No. 59). Before the invention of printing the Church possessed other means of securing the veracity of the episcopal teaching authority, e.g., in the obligation imposed upon candidates for orders to memorize many of the doctrines.

75. The Internal Grounds in Favor of Our Thesis. — The place which as a matter of fact the catechism does occupy in catechetical teaching, has also many strong reasons in its favor. No advantage would accrue from depriving the catechism of this position, assigning the leading rôle in catechetical instruction to Bible History, in order, it is asserted, to return to the earlier practice of Christian antiquity. Nor would any benefit be derived from leaving the catechist entirely free to choose the topics of instruction.

1. We may draw a first argument from the long practice of the past and the results it produced.

Just at the time when the great Protestant upheaval shook the Church, and the dire need of more thorough religious instruction for Catholics was realized, the catechism originated in the form it has preserved to this very day. And it came into existence there first of all where the faith was threatened most. Spontaneously the catechism became the providential means to instruct the young and the people alike. And the future proved the wisdom of this action. Through his catechism Bl. Canisius became the "mallet of heretics."

In our own day errors have not decreased in number; it is of great moment that religious instruction meet them with a clear-cut, accurate presentation of Christian Doctrine, such as only the catechism can furnish in its abstract formulas.

2. A comparison with the "Roman Catechism" offers further proofs.

(a) Why was this catechism introduced? In order to secure thoroughness in religious instruction, both in the pulpit and the school, although that thoroughness aimed at in scientific theology was never intended. For lack of a definite summary of the subject-matter it might easily happen that some important doctrines would not receive due attention, while others, less important, would be emphasized.

(b) Moreover, unity, and (c) purity of doctrine could be attained only by the concise presentation of the catechism. Confusion and error might easily result, were the teacher left free in his choice of matter, and the way of treating it. Lastly, (d) the reverence due the magisterium of the Church would be endangered, whilst now the qualities enumerated above, and especially its unity, make the catechism stand forth prominently as an emanation from higher authority.

3. Moreover, there is the didactic need of a precise, clear-cut presentation of doctrines of faith, together with great conciseness, so that they may be correctly understood and easily fixed in the memory. In a historical presentation of faith this would be impossible; for in the end it would be necessary to formulate, after the manner of the catechism, the doctrinal contents of Bible History, just as the Councils were forced to formulate exact definitions, although the Bible was also in the hands of heretics.

4. Finally, practical reasons militate against a fundamental change in catechetical instruction. Without a well-founded prospect of great benefits no alteration in traditional methods should be countenanced: it is obviously beneficial that the children be instructed in the same way as their parents, so that the latter at least by their supervision may co-operate with the catechist. Besides, the preacher in the pulpit must often draw upon the catechism. The confusion engendered by far-reaching changes in religious instruction came always to the fore wherever a revised catechism was introduced.

Therefore, as long as we have not at our disposal a "historical" catechism possessing all the good points of the older books, together with marked improvements, it is the part of wisdom not to strive for a change, even if for the nonce we leave out of consideration the will of the episcopate in this matter. Whatever benefits may be reaped from a more thorough use of Holy Writ can be incorporated by the catechist in his teaching, without introducing on that account any changes in the catechism itself.

A further confirmation of our arguments is found in the solution of the objections urged against this principle.

76. Refutation of Objections. — Several objections, some of which we have met already, are urged against our principle. Some of them are well founded; yet they cannot displace the catechism from the position which rightfully belongs to it.

1. It is said: Catechization in the primitive Church was characterized by the preponderance of the biblical-historical method: this should remain our model.

We answer: (a) Granting the premise, the conclusion does not necessarily follow: changes, fully warranted by the times, have occurred in the way of spreading the Gospel. Thus, when a particular point of faith was attacked, the Church at once defined it more accurately, and made clear the grounds on which it rested. A development of this kind would naturally react on the instruction of youth, which must keep pace with the times. Hence our present type of catechism is the outcome of a constant natural evolution. To give it up for a return to more primitive methods were not a sign of progress but of retrogression. We firmly believe that any concession in this regard would only increase the intellectual chaos already so prevalent; light and order can come only from uncompromising firmness, clear concepts, and a return to the elementary laws of thought.

(b) But even the premise is not altogether proof against criticism, for it is untrue that primitive catechization was confined to instruction in Bible History. When the Apostles argued against the Jews, they naturally had recourse to the Bible. But do not their epistles, on the other side, call to mind, by their exact formulation of doctrines, the crisp statements of our own catechisms? (Compare No. 61.) And as we know already, the formulas that have gone into the make-up of our catechisms, have come down to us from remote antiquity. If St. Augustine offers us some examples of historical catechization, we have, on the other side, St. Cyril of Jerusalem to prove that the historical method did not by any means enjoy a monopoly.

Both parts of the objection fail therefore to carry conviction.

2. Another objection is thus stated: Not the catechism, but the catechist, is all-important in catechization. To a certain extent this is very true, and is admitted by Bishop von Leonrod of Eichstätt, who, although one of the most thoroughgoing supporters of our theory, yet writes: "Of prime importance for fruitful religious instruction is the catechist. Even a flawless catechism remains a dead letter, unless the catechist breathe life into it." How is this to be understood?

The catechist remains the important factor as far as the educational part of catechization is concerned:

life is imparted only by a living being. He is also an important factor in the instruction itself, when it comes to a vivid presentation and exposition of the subject-matter required for correct understanding, and assimilation fruitful in practical results. But all this does not conflict with the fundamental position of the catechism. The case is somewhat similar to the exegetical treatment of Holy Writ in the homily: the preacher must be a capable exegete, yet from the standpoint of authority he remains subject to Holy Writ. In the same manner the catechist finds himself in a subordinate position with respect to the episcopal teaching as propounded in the catechism.

3. When the above considerations are kept in mind, the answers to other difficulties often propounded in the form of aphorisms will come readily to hand.

"All these objections have their origin in a wrong conception of the principle that the knowledge of faith should come not through a dead book, but through the living magisterium of the Church. The principle is incontrovertible, but it means: the knowledge of our faith comes to us, not through Holy Writ alone, but through Holy Writ explained and illumined by the teaching Church. . . . It is well to guard against exaggerations. The catechist and his position do not lose in dignity when his catechization appears what it is and ought to be: a correctly understood exegesis of the official ecclesiastical textbook: the catechism. The method he follows may be analytical or synthetical, according to the requirements of the case."

77. Practical Conclusions. — 1. The catechist himself should cultivate a high regard for the catechism, and lead the children to look upon it not as an ordinary schoolbook, but as the official textbook of the Church.

And how can the catechist manifest his esteem for the catechism?

(*a*) He should know it by heart. (*b*) He should be firmly convinced that by adhering to the catechism he does not lower his intellectual dignity, but raises himself to a higher plane, so that he needs to concentrate all his strength on meeting the requirements of his high office.

> Bishop von Leonrod writes on this subject: "The catechist and the catechism should move on the same plane. The catechism could not adapt itself to the level of the catechist's theological training, for thus the door would be thrown wide open to subjectivism, and the catechism in most cases would lose considerably. But conversely, the catechist should spare no pains to adapt himself to the diocesan catechism, so that both may be perfect." Hence the need of thorough dogmatical training; hence also "the laudable custom of the ablest catechists, when preparing their lessons, of reviewing the dogmatic treatise relating to it." Thus they gain a clear insight into the doctrines, and their interrelations; in a few well-chosen words they can analyze and explain to the children, according to their age and capacity, the questions and answers of the catechism.

(*c*) The catechist must not arbitrarily deviate from the text of the catechism, altering and inverting its parts. He should on the contrary adhere to it as a safe foundation and guide: a guide in so far that the catechist should follow it as regards the contents and their orderly arrangement; a foundation, not as a starting-point but as the end is a foundation, viz., the comprehension of the truths of the catechism is the end which the catechist must never lose sight of.

(*d*) When the catechist takes this view of his own position with regard to the catechism, then his teaching will spontaneously fill the children with reverence for the same.

2. When the catechist and the secular teacher both give religious instruction, the catechist should reserve for himself the teaching of the catechism. It would indeed be better yet, as we shall show further on, if the catechism and Bible History were taught by the catechist exclusively.

3. Above we cautioned the catechist against being a mere "questioner." And this warning can no longer be open to misunderstanding. His duty consists not only in explaining the catechism; he must know how to work upon the heart. He should see to it not merely that the text is memorized, but that the children grasp divine truth and warmly embrace it. With this restriction borne in mind, the catechism remains, however, the foundation and center of catechetical instruction.

§ II. BIBLE HISTORY

78. Historical Notions. — By "Bible History" we understand at present not the whole Bible, nor a complete survey of the history of revelation, but a compendium of Holy Writ, a synopsis of the history of revelation, dealing with the salient facts of salvation, from the creation of the world to the foundation of the Church, in a manner adapted to the capacity of the children.

In Part I we have already pointed out at length (Nos. 13, 18, 27) how the primitive Church put the Bible to use in catechetical instruction; how the Middle Ages fully realized its importance for the Christian training of youth and adult alike, and emphasized its teaching in graphic representations. Christian antiquity and the Middle Ages did not have at their disposal, however, a school manual of Bible History, but the many other means used to inculcate a thorough knowledge of Holy Writ supplied the want very fully.

During the long period from the Reformation to the nineteenth century Bible History as a special textbook for children is also unknown: it is largely digested in the catechism, whose short questions and answers condense whole chapters of the Bible, although not following any historical order.

The use of Bible History as a schoolbook is of very recent date, and began after Gruber, Overberg, and Hirscher had pointed out the importance of the historical side of catechization.

Well written Bible Histories in German are numerous. The bibliography appended to Messmer-Spirago (p. 574), and to the article on Christian Doctrine in the Catholic Encyclopedia, vol. V, p. 88, gives those most used in English-speaking countries.

SIXTH PRINCIPLE. — *The second object of catechetical instruction is Bible History, which constitutes a most useful and a necessary complement of the same. Hence it should be intimately combined with the catechism. Besides it offers another great advantage: it is of great value as an educational factor in catechization.*

79. Necessity of Bible History. — No one denies that Bible History is an important branch of religious teaching, while it is at the same time a valuable help in catechismal instruction, just as Holy Writ is a copious source of material for preaching. It remains to be explained in what way Bible History is a *most necessary* complement of the catechism.

Without the help of Bible History the doctrine of salvation can scarcely be grasped aright. For this doctrine is at the same time the history of salvation: it is offered to us in historical events and is embodied in concrete facts.

Suffice it to call to mind the revelation of the Blessed Trinity at the baptism of Christ; or the manifestation of the powers and gifts of the Holy Ghost on Pentecost. The practical foundations of faith, such as, e.g., the doctrine of the Cross, of humility, are brought out with characteristic emphasis in biblical facts. The justice of God, the consequences of sin, are best understood from the impressive descriptions of divine wrath found in Scripture. Our knowledge of the work of Redemption would be very meager if we knew nothing of the life of Christ in its historical setting. And even those passages which have only a prototypical meaning, such as the rite of the Paschal supper, how much they contribute toward a fuller understanding of the most important doctrines of salvation!

In the sense that catechetical instruction should go hand in hand with Bible History, we may refer to the former as historical. This is not intended to imply, however, that it should limit itself to historical instruction or make the latter the central starting-point. "By confining himself to a historical presentation, the catechist would scarcely succeed in inculcating the fundamental doctrines of faith in all their completeness, in expounding the several notions and dogmas with distinctness and clarity; and yet this is of paramount importance in our day, if Catholics are to meet the innumerable attacks and distortions leveled against them by unbelief and heresy. On the other side the historical method must needs also give rise to many repetitions."

From the foregoing the mutual relations of catechism and Bible History ought to be clear: both are necessary, but the dangers threatening faith from flabbiness and vagueness of thought and from the prevalent confusion of ideas make more imperative than ever a clear catechismal formulation of the doctrines of faith and morality which form the groundwork of catechetical instruction. Any change in this regard would but contribute to the general disorder. That Bible History is in no way slighted in our plan, shall appear from the following.

80. The Relation between Bible History and the Catechism may be stated as follows:

1. Bible History precedes the catechism, for which it paves the way. It is preferable to start out the youngest pupils with Bible History.

2. Bible History offers the best possible commentary of the catechism. For how could one convey a better idea of God's attributes than through the medium of the descriptions found in Holy Writ? For instance, God's omnipotence as shown in Creation; His Providence in the history of Joseph; His love in the life and sufferings of Jesus Christ. And this holds also in general for all instruction in Christian Doctrine, as well as for the preaching intended for adults. The preacher, and even more so the catechist, must bear in mind the rule: "In announcing God's word, human life and the visible phenomena of nature should be drawn upon as much as possible, that through them the mind may be led to grasp the supernatural. The priest, moreover, should take into consideration the nature of the lower cognitional faculties, and bend all his energies towards

making them useful adjuncts for the easy, distinct, clear, vivid intellectual comprehension of truth." The whole history of Revelation is a rich storehouse of varied means for the furtherance of this end.

The judicious use of Bible History is well explained by Bossuet in the pastoral letter which introduces his catechism to his diocese: "Combine with your instructions historical narratives from Holy Writ or from other reliable sources. Experience teaches that these exercise an influence all their own; while keeping up attention, they have always proven the chosen means to make the children learn religious truths lovingly and willingly. When therefore you wish to instruct them concerning a mystery or a sacrament, let your instruction be preceded by the recital of the circumstances in which the mystery took place. . . . Be careful to present the facts clearly and vividly. Endeavor to captivate the senses of the children (the imagination and the lower cognitional faculties) to reach through them their minds and hearts."

3. From the above it is clear that Bible History makes catechization attractive and interesting.

4. Holy Writ furnishes the most convincing arguments, while these are at the same time easily grasped by the child. The mere pointing out of the fact that a given doctrine is the teaching of Christ surpasses all other argumentation.

5. Finally, from a psychological standpoint, Bible History is an excellent help in stamping a truth permanently upon the mind. When an abstractedly stated doctrine is presented anew in concrete form, taking on flesh and blood and moving in concrete surroundings, it will not so easily fade from memory, or at least it will be easily recalled to mind.

81. The Importance of Bible History for Catechization in General. — Bible History not only affords an indispensable help in catechization; it is of paramount value for the second and highest object of catechization: the religious training, the formation of the heart after Christian ideals. Here we may well recall the text: "All Scripture inspired by God is profitable to teach, to reprove, to correct, to instruct in justice, that the man of God may be perfect, furnished to every good work." II Tim. 3, 16–17. The Imitation of Christ contains a chapter entitled: "That the Body of Christ and Holy Scripture are most necessary to the Faithful Soul." This juxtaposition of Holy Writ and the Holy Eucharist rests on good grounds: "Detained in the prison of this body, I confess myself in need of two things, light and food. Therefore Thou hast given to me infirm man Thy Sacred Body for the refection of my mind and body, and Thou has put Thy word a light for my feet. Without these two I cannot live well; for the word of God is the light of my soul and Thy Sacrament is the Bread of life."

The efficacy of the word of Holy Writ may be compared to the Sacramentals: it has a power and unction superior to any book of piety. Scriptural language imparts a peculiar unction to the discourse both in preaching and catechization. Experience testifies that the stimulating grace of the Holy Ghost is bound up with it in a particular manner. Its narrations abound in plain and vivid characterizations; they are simple and unaffected, and hence well calculated to win the heart. Its great examples of virtue appeal strongly to the hearts of children: Samuel, Tobias. Awe-inspiring is the history of the forty-two young men revolting against Eliseus. All this is especially applicable to the life pictures of the Son of God as delineated in the New Testament.

And since it has become necessary to arouse in our Christian people in general renewed love for the word of God, in order to make Holy Scripture once more a household book, it seems that this end can be attained most easily by teaching Bible History to the children.

82. Conclusions. — From the foregoing we may conclude:

1. That catechization and Bible History should not be juxtaposed, but closely interwoven and combined. Let biblical narrations be adduced in the teaching of the catechism. Whenever possible, let historical scenes lead up to abstract doctrines, or let the latter be explained by a biblical event. In the treatment of Bible History let stress be laid on the dogmatical and ethical doctrines contained therein, if possible by using the words of the catechism, which is thus brought into relation with the Bible. How to proceed in detail shall be explained more at length in the chapter on Method.

2. It is regrettable that sometimes instruction in Bible History is left completely to lay-teachers. Bible History suffers from the fact that not the priest but a lay-person expounds it; however competent the latter may be, he does not possess the authority of the priest, and as a rule he is handicapped for that reason in trying to instil into the minds of children a high regard for the Bible. Moreover, it is scarcely possible for a layman, even when experienced in methodical questioning, to treat religious matters, on their affective side especially, with that warmth of feeling proper to

and becoming one of spiritual calling. And when the help of the lay-teacher must be invoked in catechization, it is a moot point whether it might not be well to entrust him with the memorizing and testing part, while the priest reserves for himself the necessary explanations and ascetical considerations.

83. Two Questions. — Extent of biblical instruction, and its relation to "liberal" exegesis.

1. Since Holy Writ is of such great import for religious instruction, should it not be given to the children in the unabridged original? We answer: precisely because of its great importance, only well-chosen selections should be given to children. For Holy Writ contains much that is unsuited for youth and is intended only for mature readers and married persons. Of late frequent complaints have been uttered by unbelievers against the educational value of Holy Writ, and unfortunately they are justified to a certain extent: non-Catholic teachers have inconsiderately allowed children free access to the complete text of Holy Writ, and from the reading of passages not intended for them abuses have followed. On the other side, the question arises whether the Old Testament should not be excluded altogether from biblical instruction intended for children? For why should our Christian children be concerned with the Jewish race? We answer: the Old Testament is not the ordinary history of an ordinary nation, but it is a divine book, with a universal appeal because of that. God intended it to be written for the whole human race. It is true, God revealed Himself directly to His chosen people, but to the end that this revelation should become the property

of all mankind. Before the coming of Christ Holy Writ was directly the property of the Jews; but through them it was to become the possession of the whole human family. Since Christ's coming Holy Writ is the property of the Church. Christ gave it to her and she has become the heir of the synagog; hence it is true to say that even the books of the Old Testament belong, not to the Jews but to the Christians, and mankind should receive them from the Church. Besides, the history of the Old Law is necessary for the understanding of Christianity and its teachings.

2. For some years past catechists have also become concerned over the problem of what stand to take with regard to "progressive" Bible exegesis. Four years ago an exegete, not a catechist, propounded the question: Shall we, in teaching Bible History, take account of the results of progressive exegesis? And he answered: Progressive exegesis does not meet with general approval in higher ecclesiastical circles. This puts a definite restriction on its practical extension. The progressive catechist also finds himself hemmed in by these limitations. . . . In so far as on that account progressive exegesis must be carried out in practice with some reserve, I would give a new turn to the old motto: dare while you must, and have it read: you must dare.

(*a*) The above was written before the important declarations of Pius X and the far-reaching decisions of the Bible Commission. Therefore it need not arrest us further. It is well to note, however: (*a*) there can be no question of a "must," i.e., we must follow progressive exegesis, even if no one had given vent to any suspicion regarding the agreement between progressive exegesis and the decisions and the practice of the ecclesiastical magisterium. For in the first place progressive exegetes are not at one amongst themselves, and therefore the subject is not ripe for practical use. The author of the above mottoes has replied that there was complete agreement in all essential points; but in the end he admitted, however: "It seems clear to us that the ground must be further prepared before theories can be translated into practice, especially by teachers." The teacher, and also the catechist, is better justified than any one in adopting a critical attitude towards all innovations, since undue haste might endanger certitude and jeopardize authority.

(b) It proves very little in favor of progressive exegesis when, in order to buttress its claims, it ever and anon points out "difficulties" which traditional Bible study was aware of long ago, and has solved satisfactorily. Of this any one can convince himself by reading attentively any extensive commentary written in the traditional spirit.

It will then be easily seen that the difficulties with which traditional exegesis cannot cope are not very formidable.

(c) The catechist and pastor conscious of his responsibility will bide his time in making use of the results of progressive exegesis for still another reason: as long as all ecclesiastical pronouncements lay stress on the inerrancy of Holy Writ, while the protagonists of progressive exegesis are chiefly interested in pointing out the possibility of error, it is wholly impossible to get around the question. Whom shall I follow? Who is the right interpreter? The answer has never been in doubt in the Catholic Church. And only recently Leo XIII, in the Encyclical of November 18, 1893, "Providentissimus Deus," has emphasized it anew. Pius X has confirmed and sanctioned it in the chapters on Bible interpretation of the decree "Lamentabili sane exitu," in the Encyclical "Pascendi Dominici gregis," in the Motu Proprio of November 18, 1907. In the past few years the Biblical Commission has published definite answers to much-debated questions. That the catechist and pastor should hold fast to these is evident from the few preceding remarks. The answers of most far-reaching importance for the present day are those concerning the Gospel of St. John, and the three first chapters of Genesis.[1]

§ III. COMPLEMENTARY INSTRUCTION

SEVENTH PRINCIPLE. — *Besides catechism and Bible History, catechization should also include, as far as possible, the study of Liturgy, Church History, and sacred hymns.*

A. LITURGY

84. The Participation of the Faithful in the whole liturgy of the Church is of the greatest importance for the Christian life. In the introduction to the Motu Proprio on Church Music, Pius X expresses himself thus: "It is our sincerest desire to see a true Christian spirit blossom forth and kept alive in the hearts of the faithful; hence we deem it necessary to foster with the utmost care holiness and decorum in God's house. For there our Christian people gather to imbibe the

---

[1] All these decisions may be found in the *Acta Apostolicae Sedis*, and also in the American Ecclesiastical Review, since 1902.

Christian life at its primal and necessary sources, by active participation in the divine mysteries, and the public and solemn sharing in the prayers of the Church." These words carry great weight: the primary and indispensable source of Christian life, we are told, is "the active participation in the holy mysteries and the public and solemn prayers of the Church." Hence it follows that the pastor and catechist charged with the task of awakening and fostering Christian life in the child, should consider it their primary duty to train the children for active participation in divine service and the liturgical mysteries of the Church.

Is this done? As far as essentials are concerned, yes. Assistance at Holy Mass, reception of the Sacraments of Confession, Holy Eucharist, Confirmation, are among the essential aims for which catechetical instruction strives, and they are duly adverted to in the catechism. We shall treat of them more in detail in Special Catechetics. However, when the essentials have been attended to, more should be attempted: the people should be enabled to assist actively and with attention at the liturgical functions. What can catechization effect in this regard?

85. Introduction into the Ecclesiastical Year. — Every year the Catholic celebrates his holy seasons; he lives through the ecclesiastical year, and all too often his knowledge of it is very limited. He should at least be informed about the meaning of the principal feasts. What can the catechist do to prepare the ground? The catechism prescribed by Pius X for the province of Rome contains an "Instruction on the Feasts of Our Lord, the Bl. Virgin and the Saints."

A similar chapter would be very desirable in every catechism. Whether or no he have at his disposal a catechism thus arranged, let the catechist bear in mind the following:

1. At the approach of a liturgical season, or a great feast, he should take a little time, e.g., ten minutes, to explain to the children the meaning of the feast or the season. This could be done for Advent, Christmas, Lent. Let him try particularly to gain the heart of the child, by pointing out, e.g., at the beginning of Advent, how all of us, children also, would be supremely unhappy without the Saviour; how we owe everything to Him; how fervently we should pray, therefore, that the Saviour may come into our hearts with His grace and His love, to abide there always.

2. The explanation of the Sunday and feast-day pericopes is very helpful in this regard. In these the spirit of the day is often beautifully expressed. As a rule the Gospels will have to be used, since the epistles are too difficult for children, except on those days when the mystery of the feast is related in the epistle itself, as, e.g., on the feast of the Ascension, the martyrdom of St. Stephen. In many places it is customary to devote from ten to fifteen minutes on Saturday or in the last instruction before Sunday to an explanation of the Gospel for the children of the higher grades.

3. Before certain feast-days it is well to explain the distinctive liturgical functions connected with them, e.g., the blessing of candles and the procession on the feast of the Purification; the blessing of Ashes; the ceremonies of Holy Week, the procession of Corpus Christi.

4. The explanation and practice of Church hymns adapted to the various seasons, such as hymns for Advent, Christmas, etc., is also a great aid.

Recent attempts to facilitate the understanding of the ecclesiastical year by means of apposite pictures must be hailed with joy. A publication to be warmly recommended is "The Catholic Ecclesiastical Year in Pictures" (60 prints in color), issued with the co-operation of the catechetical societies of Vienna and Munich by Dr. Ulrich Schmid (E. A. Seeman, Leipzig). An explanation of the pictures was written by Ign. Seipel, professor of theology in Salzburg.

86. Holy Places and Sacred Objects. — The children should be familiarized with the church, its contents and belongings, the sacristy, tower, bells, baptismal font, pulpit, confessionals, cemetery, chapels, vestments, vessels, liturgical statues, such as Stations of the Cross, and liturgical books.

The interior life of the faithful would be largely benefited, if they understood, to some extent at least, the meaning of the altar and all that pertains to it; the vestments of the priest at the altar; what books he uses, at the altar, for baptism, for funerals, etc.

How is this instruction to be given? Primarily by showing the things explained. When possible, let the catechist take the children to church, or let him bring the objects from the church to show and explain them. When this cannot be done, let him use pictures for that purpose.

Most favorably known are the "Liturgical Wall Pictures for Religious Instruction" by Reich and Jordan, explanation by H. Swoboda, professor of theology (Vienna, H. Kirsch).

87. The Most Important Liturgical Actions. — Among the ceremonies proper to the priest only, those that recur oftenest, and attract the attention of the children, should be explained: e.g., the various inclinations, the lifting up of the eyes and hands, the position of the hands on the altar, the kissing of the altar.

When explaining what the children themselves should do when praying, e.g., making the sign of the Cross in the twofold manner, striking the breast, folding the hands, genuflecting before the tabernacle on one knee, and on two knees before the Blessed Sacrament exposed, — the catechist should: (*a*) show the children how to perform these actions. They should be practised: the children may be taken to church, and taught how to genuflect, etc.; (*b*) he should watch the children during practice and correct mistakes; (*c*) he should make them realize the spirit informing those actions, by explaining the meaning of the Sign of the Cross, of the genuflection, etc., telling them what feelings to excite in their hearts meanwhile.

And, of course, special attention should be paid in catechization to those liturgical actions connected with the dispensing and reception of the Sacraments, e.g., the right manner of going to confession, the right behavior at the Holy Table; also the manner of receiving Extreme Unction.

88. The Most Important Sacramentals. — Ecclesiastical Persons. — Scarcely enough time will be available for the explanation of the Sacramentals but seldom used: consecration of a church, cornerstone laying, etc. Those of more frequent occurrence should not be passed over: Holy Water, blessing of food before meals, of medals, rosaries, houses, and St. Blase's blessing, the funeral rites, the tolling of bells at funerals.

Some of these liturgical functions may be performed advantageously in the catechism class itself: blessing of water, of rosaries, of the children. Others are best explained before or after the function has taken place in church. It is surely not demanding too much to expect that the children, on leaving school to enter upon their life-work, should be familiar with the name and the office of the Pope, the bishop, the pastor, the assistant; that they should know what is meant by a diocese, an archdiocese, a cardinal, a nuntio, an Apostolic delegate. Children should also be shown the pictures of these ecclesiastical dignitaries.

89. When to Give Liturgical Instruction. — How shall we find the time to treat these numerous topics? A thorough systematic instruction in liturgical matters is scarcely practical anywhere. It is possible, however, whenever occasion offers in the ordinary course of catechization, to make use of the Liturgy by way of illustration or application of the doctrinal teaching, or also for the purpose of fostering devotion. Liturgical teaching, therefore, is more in the nature of occasional instruction.

EXAMPLES. — We have already called attention to the ecclesiastical year. When speaking of the Church, there is ample opportunity for introducing occasional explanations concerning ecclesiastical persons: priests, bishops, archbishops, cardinals, Pope. When speaking of death, reference may be made to the funeral rites. Holy Communion calls for an explanation of the Viaticum; Extreme Unction for an explanation of the rites used in its administration.

B. CHURCH HISTORY

90. Why Should it be Taught? — Many catechisms give a summary of Church History in the guise of an appendix, as do the catechism of Deharbe, and the one prescribed by Pius X for the province of Rome. The Austrian catechism does not have this supplement, but the catechists are exhorted to pay special attention to Church History in the higher school grades.

The reason is that the contents of Church History are eminently calculated to deepen the religious life of the child. For (a) in Church History we are brought face to face with the continuation of Christ's Kingdom on earth until our own day. From the beginning of the world until the institution of the Church the history of God's dealings with mankind is related in the Bible. All subsequent events find their place in Church History, which consequently deals with events in some sense equally supernatural as those in the Bible. (b) It is therefore well adapted to arouse in the children enthusiasm for the faith, and to strengthen them in it. Church History affords a palpable proof of the truth of Christianity. Holy Writ sets forth the great blessings to come through the Church, and Church History shows the fulfilment of these prophecies: in the work of the Spirit of Truth keeping the Church free from all error in the midst of violent conflicts of opinion; in the strength of supernatural grace which the Lord provides in His Sacraments and brings to full fruition in the exalted lives of His Saints; in the divine protection which has always shielded the Church during all attacks and amidst the most virulent tempests. Hence

(c) Church History is an eminently edifying study: the admirable examples of the Saints, especially the younger among them, must needs arouse the children to imitation of their virtues. Finally (d) Church History gives the children a deeper insight into ecclesiastical institutions: orders, missions, ecclesiastical precepts, and fills them with love for their common mother.

91. How is Church History to be Taught? — We may distinguish two ways of proceeding:

(a) The non-systematic teaching consists in this: that the teacher occasionally refers to an event, to the life of a saint or some trait of character, by way of illustration or confirmation of the truths explained, or for the purpose of increasing devotion. This course may be followed in the common schools from the lower grades on.

For example, when explaining the doctrine of the Immaculate Conception, reference may be made to the apparitions in Lourdes. In the case of the Infallibility of the Pope the Vatican Council may be called to mind. When dwelling on chastity, quote the example of St. Aloysius. When local, diocesan, or national (ecclesiastical) feasts are celebrated, relate the history of the saint in question: St. Nicholas, St. Martin, St. John Nepomucene, the patron of the parish. In this wise the children are gradually familiarized with a short Church History in character sketches.

(b) In accordance with the prescriptions of many bishops, Church History is taught systematically during the last school year. Even if authoritative direction be lacking, it is nevertheless advisable that a few hours be devoted to this subject, in as far as the time at the teacher's disposal may allow. The summary contained in some catechisms may be used as a guide, or some special book may be procured for the purpose.

A good school manual of Church History in English is: Church History for the Use of Schools, adapted from the original of L. C. Businger, by Rev. R. Brennan. The volume, however, ought to be brought up to date. (Benziger Bros.) Also: Compendium of Church History by Sisters of Notre Dame; Father MacCaffrey's History of the Catholic Church: Gill & Son, Dublin.

As for the method: let the manner of teaching be vivid and free; hence the reading of the lesson should not come first. The teacher should strive to inspire the child with enthusiasm for the Church by presenting to him an attractive series of vividly drawn pictures, not a mass of dry dates and facts. Whenever possible, use visual helps: pictures of persons and events, geographical charts for the identification of places met with in the narrative. In memorizing and reviewing, do not insist overmuch on lifeless dates: it kills interest. And let the teacher keep this advice well in mind: always make the subject under consideration serve as an illustration or confirmation of some doctrine studied in the catechism, or present it as an example to be imitated, so that the study of Church History always tends to strengthen the children in their faith and devotion.

C. CHURCH HYMNS

92. Why Should the Teaching of Sacred Hymns be Fostered in Catechization? — Considered in itself this topic ought to have found a place in our treatment of the Liturgy (No. 84, ff.). But because of its importance we devote a special paragraph to it.

By Church hymns we understand in the first place religious songs in the vernacular, many of which are of great antiquity. Outside of the liturgical High

Mass and solemn Vespers they may be sung by the congregation in church. We include also amongst them the most common choir melodies such as the Kyrie, Gloria, Credo, Sanctus, Agnus Dei, Tantum Ergo, Vesper Psalms. The Holy Father in his Motu Proprio of November 22, 1903, writes: "The Gregorian chant is to be restored especially amongst the people, so that Christians may once more, after the manner of their forefathers, participate in the sacred liturgy." The explanation and the practice of ecclesiastical chant in catechization should serve a threefold purpose:

1. Sacred songs should prove useful in catechization and enhance its value. Although this is not the main end in view, it should not be overlooked. The chant imparts to religious instruction a certain unction and relish, and makes it more interesting. Unction is given to the teaching when now and then, instead of a prayer in conformity with the ecclesiastical season, or in the midst of the lesson, an appropriate hymn is introduced; e.g., when the Nativity is spoken of, a Christmas hymn is in order; when God's attributes are explained, the Te Deum seems called for. Such practices awaken and foster lofty religious feelings in the children. And the chant gives relish to the instruction when the latter is interspersed with songs for the sake of variety and animation.

This use of religious songs as advocated above is not by any means an innovation. The school curriculum prepared in the year 1586 by Ferdinand II of Tyrol with the co-operation of the Innsbruck Jesuits states: "School-teachers should familiarize their charges with the old Catholic Church songs as found printed in a special volume. They should practise them and have them sung in church as well as in school, and in accordance with the season, instead of the usual prayer."

2. The principal purpose is indicated in the word itself: "Church" hymns: we refer, not to school songs, but to Church songs. And the children should learn them so as to be able to render them at divine services during childhood and in later years. Their importance should not be underestimated, for congregational singing in church is of great value. Good Church Music renders divine services (*a*) more fruitful: "Church Music must render the words of the sacred liturgy more intelligible, arousing Christians more readily to faith and devotion, so that they receive in greater abundance the grace which flows from the sacred mysteries." Thus writes Pius X in his Motu Proprio of November 22, 1903. Moreover, (*b*) it makes divine services more attractive, and not a few who are inclined to be indifferent may thus be brought back to church, where divine grace may influence them to a change of life. Truly apostolic men, therefore, are deeply interested in the restoration of Church Music.

The main thing when assisting at Mass is the deep silent devotion of the heart, which from time to time only breaks forth in song. Hence the people should be given time to sing as well as to pray.

3. A somewhat more remote reason, which, however, deserves consideration here, for fostering the cultivation of Church Music, is: its influence on the religious and moral life of the people as a whole. Good patriotic and popular songs ought to be diffused more widely amongst the people. They would insensibly

supplant the frivolous and ribald songs which work greater harm than is often realized.

The excellent "Speculum catechismi" of Innsbruck (1588) complains: "While heretics have preserved the old Catholic Church Music and melodies, they have substituted a heretical for the Catholic text." Hence "these ancient songs and melodies have been more and more neglected by Catholics." Therefore, together with the new school curriculum of Ferdinand II, a new hymn book is published "so that the former chant may be reintroduced and restored, and anything smacking of heresy or frivolity, licentiousness or scandal, be done away with, so that mind and heart may be drawn to the love and fear of God."

93. How to Proceed. — Let the catechist first of all convince himself that the above-mentioned end: the participation of the people in the liturgy and chant, is not unattainable. Of course it cannot be attained in one bound, and in large city parishes with a constantly shifting population it may only be partly realized. But steady care devoted to singing in catechism classes will secure the realization of what is attainable. Despite initial drawbacks, results will soon be apparent with children. Begin with the simple, more easily grasped melodies and remember the following:

1. The children should be trained to pronounce the text — whether Latin or vernacular — correctly. For the text is all-important in church songs.

2. Many hymns, or at least stanzas, should be learned by heart, not excepting the words of the Gloria, Credo, etc. This is necessary to prevent that the singing be given up when the children have grown into adults who do not always bring their books to church.

3. The text of the chant ought to be explained to

the children, and this can be done whenever a passage in the catechism leads up to it; e.g., an explanation of the Lauda Sion would be timely when the Holy Eucharist is treated of. Even a few words might be added about the history of the better-known chants.

4. The all-important point is frequent practice. The first practice might take place at the close of the day's schoolwork.

5. Choose the songs to be learned with a view to their practical value for church use. You will have too little time at your disposal for many others besides these.

. . . .

We realize, of course, that at present it is scarcely possible fully to carry out the above outlined program, and one of the great reasons for our inability to do so is the lack of training in the catechist. But the only consistent conclusion in presence of this matter-of-fact situation should be: we must devote more care than we have done thus far to this all-important matter so close to the heart of the Holy Father.

CHAPTER II

THE CATECHETICAL METHOD

¶ 4.

PRELIMINARY Notions. — We have explained first the end, then the object of catechetical instruction. Presently we must examine in what way the catechist should proceed: what road shall he take, so that the subject-matter — the complexus of revealed truths — may be so impressed upon the minds and hearts of the children that the direct end explained in the first chapter may thereby be attained? This is the question of the method to be followed in catechetical instruction.

A method, in general, is a fixed, deliberately selected manner of proceeding. "Fixed," i.e., not chosen for some incidental occasion; a method must be of general application. "Deliberately selected": where there is no choice, there is no method. If the choice were not made with a definite end in view, but in a haphazard manner, we might call it a way of doing, but not a method, for the former lacks objectivity and proceeds from personal impulse.

In the general definition given above, the word "method" may be used for every established, intentionally chosen manner of procedure: educational method, writing method, etc. We are here concerned with the teaching method.

The teaching method or didactic method is then a fixed, deliberately selected way of teaching. It may be taken in a wider or in a more restricted meaning, as applying to one study as a whole, e.g., geography, or to one particular lesson. Let us apply the above to catechization.

95. The Catechetical Method is the fixed, deliberately selected manner of proceeding in catechetical instruction. It may be understood in a twofold sense:

In a wider sense it means the manner of proceeding according to certain principles, and with the end in view of conveying to the child mind the sum total of catechetical truth. It is in this sense that we shall treat of method in this chapter.

In a more restricted meaning it is the fixed, deliberately selected manner of proceeding in a single lesson; and the method will then vary as the lesson is concerned with the catechism, Bible History, or any other object of a complementary course. This subject shall be treated more in detail in the last part of this volume under the heading: Special Catechetics. Yet it is impossible to draw a sharp line of demarcation between general and special methodology.

This third chapter is concerned — and divided accordingly — with the solution of two questions:

1. How should the catechetical matter be selected and arranged with regard to the various school grades? It is the question of the program of studies.

2. This point settled, how shall the matter be treated? — the question of the catechetical teaching method.

§ I. THE PROGRAM OF STUDIES, OR SELECTION AND SYSTEMATIC CLASSIFICATION OF THE MATTER

96. Necessity of a Program. — By program of studies we understand an efficient division of the matter so as to adapt it to the age of the pupils.

1. The need of such a program appears clearly from the differences in age among school children. For obviously it would not do to divide mechanically the instructions designed for children from six to fourteen years into eight equally proportioned parts. This would no longer be a program, for the latter must carefully take into consideration the requirements of various ages.

What are these requirements, or from what viewpoint should the eight school grades be grouped so as to obtain a well-balanced division of the matter according to age?

A division universal in its application, no matter how the school may be organized, is the one founded on the general knowledge and ability of the child. And we may distinguish at once two classes: the first class includes all the children who are proficient in reading and writing and whose mental development is fairly advanced. The second class includes all those who are only beginning to acquire, or have very incompletely acquired, this proficiency. When we now divide the first class into two groups, we obtain a practical basis for a good program of studies, as subsequent developments will show. The oldest children, in the seventh and eighth grades, are distinguished from the lower and intermediate grades by the fact that they stand on the threshold of life; hence catechization should prepare them for this important step. And it is well to remember here that for many a youth of our day, the first lapse from virtue occurs at the time he finishes school. The work of the catechist and pastor is therefore by no means at an end when the child has left school for good.

A grouping adopted by many catechists, and under given circumstances a very good one, is arranged with a view to the reception of the Sacraments. The first division comprises the children of the first, second, and even third grades who have not yet received the Sacraments, and are not being directly prepared for their reception. The intermediate division, the third and fourth grades, or the fourth and fifth, comprises those children who should receive the Sacraments, and must consequently be prepared for their reception. The highest division includes the highest grades: from the fifth to the eighth or from the sixth to the eighth, or all the children who have made their First Communion.

This grouping presented some difficulties even before the Pope's decree on early First Communion. The age requirements for First Communion differed so much in various dioceses that it was impossible to frame a program adapted to all cases. And since the decree of Pius X this arrangement no longer offers any advantages, because the lower grades can no longer be considered as embracing those excluded from the reception of the Sacraments.

2. Other reasons necessitating a well-defined program of studies are: it makes for order in the instructions, so that no important points are left out or slurred over, while non-essentials receive extended treatment. Moreover, only a definite program can secure uniformity of instruction in various places. At least all the schools of one diocese should adhere to one plan, so

that the children may not suffer a set-back when moving from one school to another. The plan also saves the teacher much time, and compels a careful preparation. "What the plan of a house is to the builder, the program of studies is to the catechist." Usually the program is prescribed by the bishop, or by all the bishops of a province. In the latter case it is as a rule rather general in outline, and leaves the catechist much freedom. In many dioceses, however, such a graded course of instruction is lacking.

EIGHTH PRINCIPLE. — *The three branches of the catechetical subject-matter should not be taught one after the other, but simultaneously, i.e., Catechism, Bible History, and complementary, instruction should not follow in chronological succession, but should interpenetrate one another.*

97. General Notions. — We had reached this conclusion before and from another standpoint. The central position of the catechism, the peculiar aptness of Bible History for the explanation of catechismal truths, and even the external reason that time is lacking for a detailed treatment of complementary instruction, all favor the simultaneous teaching by mutual interpenetration of the three branches. But because of the obvious methodical value of this conclusion it becomes necessary here to formulate it as a principle. Further proof is not required, but the following remarks must be kept in mind to grasp its correct meaning: When we favor a simultaneous treatment of all three branches, we do not mean that about one-third of the time should be devoted to each. Nor do we mean that the mutual relation of the three branches should remain identical for all ages. In how far one branch should take precedence over another is to be decided in connection with the age and the intellectual maturity of the pupils. Hence in the practical application of the above thesis regard must be had to all these conditions.

> NINTH PRINCIPLE. — *Elementary catechization, i.e., catechization in the lower grades, should be imparted primarily by means of Bible History. In selecting the matter, confine yourself to what is required for these catechumens.*

98. Proof of the First Part. — In the first part of this thesis we ascribe to Bible History in the elementary grades a rôle which we ourselves have claimed above for the catechism. How can we justify this stand?

"As young plants require very special care, so that they may take root and grow, — a care no longer bestowed upon older plants — so also special attention should be devoted to the children of the lower grades." It is this special solicitude which finds expression in our thesis. It will be sufficient to keep in mind the following two points in order to understand the meaning and the correctness of the first part of the thesis, viz., the end of elementary catechization, and the mental aptitudes of the youngest children.

1. The aim of primary catechetical instruction is twofold: first, the children must be trained to serve the Lord in sanctity and justice from their tenderest years. "They should be so instructed and trained as if they were to be called from the lower school grades to enter eternal life." The second aim is to fit them for the work of the higher grades. Hence they should be equipped with that preliminary knowledge which is indispensable for a profitable acquisition of future

truths, and their hearts should be trained into habits that may be strengthened later on and remain with them through life. Hence a twofold end, each important in itself, and not easy of attainment.

"The main doctrines are to be clothed in a garment that fits the child at present and shall be ample enough to fit it when it has grown older. An accomplished catechist is he who succeeds in happily combining those two requirements and carrying out this double task." (Mey)

2. What of the intellectual powers of these six to eight year old children? Reason at this age is little developed. It is difficult for them to grasp abstract truths, to understand things which they cannot see or touch. The heart, however, at this time is uncommonly plastic and receptive towards every noble feeling. It is not hardened by personal sin; baptismal innocence, in most cases still unmarred, renders it peculiarly susceptible to the seed of God's word and to devout feelings. And it is not only susceptible, but the good impressions made are permanent: whatever is deposited in the child's heart at this early age, takes deep root, and proves a permanent acquisition.

3. When we combine these two facts, and ask, Are the religious formulas of the catechism appropriate food for the mind and heart of the child at this age, a nourishment adapted to his condition and giving promise of further development? we are compelled to answer: the catechism is as yet not the right kind of mental pabulum for those children, but Bible History is. And indeed (a) the religious truths which the children should learn can scarcely be conveyed to their minds in their abstract form. But they can easily

grasp those doctrines when presented to them through the medium of Bible History. For instance, the attributes of God, His greatness, His omnipotence, goodness, mercy, can hardly be made intelligible to these children even by the most clearly explained definitions. But they are brought home to them in the recital of the Creation of the world and man, the blessings bestowed upon our first parents, the fall, and the promise of a Redeemer. These vivid and impressive historical narratives furnish at the same time the best possible foundation for the future development of the correct abstract notions as contained in the catechism, which the pupil must acquire in the higher grades.

(b) It is also easier to influence the heart through Bible History than through the catechism. Why? Because the comprehension of the catechismal formulas is very hard for them; hence the danger that because of this hardship the child may grow averse to all religious teaching. And if this occur, how shall the child be trained to love God and His doctrines and the Christian life? Bible History, however, in the hands of a competent teacher, will arouse interest, joy, readiness to listen, beget enthusiasm for the examples of virtue and aversion for sin, and in this manner lead to the fulfilment of the twofold purpose we have in view (Nos. 80–81).

(c) Finally, an external reason militates in favor of Bible History in the lower grades. In many schools not enough time is left for a thorough study of the whole Bible History; the teacher must mostly be satisfied with some references to sundry facts or events adduced in explanation of the catechism. Therefore the best possible use should be made of the opportunity afforded in the lower grades.

Moreover, experience has decided in favor of this practice. There is scarcely an experienced catechist who makes use of the catechism in the lower grades. In various programs of study the catechism is at times still mentioned before Bible History, but practically the course is so shaped that special emphasis is laid on Bible History.

99. More Detailed Description of the Matter for the Lower Grades. — 1. The norm for the selection of the subject-matter may also be deduced from the end aimed at in primary instruction as explained above (No. 98, 1). Both for the training of children to a Christian life and for the foundation of future instruction, it is necessary that their mind and heart should be deeply imbued with religious truth. And this end can only be attained when the catechist limits his teaching to those verities indispensable for a Christian life, and devotes all his efforts to inculcating these essentials thoroughly. *Non multa sed multum*, applies also in this case.

Mey writes: "Only the essentials are necessary, but let these be given thoroughly, clearly, distinctly. Leave out whatever renders impossible or even difficult for beginners a complete understanding of the subject. Follow the advice of St. Augustine in his treatise On the Catechization of the Ignorant." Hence Mey would do away with the history of Joseph in the lower grades, for whatever in it points to the Redemption is already too difficult for these children; whatever is contained in it besides that is secondary, and "when in primary instruction these secondary details are forced into the main picture, they lead the children into confusion, and prevent them from seizing upon the main outlines."

The catechist, therefore, should not give in to the temptation of making a brilliant showing with his pupils in examinations, loading down their memories for that purpose with a mass of prayers, mottoes, and songs. Gruber and Mey are models of conciseness and show us how to avoid cramming the child's mind with ill-understood and unappreciated memory matter.

2. The few points that are explained should not of course be treated in a haphazard manner: what is necessary for the Christian life, that should be chosen. What is this in a concrete form? The practice of the Church tells us: the four ancient catechismal formulas (Creed, Sacraments, Decalog, Lord's Prayer), with the truths and commandments set forth in them, should essentially be taught even to the youngest children.

Are to be recommended for the very first instructions: the Sign of the Cross and the prayers already known to the children. In this wise the transition is most easily made from what they are familiar with to the new truths now to be acquired.

From Bible History should be taken: the Creation of the world, corresponding to the first article of the Creed, while God's omnipotence, wisdom, goodness can be more especially dwelt upon in connection with it. The fall of man, the promise of a Redeemer and His coming: these correspond to the second and third articles of the Creed; in connection with the Annunciation, the Ave Maria may be explained. The prominent events in the life of Christ should be dwelt upon: His infancy and baptism, and in connection therewith give an outline of the Sacrament of baptism. Also His teaching concerning the two great commandments of the love of God and our neighbor, which are further developed in the Ten Commandments. Then, Christ's doctrine on prayer, together with the Our Father. Then, Jesus as the friend of children should be sketched; also, the Last Supper and the institution of the Holy Eucharist, with Confession, since according to the teaching of Pius X these children should be admitted to First Communion. Finally, the Passion of Christ, His Resurrection and Ascension, and the descent of the Holy Ghost. — From this enumeration it may be seen how, taking Bible History as a guide, the important points of the four catechetical formulas may be gone through with the children. And in so doing the catechism is not lost sight of, since the truths taught have prepared the ground for further catechetical instruction. How? Because of the simple explanation and memorizing of the four catechetical formulas; besides, also, because the essentials of Bible History have been given to the children in the words of the catechism. E.g., after relating the biblical account of the Creation, the question may be asked: What did God create? And the answer should be: God is the Creator of heaven and earth and all things. Finally, the children in the second and third grades may be given a catechism, thus enabling them to learn more easily the answers to the questions asked in connection with Bible History. Naturally a very limited selection will have to be made. In the first grade concert repetition of the answers, and other means will have to take the place of the book.

For complementary instruction: besides the teaching of the Lord's Prayer, Hail Mary, Creed, Decalog, Evening and Morning Prayers, prayer to the Guardian Angel, Doxology, Salve Regina, etc., attention should also be paid to the manner of attending church, folding the hands, genuflecting; visual instruction should be given about the altar, chalice, the important parts of Mass, e.g., why the priest lifts up the Host and chalice; the great feasts of the ecclesiastical year should be mentioned, and some hymns, especially for Christmas, should be learned.

The complexus of catechetical matter for the lower grades we shall designate as: the fundamental catechism, and the next thesis also applies to it.

100. Concluding Remarks anent the Youngest Children. — Many of the methodical rules given further on in this third chapter are also applicable to the lower grades. Their right use will not present any special difficulty as far as the questions hitherto explained are concerned. It may be added here that older children, especially brothers and sisters, should be led to take an interest in the instruction of the younger ones.

There have been periods in which the catechization of the younger children was direly neglected. Gruber gives vent to frequent complaints in this regard. May those times never return! For we should never forget that even in their tenderest years children are entitled to enjoy the supernatural treasures; nay, that God desires especially to be honored by His little ones. The zealous catechist will therefore leave no stone unturned to secure for the Lord this agreeable morning oblation of a pious Christian youth. Since the First

Communion decree of August 8, 1910, the zealous catechist, besides many motives to spur him on to fervent endeavors in behalf of the little ones, has been given a secure direction for his work in the lower grades, based as it is on the clearly manifested will of the Holy Father.

The very special interest which Pius X has taken in the younger children will no doubt call forth a rich catechetical literature for their benefit. And indeed, quite a number of such elementary booklets have already come from the press.

TENTH PRINCIPLE. — *In the higher grades the catechist should not treat a special part of the catechism each year; but he should endeavor to go through the whole catechism, at least in its main lines, every two years. The fundamental catechism, however, i.e., those truths which make up the essential content of Christian Doctrine, should be treated or reviewed every year.*

101. Explanation. — It were wrong to treat every year but one main section of the catechism, as scientific theology is bound to do by dividing its subject-matter into several tracts. It is to this practice, which has recently been advocated once more, that we oppose the first part of the above thesis. Thereafter, the intermediate or large catechism should be gone through twice during the last four to five years of the school curriculum.

The small catechism, in so far as it can be used in the lower grades in connection with Bible Stories, should be gone through in one year, always remembering that Bible History ranks first at this age, and that the subjects taken from it must be restricted in number, as explained above (No. 99).

Our proposition needs to be well understood. The reviewing should not be a mere verbal repetition of what was said before; but the second time every subject should be gone into more deeply, so that a more thorough comprehension results. The spiritual progress of the child requires this, and also the necessity of keeping the child's interest in the subject alive. This didactic method is known as the teaching in *concentric circles*. In line with this, many questions in some catechisms are marked with an asterisk: these should be adverted to only in the second treatment of the matter. We call special attention to the clause in the above thesis: "at least in its main lines." Where lack of time prevents the study of the whole catechism in this manner, the matter should not be spread over more than two or three years, and then, while full time is devoted to the more important truths, the less fundamental doctrines should be cursorily treated.

The "fundamental catechism" mentioned in the second part of the thesis embraces all those truths whose knowledge and practice are indispensable to a Christian and to all Christian life. It is a synopsis of the most necessary truths of the catechism, and coincides with what we have already found to be the primary requisites for the Christian life (No. 99). In the lower grades nothing but the fundamental catechism is taught, and that after the manner already explained (No. 98), i.e., by means of Bible Stories. When reviewing the matter, the teaching may be gone deeper into, and this can be done by adducing new examples from Holy Writ. In the higher grades the teacher should review extensively whatever may not have received thorough treatment in the first school years. Moreover, whenever opportunity offers, he should not fail to direct attention to those fundamental truths.

102. Proof of the First Part of the Thesis. — The "concentric method" is favored by the best programs, founded on long experience. Moreover, internal reasons favor it also.

1. Even if we aimed merely at imparting a thorough knowledge, we should have to adopt this concentric method, — although perhaps theoretically opposed to it, — for we must take into account the psychological law that with adults, and more so with children, an object presented to the mind for the first time is grasped only in its external outline. It is only slowly and after repeated efforts that its deeper and essential characteristics are finally comprehended.

When a child is to be taught geography, a map is first drawn on the blackboard, and the child is told to copy it. In this manner he is enabled, by visual impressions, to build up a complex mental picture; it becomes an easy matter then to introduce the characteristics of countries and peoples into this fundamental outline of the physical layout of the various countries. The art of the religious teacher consists also in imparting this general outline of faith during the time at his disposal, filling in the sketch by the gradual addition of colors and tints, as the child advances in knowledge.

The principal reason in favor of the method we advocate is: it makes for a deeper, more thorough comprehension than can be expected from a single study of the matter. Even when the teacher succeeds in giving the children a clear grasp of the subject in a first explanation, the full import of a given doctrine will be clearer to a ten year old, and more so to a twelve or thirteen year old pupil than to an eight year old one. And a further reason why we require a twice-repeated study of the catechism lies in the evident divergences noted in children from nine to twelve, and from twelve to fourteen years of age.

2. Catechization, however, does not stop at imparting knowledge to the children; care should be taken that Christian Doctrine be memorized and deeply impressed upon the heart. Frequent reviews and explanations, with applications to the various states of life, are necessary to attain this end.

3. A practical reason militating against piecemeal teaching is the fact that not a few children change their abode more or less frequently. For such there is great danger of their never being instructed in the whole Christian Doctrine, if in a relatively short space of time it cannot be given to them in its entirety.

103. Proof of the Second Part of the Thesis. — Our claim that the fundamental catechism should be gone through every year is based on the fact that many children, after leaving school, forget much of the religious instruction they have received. The consequences will be deplorable, unless at least the great truths of Christianity can be stamped indelibly upon the mind and heart. But this end is only gained by frequent reviewing, not of course by mere mechanical repetition. It is therefore not too much to demand that the cardinal doctrines of faith and morals be presented to the child every year; that moreover his attention be called to them on every appropriate occasion, that his whole life may be molded upon supernatural tenets and informed by supernatural motives.

The special subject-matter then for the primary department is the fundamental catechism taught in Bible Stories. The objection may here be raised: is it not a didactic mistake to treat the same matter repeatedly, as the interest of the children is bound to flag? This objection will be met more in detail further on (No. 105). A provisional remark may, however, find place here: even if the children of the lower grades are together in one room, one need not be overmuch concerned about their attention falling off. An experienced theoretical and practical writer testifies: any one who has dealt with children knows how necessary it is to repeat the same thing frequently in the same manner. The words of St. Paul: "To write the same things to you to me indeed is not wearisome, but to you is necessary" (Philip. 3, 1), may be applied to every school as a whole, but especially to the lower grades. The catechist, however, must guard against expecting more of the children than their age and mental development warrant. Although the subject-matter remains identical, the results will differ from year to year.

104. Concentration. — Of late "concentration" has been opposed to the concentric method. It has been proposed that, while Bible Stories keep their place in the lower grades, the catechism be divided in such fashion among the higher grades that it need be gone through but once. Thus, e.g., in the fourth grade: the Commandments of God, of the Church, and confession; in the fifth, the other Sacraments, the sacramentals, and prayer; in the sixth, the lessons on faith, with more exhaustive instruction on the Sacraments; in the seventh, Church History, the Sacrament of Matrimony, the doctrines of grace, virtue, Christian perfection. And concentration is recommended to provide for the needed reviewing, and in such a manner that the teacher needs frequently to revert to those doctrinal points which are intimately related to the newly learned truths.

A concrete example of the concentration method: "the ninth article of the Creed shows us the foundation and development of the Church beginning on the day of Pentecost. It is impossible to think of our Church without the offices of teacher, priest, and shepherd, found in her only. Her teaching office is grounded on a faith infallible in its source. Here is the place to treat the infallibility of the Church, to explain and prove the notion and object of faith, Holy Writ and Tradition. . . . Here also the sacrament of Holy Orders may be treated appropriately. . . . It is equally appropriate to treat of the seven Sacraments in general, and also of the sacramentals. . . . And are not also the commandments of God and the precepts of the Church kindred subjects that may be explained in connection with the ninth article?"

But any one can easily see that such attempts rest on a mere subjective basis, and may undergo a number of variations to suit individual tastes; for points of contact may be detected between even the most disparate doctrines. Why, e.g., not treat in connection with the ninth article, of prayer, that strong weapon of the Church? Why not treat of the Church as the guardian of the commandments of God? Thus we would have explained the whole catechism in connection with the ninth article! If this suggestion were acted upon, the result would exceed even the expectations of the defenders of "concentration"! — Does this imply that we must unreservedly reject this theory?

Whatever it contains of value should be retained. There is no irreconcilable opposition between it and our theory; nor is it a new discovery in any way, for it has been practised of old by all expert teachers. The older pedagogy was deeply interested in concentration: it insisted that all education should be unified, not in a mechanical manner, but after the fashion of a living organism. Thus we have the twofold concentration of which we hear much nowadays: concentration in the ethical sense, consisting in this, that a uniform direction towards a higher ideal of moral perfection is given to various branches of study; and logical concentration, which seeks to connect inherently related doctrines. The old requirement that all education tend towards the upbuilding of a thoroughly Christian character is the most thoroughgoing realization of ethical concentration; and what we have said above concerning the interpenetration of all branches of catechetical instruction, nay our very upholding of concentric teaching, is partly grounded on the principle of logical concentration: the child is entitled, not to detached parts, but to a consistent whole, divided and integrated as the child's age may demand.

It seems impossible to us to cast aside the concentric method in the teaching of adults, and especially so in the common school, when dealing with growing children whose mental powers and experiences undergo a continual evolution.

105. Objections. — Opposition to the method we champion is at times very sharp. Some of the weightiest arguments urged against us are:

1. The concentric method deadens interest and creates tedium, because the children are ever poring over the same matter. Good ground for this objection may be found at times in the mechanical method and the slipshod work of many teachers. Instructors of this kind, however, would not attain better results with any other method. We do not favor mechanical repetition, but insist that the verities already learned should constitute the foundation on which to rear the

remaining parts of the edifice of Christian truth; and this should be done by more comprehensive explanations leading to a deeper insight.

For would it not be a deplorable admission in this day of "psychological methods" to manifest so little confidence in the teaching art as to grant that the reviewing of a study after one or two years must prove irksome? Were our Christian people ever heard to complain about the wearisome yearly recurrence of the festivals, and the great mysteries they commemorate? And is it not an attested fact that truths well understood never pall, any more than classical works of art? If evil there be, it cannot result from the concentric method: let Christian Doctrine be presented to the children with inspiring warmth and supernatural persuasiveness, and no fear need be entertained about the irksomeness of frequent reviews.

And we hope it does not savor of injustice to remark that our critics seem to project the blasé disposition of modern adults into the minds of children. Yet when tradesmen and their apprentices do not deem it tiresome to be intent constantly on their selfsame tasks, why should not our immeasurably higher supernatural concerns stand a repeated examination into their manifold motives, shadings, and applications?

And more: when in profane learning the principle holds good: not many things but much, we should not lose sight, especially in catechization, of the fact that quantitative increase and new matter at best only stimulate curiosity, but cannot make for solid spirituality. The latter is built on an ever-deepening insight into the treasures of divine wisdom, and this seems impossible of attainment without recourse to the concentric method.

2. Others base their opposition on this, that the concentric method overburdens the program, since the whole subject-matter is to be absolved in a relatively short space of time. Hence thorough treatment is sacrificed to haste and the result is the opposite of the great advantages claimed for the method.

These evil features are liable to creep into any school if the time devoted to the catechism is very limited, and the latter is perhaps gone through in its entirety every year for six or seven years in succession. But the consistent conclusion to be drawn therefrom is not that the concentric method should be rejected, but that the teaching should be confined to the essential truths. Hence our thesis says: "at least in its main lines."

3. The objection that the concentric method is opposed to the psychological law according to which the pupil must be led from the individual and concrete to the general, while the concentric method follows an opposite course, may provisionally be answered thus: the psychological method, in as far as it is indeed psychological, must harmonize with the other laws of the mind, e.g., with the one that human reason attains a thorough knowledge of the inner nature of an object only through repeated efforts of thought and comparison. How in this case this apparent contradiction may be solved is explained further on more exhaustively.

. . . .

Before giving some practical hints on where to find well-digested programs, or how to make them up for one's self (No. 108), it is necessary to state another principle, in answer to the question: Are there not in Christian Doctrine a number of points, either so unpractical or so difficult of understanding as to make it advisable to leave them out of the common school curriculum?

Eleventh Principle. — *No important part of Christian Doctrine should be passed over in catechetical instruction, even when it proves difficult of understanding, or has no immediate practical bearing for the children.*

106. Meaning of the Thesis. — An erroneous and pernicious view, already formerly combated by Gruber, presently comes to the fore again: many catechetical doctrines are injurious to children, or at least they are ill-understood and altogether unpractical; they should be left out of the program. We know how Rousseau would prevent the child from being taught any religious truth until he reaches his adolescence. "In his fifteenth year my pupil should be unaware that he has a soul; perhaps it is too early for him to know it in his eighteenth year, for in case he learns it earlier than is necessary there is danger that he may never know." That Christ taught differently concerning children, and that God Himself manifested His will in their regard in the fourth commandment, did not of course impress Rousseau in any way. But it is rather strange that sundry catechists should be found defending views which must necessarily lead to the same consequences. Even Hirscher has not altogether freed himself from this erroneous tendency, holding as he does, that "image of God, original sin, legislative authority of the rulers of the Church, capital sin, etc.," are so many obscure or unpractical and hence unnecessary notions for children.

Our thesis is directed against such views. Yet it must be borne in mind that we do not insist on treating everything contained in the catechism in the same exhaustive manner. For lack of time will compel us to pass over much already contained in the fundamental truths, as we have clearly shown in answering the objection raised against the concentric method. But none of the fundamental truths themselves should be withheld from the children.

107. Proof of Our Thesis.

1. Granting the principle of our opponents to be right, that nothing should be taught the children which they cannot fully comprehend, we must conclude that an extremely small number of supernatural truths is to be offered to them, since most of these are beyond the reach not only of children but of adults as well. From this false conclusion we argue that the premise is unsound. Why, is explained shortly.

2. It is said: the child should not be taught what he cannot grasp. We answer: if indeed a truth were altogether incomprehensible, it were superfluous to attempt learning it. But this is not the case with revealed truths. As a matter of fact they cannot be fully comprehended: God and His infinite truths cannot be exhausted by a finite intelligence. What we learn of the mysteries of faith is largely by analogy, example, parable. But this incomplete knowledge, even in the case of the child, is such that we may rest satisfied with it. Nay, this very limitation of the child's intellectual powers is a distinct advantage in realizing the chief aim of all catechetical instruction: the upbuilding of a life of faith. For, (*a*) from his very nature, and experience confirms this view, the child is not handicapped by intellectual pride, and faith can grow unhampered in his soul; (*b*) experience also teaches that this faith, if but imperfectly compre-

hended, becomes so firmly rooted as to blossom forth in practical results that might well be envied by many an adult. And this is true even of the deepest mysteries: God's greatness and ubiquity, the Holy Eucharist, original sin, the death of Christ, etc., arouse most lively emotions in young hearts.

"Teach the truth with conviction," warns Jungmann, "and every day you shall witness the fulfilment of the prophetic words: 'Out of the mouth of infants and of sucklings thou hast perfected praise because of thy enemies' (Ps. 8, 3); and 'Wisdom,' i.e., not proud human science, but the grace from above infused in the soul, 'Wisdom openeth the mouth of the dumb and made the tongues of infants eloquent.' Wisd. 10, 21. Let us never indulge the idea, so often taking stealthily possession of the mind, which would make deep theological speculation the test of faith, and is inclined to regard mere human, natural knowledge of religious matters as the gauge of Christian understanding, love and life." From personal experience Beda Weber answers the question: what steadied his faith amidst the vicissitudes of life, the fearful stress of onsetting doubt, the crushing weight of bad example. "The grace of God which in my tenth year was infused into my soul through Christ's Body and Blood unto knowledge and sanctification, became my teacher, brought peace to my soul, and was my only salvation." Many testimonials of this kind have been written; innumerable are the unprinted, living proofs to the effect that the grace of God opens the child's soul for the appreciation of faith's deepest mysteries.

Christian teachers have known this right along, and for this reason they relied first on divine grace, and then on human ability. St. Augustine puts forth the most sublime truths in his catechization for beginners; Bossuet requests parents to teach their children, as soon as they begin to speak, about God the Creator, the divine Trinity, God's omnipresence, omniscience, the Incarnation, etc. Alban Stolz also requires that "as soon as the child is able to talk, he should be trained to devotion. In young children baptismal grace, like a tender plant, thirsts after the devotional in prayer, divine service, and instruction."

3. The second objection raised against our proposition is thus formulated: many doctrines of the catechism, e.g., Extreme Unction, Holy Orders, Matrimony, Precepts of the Church, are of no practical value for children, and become binding only in the future; why treat of them in the catechism?

Answer: We do not ask that the children be taught everything that is said in sermons for adults concerning the duties of their respective state of life. But on the other side it is erroneous to hold that the explanation of duties which the child shall have to fulfil only later on, is altogether superfluous. Such teaching is necessary in order that (a) in later life these commandments may be fulfilled all the more surely. In purely natural matters the impressions of childhood remain quite ineffaceable; and the children's future religious and moral life is all the more intimately bound up with their early knowledge and realization of the binding force of the commandments. "Many a one besides myself," writes Overberg, "has learned through long experience that common people with the fear of God are quick, as soon as they are warned, to recognize as wrong and to avoid anything sinful, in case they have learned in their youth to look upon it as such. But if this has not been impressed on them, it is frequently difficult and even impossible to make them realize the danger. Any one who has had that experience will understand why after each of the Ten Commandments I have given a table of the sins oftenest committed against each."

(b) There is another very practical reason why even those doctrines that become binding only in later life should not be neglected in the catechization of children: to reserve such teaching for sermons only, shows a woful lack of acquaintance with real life. Very much would thus be left to chance: for who can guarantee regular attendance at sermons, even when overlooking for the nonce the all too frequent unwillingness of adults to be instructed? And how could even the most zealous preacher impart that thorough knowledge of our duties which can be so easily inculcated through a well-ordered program? Does not the priest know from experience how little regard is often paid by Christians to the duties of their state of life? How seldom do people accuse themselves on this subject in the confessional, and yet how frequent and grave are the transgressions! Whence is this? When the children hear little about these duties, they scarcely realize later on that any sin is committed by neglecting them. It is therefore wrong to begin the instruction on the commandments and duties only when they become binding. Moreover, human passions grow stronger all unseen, unless their growth be forestalled by timely instruction, thus repressing them before they have really come in conflict with duty. A deplorable example is found in mixed marriages. Now if we neglect to instruct the children on this subject, — we refer of course to instruction adapted to their age, — the results in the course of time are bound to be still more deplorable.

(*c*) From all this it follows very clearly that the premise of our opponents: certain doctrines are quite unpractical for children, is altogether false. Indirectly, i.e., for later life, they are of great practical value. Moreover, they are even directly beneficial to the children at their present age. For the child is thus impressed with the conviction that he stands in presence of a divine doctrine, although it is to be carried out only later in life. He has also learned to make acts of faith, of submission to the divine will, and of firm purpose faithfully to perform his duties through life. Thus, e.g., when explaining the Sacrament of Matrimony, the children may be told that because of the sacred duties devolving upon parents, God has instituted a special Sacrament for them; that at the same time He has thus shown his special love for children, because on their account He gave their parents so many graces. Is not this calculated to increase the respect of children for their parents, their love for God, their gratefulness towards Him?

4. We conclude our argumentation with two authoritative testimonies: Leo XIII in his Encyclical on Freemasonry of April 20, 1884, expressly demands that our youth be warned against the danger of falling into the clutches of this secret society.

"Parents, teachers, pastors should zealously endeavor, whenever opportunity offers in religious instruction, to warn children about the true character of this sect, so that they may learn in time to guard against the manifold wiles and deceptions by which those who work for its increase try to ensnare the unwary. Nay, those who prepare the children for the reception of the Sacraments would do well to lead each one to make the firm resolution never to join a society without the knowledge of their parents or the advice of their pastor or confessor."

This is the language of an experienced shepherd mindful of hard facts, irrespective of any didactic theories.

Mixed marriages constituted one of the chief topics of deliberation at the provincial Council of Melbourne, Australia, 1869. Besides the decrees, the bishops present also published a pastoral letter wherein we read: "The frequency of such marriages is a foul blot on the good name of our Catholic people. . . . Hence, if our youth were frequently and freely instructed as they should be, by their parents and pastors, about the mind and the teaching of the Church concerning such unions, this evil would occur less frequently than is the case at present." Because of the resulting mixed marriages, the most zealous shepherds of souls unqualifiedly condemn the pernicious practice of postponing instruction on this head until such time as it can be understood and becomes of practical value.

. . . .

In conclusion a few words must be added in answer to the question:

108. Where can a Thorough Program of Studies be Found?

In most dioceses such a program is prescribed by the bishop. The young catechist and theologian should acquire the issues of the diocesan paper in which are published the program and other catechetical norms. In the absence of such an official plan, or in case the one prescribed cannot be carried out in some particular school because of extraordinary untoward circumstances, the catechist himself or all the catechists of a given district should elaborate one. Sketches are found in most catechetical manuals, and it is obviously preferable to follow closely those best adapted to the diocese in question. Since the publication of Pope Pius' First Communion Decree some dioceses have introduced new, temporary programs, because catechetical instruction must henceforth take into account this early First Communion. The catechist, therefore, should keep informed about the latest measures emanating from ecclesiastical authority.

Graded programs adapted to American schools and conditions are found in: Spirago-Messmer: Method of Christian Doctrine, p. 155 ff.; the "Course of Christian Doctrine," published by the Dolphin Press, Philadelphia, Pa., 1904, is also very valuable.

In a well-organized school with at least three classes no difficulty will be experienced in carrying out the plan we have sketched. We called for three stages in religious instruction, and no class will embrace more than one stage. In a school with only two classes one may proceed by taking together the three first grades as the lower division, dividing the upper division into two grades.

When there is only one class in the school, the work is slightly more complicated. At times provision is made for organizing three divisions: it would be easier to have only two, but in that case the catechist must pay even more attention to the differences in age when testing the children than in teaching them. We shall have more to say further on about schools with only one class (Nos. 110–111). Whatever the complexion of the school may be, this should be remembered: in the first three (or two years, according to circumstances) teach the fundamental catechism by means of Bible Stories. Then go through the intermediate or higher catechisms twice, the first time in the two intermediate years, the second time, with more details, in the two or three last years of the school curriculum.

. . . .

The program, considered thus far in its more restricted meaning, does not offer a detailed division of the subject-matter. This is called for, however, and what we have to suggest in this regard follows quite naturally from the above, and can be summed up in the following

TWELFTH PRINCIPLE. — *In order to ensure completely the end of catechetical instruction, the catechist must, moreover, plan the amount of matter to be explained every month and week, and divide accordingly the time at his disposal.*

109. This More Detailed Schedule is distinguished from the program in this, that the latter distributes the matter according to the children's age, whilst the former assigns this same matter in detail to each month, week, and hour.

Ecclesiastical authorities, even when they prescribe a program, seldom lay down a time schedule, or at most prescribe what is to be taught in a month, but do not go into the details of the weekly or hourly task. A general uniform plan of this kind, however, offers this great advantage in large cities and industrial conglomerations, that, with a sometimes rather frequent change of domicile, the children nevertheless can make steady, uninterrupted progress in the catechism. Where such a definite plan does not exist, the catechist himself should draw up one. Otherwise his instructions are likely to be given in a haphazard way, any program notwithstanding. Sundry important points will be slurred over, while others will be unnecessarily elaborated. With the help of his schedule, however, the catechist is bound to exercise self-control, and facilitates at the same time the conscientious preparation of his lesson.

How should the catechist proceed in making up his schedule? He should not strive after a mechanical division of the matter in parts of equal length; but he should take into consideration (a) the relative importance of various doctrines, for more time must be devoted to the essentials (compare thirteenth principle); (b) the reviewing of a doctrine requires less time than the initial explanation of the same. Climatic conditions, the cold of winter and the heat of summer, must be taken into consideration, and the explanation of important doctrines should not be set for a time when interruptions in the instruction may be expected; (c) let the catechist write out his whole schedule in the form of a comprehensive table, indicating thereon not merely the number, but also a synopsis of the doctrines, so that at all times he may have before him a complete schema of the subject.

110. Time Schedule. — The days, and the time of the day to be set apart for catechetical instruction, should be carefully selected. What is meant by such a time schedule may be seen from the following:

(*a*) In the case of small children it is advisable to spread the instruction over several half-hours. They become quickly tired and distracted, and hence also profane pedagogy has introduced more and more half-hour periods. Of course the prudent catechist will always take the general arrangements of the school into consideration.

(*b*) The morning hours are preferable, especially those that do not immediately follow upon exhausting lessons. Experimental demonstrations claim to prove that the children are most alert during the first hour of study; their efficiency slightly increases during the second hour, to decrease right thereafter. The following general rules may be recommended in practice: let catechetical instruction be given during the first hour of the session or during the hour following a protracted recess.

(*c*) The hours for catechetical instruction should be spread uniformly over the week, e.g., Monday, Wednesday, Friday; not Monday, Tuesday, Wednesday.

(*d*) In schools with one class only, the making-up of a schedule presents greater difficulties. In some places the custom exists of devoting about ten minutes to the smaller children, twenty minutes to the intermediate grades, and thirty minutes to the higher grades. In case only two grades are represented in one class, each may be given an equal amount of time. For further guidance the following hints may be useful:

111. How to Proceed in One-class Schools, and in general in classes including divisions of various ages. — The ideal should be to have all divisions profit at the same time by oral instruction imparted in such a manner that both the younger and the older pupils may follow it to advantage. Two or three grades in one room present no great difficulty in this regard; but it becomes a rather serious problem when older pupils are in the room besides the lower grades. The catechist might proceed in this way: while addressing indirectly the younger pupils, many a biblical event related to them will no doubt interest the older pupils; the catechist may therefore include in his teaching many remarks intended for the latter. An occasional question may help to keep them attentive. Catechization under such conditions demands of course careful preparation. Besides, the older ones may be given written compositions, treating of the essential doctrines of the catechism, or some biblical event, or a prayer; or they may be asked to develop in writing the answer to a question, e.g., how is Sunday celebrated in the church, at home? How often are the church bells rung during the day, and why? What are the appurtenances of the altar? The catechism may also be brought into relation with other branches: what churches do you know north, or south of us? Where in Christian Doctrine do you meet the numbers 1, 2, 3, 4, 5, 7?

To keep the younger ones busy while addressing the older pupils is a more difficult task. While expounding Bible History, it is easier to keep alive their attention: sundry details or questions intended for them may be interspersed in the teaching. They are perhaps ahead of the older ones in their curiosity to learn, but their intellect is less developed. Those who are able to write may be kept busy at this task; for the others a drawing may be sketched on the blackboard (of the

Crucifix, Mount Calvary with the three Crosses, the church, steeple, altar) and the children told to copy it.

While, however, their writing or drawing must be examined, and this involves a certain amount of labor, it will generally prove more advantageous to devote this time to the careful preparation of a lesson by which all the children may profit at the same time.

§ II. THE TEACHING METHOD

112. Synopsis. — Should catechization walk its own individual way, or should it profit by profane didactic methods? In accordance with the saying: grace does not destroy nature, we may take for granted at the outset that there can be no opposition between correct catechetical methods on one side, and the didactic rules established for profane sciences on the other side. Yet we should not lose sight of the fact that catechization must not be hidebound by scientific rules. And this first of all because its object is not a scientifically systematized matter: we cannot possibly place on the same level the doctrines of Jesus Christ and the profane learning of our schools. Secondly, the catechist, while making use of profane didactic means, must also rely on the assistance of divine grace.

Among present-day didactic systems that of Willmann appears to us to be the most complete and most satisfactory on account of its correct and thoroughly grounded principles. Despite some variations in terminology, it will not be difficult to follow closely his Didactic in establishing our own norms for catechization.[1]

[1] See: Cath. Educ. Rev., Jan. 1914, p. 3 ff.

Willmann prefaces his explanation of the study course and method by a statement of those psychological and logical principles which are of prime importance in this matter.

1. The psychological analysis of the learning process tells us that the pupil grasps and assimilates a given subject gradually and not in one act. Although these stages are variously enumerated by different didacticians, they all agree in the main on three chief stages in learning and teaching: the pupil proceeds from apprehension to understanding and then to application (knowledge, understanding, ability); on the part of the teacher this threefold processus presupposes: presentation, explanation, confirmation, or fixing, making the knowledge permanent.

This succession of stages is so deeply grounded in the nature of things that we may expect to meet with it in the various directions and rules left us by teachers of all times. The requirement of the old rhetoricians: first to seek the material, then to meditate on it, and finally to express it, shows the same tripartite division, and all art proceeds in the same manner.

Hence every science requires first rich experiential matter; this must then be digested, and finally it must be correctly expressed. Even daily life demands "an open eye, sharp understanding, ability." And Holy Writ says: "A man that hath much experience shall think of many things; and he that hath learned many things, shall shew forth understanding." Ecclesias. 34, 9. The teacher, therefore, should remember that the various stages in the development of youth follow in like manner: the child (until about its tenth year) receives impressions; the boy's characteristic trait is the desire to understand; the youth (from about the sixteenth year on) is already intent on working out his plans in practice.

The Presentation: The teacher should present the object itself or its image to the senses of the pupil: objective presentation; or he may recall to the memory of the pupil objects previously perceived: reproduction, presentation in its true meaning, describing objects and circumstances, telling about events and facts.

The Explanation aims either at verbal understanding: textual explanation (exegesis, interpretation, comment, etc.); or it has in view the understanding of the essence of an object: essential explanation, showing not merely how a thing is, but why it is. Aristotle sums up the matter thus: "To know what something is, is identical with knowing why it is." While explanation in this sense (causal explanation) consists more particularly in evolving a concept, by showing either how the particular is derived from the general, or how the general is reached inductively from the particular, it seems appropriate to designate this processus by the word: development.

Permanence is secured, where knowledge is concerned, by impressing the matter on the mind; where the will is concerned, by practice. Frequent recourse must therefore be had to reviewing and supplementary explanation. The gap between the mere knowledge of truth and its practical use is bridged over by pointing out practical opportunities for the application of knowledge. Catechization has it in its power not only to lead to the utilization of knowledge, but to the practical and permanent molding of individual life, e.g., by the praying of the acts of faith, hope, and love.

At this stage questioning is most appropriately

brought into play, and a question is but a condensed statement. However, during the explanation also questions must be asked. As language in general, a query is the vehicle of intercourse between teacher and pupil.

These manifold activities of the teacher are usually called the modes of teaching.

2. But the knowledge of the psychological stages of learning is not sufficient for the right utilization of the teaching material. The latter itself must be logically developed. If it were always of a simple nature the teacher would merely have to correlate it with other knowledge. But the complex material must be analyzed first, and afterwards again synthetized: only thus can one hope to gain an insight into the mutual relations of things and ensure their comprehension. This processus is called the method of analysis and synthesis.

To avoid the confusion created by the erroneous use of these expressions, they should, in conformity with Aristotelian logic, be used only in the following meaning: "The resolution of every complex into its elements is called analysis; while synthesis is the processus from the (general, simple) principles to the conclusions derived from them, analysis is the regressive processus from the complex to the particular."

Analysis, therefore, goes from the singular, the concrete, the determined, to the general. It abstracts in concepts, generalizes in judgments, inductively establishes laws on the basis of comparison between individual facts, and regressively examines the grounds and causal connections.

Synthesis on the contrary follows a downward course, particularizing concepts, specializing judgments; it deductively applies laws to particular facts; from the cause it proceeds to its activities and effects.

Whenever we wish to comprehend an object, we use both analysis and synthesis, and for this reason they are especially valuable in the training of undeveloped minds. Their importance is clear from this, that the very mention of a didactic method calls first and foremost for the analytical and synthetical processus.

. . . .

What has been said above is summarized in the subjoined schema.

Following is the order of our exposition: as a protest against mechanical, stilted formalism, we insist

1. that all doctrines should not be treated as of equal importance. Then we advert to what must be especially taken into consideration for the first stage, and at the same time for the teaching in general, viz.,

2. catechetical perspicuity and catechetical language; then

3. we treat of questioning. Then, in connection with the second stage, we

4. treat of the explanation, and especially the analysis and synthesis, and further, because of its great importance, of

5. demonstration.

6. Some remarks about 6. impressing the truth upon the mind, and 7. applying and utilizing it, will suffice to make clear the last formal stage.

Stages of learning:	Teaching modes:	Special helps for these:
Apprehension	showing presentation in its proper meaning (description and narration)	language (is used however for all stages of instruction)
Understanding	explanation of words and things (the "how" of things) argumentation (the "why" of things)	methods of analysis and synthesis
Application in wider meaning	impression application in restricted sense practice	questioning (used throughout instruction)

A. NO MECHANICAL UNIFORMITY

THIRTEENTH PRINCIPLE. — *The catechist should devote special care to the teaching of those doctrines which are of paramount importance for the Christian life, and make sure that all children are thoroughly familiar with them.*

113. Explanation. — In the tenth thesis we required that the fundamental catechism be reviewed every year at least. Now we carry this proposition still further, for even those truths which are contained in the fundamental catechism do not all influence the Christian life to an equal extent.

That the catechist "should devote special care" to the doctrines of paramount importance for the conduct of life, means: that these should be presented in an easily understandable manner, thoroughly explained, well proved, impressed on the mind, and fittingly carried out in practice. To the teaching of these truths should be devoted more time, more lucid explanation, more thoroughness, and more frequent practice. It may happen that some children can master only the bare essentials; these, however, must never be dispensed with, and, when necessary, less weighty matters may be left out.

Our thesis is intended to counteract the practice of taking perfunctorily question after question, chapter after chapter. Some there are who adhere to this practice in perfect good faith; yet it is the outcome of a superficial conception of catechetical instruction and may have deplorable consequences.

114. Proof. — The thesis is first of all a necessary corollary of the fact that not all doctrines of faith and morals are of equal import for the Christian life: prayer, contrition for sin, reception of the Sacraments, obviously influence the Christian life more intimately than the doctrines about the choirs of Angels, Purgatory, Indulgences, etc. The former are essential to all Christian life, and indispensable for the soul's salvation; the latter, however profitable their knowledge may be, because they are God's word and therefore of infinite value, are not of equal import in the economy of salvation. What would be the consequence if all were put on the same plane? Many pupils would fail to grasp sufficiently the importance of even the capital doctrines; they would forget them readily and live in fatal ignorance of the most indispensable means of salvation. This danger can be averted only by giving a prominent place in teaching to the capital doctrines of faith.

And this holds true even on the supposition that the catechist have none but willing and intelligent children.

But the latter situation is never met with in a large class. Hence the second proof of our thesis: it embodies a duty we owe in all reason and charity also to the less endowed children. There will be found everywhere children with limited abilities, or children who, because of actual dulness or unfavorable home surroundings, can be taught only with great difficulty. As long as we cannot have continuation schools for retarded children, — and even those would not in all cases be sufficient, — the latter must at least be so far taken into consideration that those doctrines indispensable also for them be treated with the greatest care; that everything be done to secure their eternal salvation. The consequence may be that many doctrines of the catechism are only touched upon; we see no reason, however, for retreating before this conclusion, especially since a widespread pedagogical tendency favors a decrease in the quantitative amount of teaching matter.

One question remains to be answered:

115. What are those Indispensable Doctrines? — The answer is found in the teaching of moral theology concerning "the truths to be explicitly known and believed." That we must advert to actual conditions of time and place; that those truths especially which are openly attacked by unbelievers are to be more emphatically insisted upon, so that children of maturer age may be prepared to answer the more frequent and important objections, this is easily understood by every pastor, especially in communities of mixed religion. Thus Jungmann mentions as all-important: practice of the divine virtues and of contrition; prayer, reception of the sacraments necessary for every Christian; the sixth and ninth commandments. Because of present-day social conditions we must add the fourth commandment.

Generally speaking, the requirements of catechization coincide with those of homiletics. The latter, however, adds a few doctrines to the list of truths required for the Christian life, viz.: the doctrine of the Holy Ghost, of Grace, and of the Sacraments, the Church, the Christian family. Besides prayer in its restricted meaning, also the other devotions which are of great moment in the spiritual life (Holy Mass, examination of conscience, pious reading); self-sacrifice, patience, humility, purity; other virtues such as diligence, Christian solidarity in the home and society; the fear of the Lord; Liturgy; the Saints and Angels, the Blessed Virgin Mary, love of God and of our neighbor; perfect contrition proceeding from perfect love of God.

Local conditions may call for a more extensive treatment of even other doctrines: in places with adherents of various sects, the "differentiating doctrines": the Church, Sacraments, Justification; where Socialism is strongly represented, the Christian doctrine on property, authority, our present life as a trial period, God's providence, etc. These latter doctrines can be best treated when opportunity offers in connection with other points of faith: for in Socialism we are facing not any one heresy in particular, but a materialistic conception of the universe which, step for step, opposes the whole of revealed religion.

The paramount issue in catechization and in preaching, and the earnest of their salutary influence, lie herein that the children learn to refer all religious truth to Christ; that they find all their motives for action in Him; that they learn intimately to understand and love Him who is the way, the truth and the life, the beginning and the end of faith, the light of the world, Jesus Christ the same yesterday, today, and forever.

In the third part of this treatise (on Education), and also when speaking of Special Catechetics, we shall have more to say about the children's life of prayer, perfect contrition, the reception of the sacraments. One word more about the most essential topic of all:

116. The Doctrine of Jesus Christ. — When we realize that Jesus Christ stands at the center of the whole history and doctrine of salvation; that neither of them can be understood without the unconditional admission of His — the light of the world's — teaching; that the salvation of the individual and of the world can be operated only through Him; that the beatific end of all human life can be found only in Him; that therefore in Christ we have the material, formal, efficient, and final cause of our faith; — we come to understand why the Fathers of the Church were so fond of relating to Christ every event of this world.

"Jesus Christ and His Church is all in all. Jesus Christ, who is the beginning and the end of all salvation, should be recognized in all mundane happenings. His Church, in whom is all salvation, should be honored, loved, and followed everywhere. And by holding fast to this one point, an exalted religious and moral instinct becomes the one powerful driving principle of all human actions. From this viewpoint we can grasp the appropriateness of the method dear to the Fathers, who delighted in setting forth the types of the Old Testament and pointed out their realization in the New Dispensation. The aim of this method was to lead to the ONE Jesus Christ and the Church whose head He is; to consider Him as the one focus in which all rays of knowledge converge in such a manner that they enkindle the fire of pure divine love, through which only the human soul becomes agreeable to God and susceptible of true morality." (Gruber.)

Hence the obvious conclusion for us catechists of the present day, that, as the true shepherds of souls of yore, we also must lead the little ones to Christ: the children should study His doctrine and His life; the motives and intentions of His Divine Heart; they should be deeply imbued with the thought that all they must strive to attain is found through belief in Christ's doctrine, hope in the blessings promised by Him, love of whatever He loves and has shown to be worth loving by His word and example.

The catechist who has himself realized the central position of Jesus Christ in the economy of salvation, and the hidden treasures of the Saviour's heart, will gladly and effectively lead the children to the Christ who claimed the little ones for Himself in such an affectionate manner.

A few examples from Bossuet's Catechism will go to show how this correlation of individual doctrines with the Saviour may be brought about: "First lesson: On Christian Doctrine in General. Begin this lesson by pointing out the advantages of Christian instruction, because through it Christ teaches the way to eternal life. Relate to the children how the Saviour, at the age of twelve, listened to the Doctors, asked them questions and answered them (Luc. 2, 46). For in this mystery the Lord wished to sanctify the early instruction of youth, and give us an example of catechetical teaching. Moreover, one may relate to the children how the Lord lived through the remaining years of His youth, was obedient, and grew in wisdom and grace before God and men (Luc. 2, 40, 51, 52). Exhort them repeatedly to imitate the example of Christ in His infancy, and to live in intimate union with Him. . . .

Second lesson: The Sign of the Cross. Begin by showing to the children Christ on the Cross; how He blesses mankind, and teaches us that all blessings come through the Cross. . . .

Third lesson: The Mystery of the Holy Trinity. Relate the History of Christ's baptism, at which the three Divine Persons manifested themselves. . . .

The Blessed Sacrament, Holy Communion. Mary Magdalen weeps at the Saviour's grave, and seeks His body. How her heart is aglow with fervent love as she sees the living Christ in all His glory! . . . What we should do before Holy Communion, and on receiving the same. The humility and faith of the centurion when Jesus offers to go to his house (Matt. 8, 8). The faith of the woman who is convinced she shall be healed on touching his garment. Jesus is pressed on all sides by the surrounding multitudes, but only when the woman with lively faith touches Him does He feel the contact (Math. 9, 20; Luc. 8, 42). . . .

The Sacrament of Matrimony. — The marriage of the Blessed Virgin to St. Joseph. The marriage feast at Cana which the Lord sanctifies by His presence and the performance of His first miracle (John 2). The creation of the first woman (Gen. 2, 21). The marriage of the young Tobias (Tob. 7, 8)."

B. THE STAGE OF PRESENTATION

FOURTEENTH PRINCIPLE. — *In order that the children may grasp Christian Doctrine thoroughly, the catechist should 1. Strive as much as possible after perspicuity; 2. Use language adapted to the child mind. However, 3. while adapting his language and his teaching to the intellectual level of the child, he must yet be careful to present the Christian truth fully, never resting satisfied with half-truths.*

117. Perspicuity. — The thesis requires that the catechist's exposition be lucid throughout, i.e., such that the children see, if not with their eyes, at least in their imagination, that which the teacher expounds; that they grasp what he says, as clearly and easily as if it were before them. When instruction produces a distinct and vivid image in the imagination, then is it perspicuous.

The reasons which make this quality so desirable are the same as those adduced in favor of sensible helps in homiletics. Indeed, there is no difference between the intellectual faculties of children and adults: knowledge, for both, is intimately bound up with full comprehension of the object. There is only a difference of degree between the two: the child more than the adult is dependent on his senses for all knowledge and understanding; hence, if possible, even more care should be devoted to attaining lucidity in catechization than in preaching.

Since all intellectual cognition depends upon concomitant sensible activity, the latter must be all the more taken into consideration when the mind is to gain knowledge of entirely spiritual objects, as is the case in catechization. The catechist experienced in the spiritual life will also put to use this perspicuity as a valuable means of familiarizing the children with meditative prayer. When explaining a biblical type, he may let them practise contemplation in the meaning of the "Exercises": to see the person, listen to what he says, consider what he does.

The influence of good lucid instruction may be realized by analogy from the following example. Goethe writes in his "Wahrheit und Dichtung," Book I: "Children's libraries were unknown then. Aside from the *Orbis pictus* of Amos Comenius, no illustrated book of the kind came into our (children's) hands; but we frequently looked through the great Folio Bible, with pictures by Merian." Later on, in May, 1787, Goethe was near death on the gulf of Naples, the ship threatening to founder. "The ship was tossed to and fro with increasing violence; the waves became wilder, and seasickness returning amidst all this excitement, I decided to retire to my cabin below. I lay down on the bed only half conscious of my surroundings, but well aware of a certain sweet emotion which seemed to be wafted to me from the sea of Tiberias. For very clearly did the picture (of the storm on the lake) in Merian's Bible float before my mind. And thus all vivid moral sense-impressions came to the fore more strongly as man is entirely thrown back upon himself." Italian Voyage, May 16, 1787.

118. Aids for Perspicuous Teaching (Showing of the Objects Themselves, or Pictures of Them). — Perspicuity is attained first by showing the objects themselves. How this may be done in the explanation of the Liturgy, has already been told (No. 86). If, when explaining the veneration of relics, a relic is exhibited to the children, let them show their veneration by kissing the same.

A second means consists in exhibiting to them copies of things, such as statues, biblical, liturgical, historical pictures, wall maps, etc.; recently attempts have also been made at illustrating the catechism. A good copy, e.g., of St. Peter's Church, or the Temple of Jerusalem, is the next best thing to a view of the object itself.

With regard to the use of pictures, especially those illustrating subjects of Bible History, let the following remarks be borne in mind: pictures that may be given to each child, or collections of pictures in book form, will greatly help even the smallest children who cannot yet read. In that case they need not be large. When, however, they are to be shown to a whole class, they should be of considerable size.

They must be dignified representations, not surcharged with numerous unimportant details, but confined to the main object. Colored pictures should always be given preference. As a rule, let the pictures be shown, not before or during the explanation, but after it; while doing so let the catechist not walk up and down between the seats. A good explanation supposes that the catechist has himself carefully studied the picture in the first place. After this explanation the picture may remain on the wall, but not for too long a time.

Herder has published a series of some thirty colored plates illustrating the principal scenes of the Old and New Testament. The "Perry Pictures" are also very serviceable for religious instruction, and can be had at a reasonable price in small or larger sizes. Pictures cut from the profusely illustrated catalogs of our church goods houses can be used to good advantage in the explanation of the Liturgy.

119. The Blackboard. — It can be used to very good advantage in catechetical work: explanations are more readily grasped when written down on it with the important words underscored, e.g.: contrition is *general* when it embraces *all* sins. The component parts of a definition can be better impressed on the mind when they are written out, than when they are merely enumerated orally, e.g., in every sacrament we have: a visible sign,
        invisible grace,
        institution by Christ.

In general, a long enumeration, e.g., the seven sacraments, is more easily stamped on the memory when the component parts or their initials are written down.

The whole Mass may be schematized on the blackboard thus:

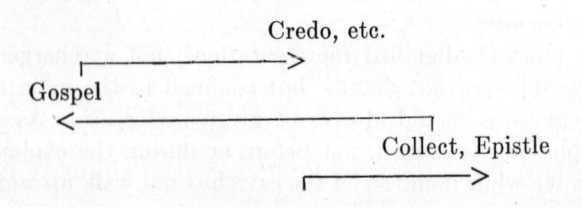

                  Credo, etc.
            ⊢————————⟶
Gospel
⟵————————————————⊣
                                   Collect, Epistle
                              ⊢————————⟶

Kyrie, Gloria
<————┐
　　　　Introit
┌—>
Introibo

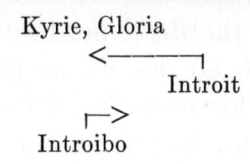

The catechist may also use the blackboard for drawing. Present-day profane didactics expects much from an intensive recourse to drawing in the school. We need not go to extremes in this matter, but the fact remains that the moderate use of it, the drawing of symbols (the eye of God, the Cross, the anchor, the heart), or of simple religious objects (crib, altar, church), contribute their not insignificant share toward making the instruction more interesting, and lending zest to the spoken word. The catechist alone need not do the drawing: he might call upon some more gifted pupils, or let the children use their own tablets for the purpose.

120. Perspicuity of Language. — Among the many means for visualizing the truth so helpful in oral instruction, special stress must be laid on the use of parables and historical material. Homiletics treats this subject at length. We content ourselves, therefore, with a few words on the use of stories in the catechism class. We have called attention before to the importance of Bible History in catechetical instruction, and what we said then may be applied to the use of historical material in general: it facilitates the understanding of the truth, and offers the best starting-point for an explanation.

Presently we have in mind only the use of stories as a help in catechization. It is evident that the story must not be too long, lest the main point: the explanation of the doctrine, be lost sight of. Do not dwell overmuch on details, as they absorb the attention of the children to the detriment of the essential doctrine. Again, historical narrations should not be unnecessarily numerous: far better to recall one event truly illustrative, couching it in lively, pithy language, and applying it effectually to the object under consideration, than to relate ten stories in succession which merely arouse curiosity.

Mey warns catechists in these words: "The collections of examples and parables, which in the catechical literature of recent years have come to exceed all other productions, are no doubt valuable helps. There is danger, however, that they may be abused. For have they not led some catechists to pay more attention to variety than to unity, to appearances than to reality? Agreeable entertainment has taken the place of clear, correct, thorough instruction. There is an intellectual greediness which no catechist can afford to satisfy. Nutritious bread, the bread of life, is what we should give the children. To sweeten it at times with a little honey is laudable; but he must above all provide healthy food, strengthening milk, not dainties."

From what sources shall we draw our historical narratives? — First of all, from Holy Writ. The grace of God is more abundantly vouchsafed with them. And the catechist need not limit himself to the Bible History manual used in the school, but can select his material from the whole range of the Scriptures. To do so he must of course be familiar himself with the sacred volume. Another source to draw from is the history of the Church, of the Saints, of Christian life in general. Stories from profane life should be avoided whenever possible. It need not be concluded, however, that profane history yields no suitable material. It does; and traits from the lives of men who as Christians played a conspicuous rôle in the world's drama, or of such as brought dishonor on the Christian name, may be used to advantage. Only, in such cases the profane should not occupy a prominent place in the narrative, but the latter should be presented irradiated by the light of faith.

Should imaginary tales be used? We answer: no.

In former times, and again in recent years, an effort has been made to substitute fairy stories, children's tales, for the stories taken from the Bible. It is a mistake to believe, and daily experience proves it, that children are more interested in "children's tales" than in the "strange, unfamiliar" stories of the Bible. No poet will ever produce anything to compare with the simple, yet impressive grandeur of biblical scenes and their stimulating power. Besides, the influence of divine grace, which generally does not accompany merely human products, is the determining factor for our favoring the Bible. And finally, an experienced teacher who makes up his stories, knows that he may easily jeopardize his authority, even when not following the eccentric method of one who wished "to complete" the story of Esau and Jacob: "One time, at Easter, Jacob had stayed in school after dismissal because he had been sick for several weeks during the winter and had failed in his examination. Esau was one class ahead of him; he received better report cards, was confirmed a year ahead of his brother, etc.!"

Reference to the example of Christ does not justify the use of made-up stories. Let us remember that when Christ spoke His parables, He addressed adults of the East, accustomed to learn deep truths by means of figurative language.

Nor can the older Christian painters, who often

gave an anachronistic setting to sacred events and persons, be adduced in favor of the above proceeding; for the catechist after all is not an art-school tyro. And let us not forget that our critical times are not to be compared with the former ages of faith.

121. The Catechetical Language, thus our thesis states further, should be adapted to the children. Which means: it should be as simple as possible, natural and easy of understanding, but always dignified.

Easy comprehension does not demand that the child be given an explanation of every familiar term: it is a mistake thus to underrate his intellectual capacity. But more often the understanding of the children is overrated, while words and expressions are used that remain a mystery to them. Hence result many false notions, sometimes comical, but often of very serious import. The psychological law of apperception, i.e., the influence exercised by notions stored in the mind on the acquisition of fresh knowledge, must be adverted to not only in the stage of explanation but also in that of perception; and this can be done especially by using expressions which correlate new objects with others already familiar to the children.

"The instruction of the younger catechumens must be as simple, as natural, and as plain as possible. This every one acknowledges, and the rule seems almost superfluous! Yet it is carried out only with great difficulty. In his first letter to the Corinthians, when speaking of the supernatural gift of tongues vouchsafed by the Holy Ghost, St. Paul says: 'I thank my God I speak with all your tongues; but in the church I would rather speak five words with my understanding, that I may instruct others also, than ten thousand words in a tongue.' This text may be applied to catechization both in the lower and in the higher grades. For in the schoolroom five words clearly grasped are worth more than ten thousand words not understood by the children. And these five words, how hard it is at times to find them! Thorough mastering of the truth, deep insight into the thing itself often point the way; for in religious matters the deepest not infrequently is the simplest." (Mey.)

However, no matter how simple, the language of the catechist must always remain dignified because of the sublime truths it conveys. Let the catechist be on his guard against the fallacy that would identify trivial with popular expressions. The catechist should also avoid the use of dialect, and he should never imitate the mistakes in expression which children may make. The latter, however, may be allowed the use of colloquial terms — although the practice should be gradually discountenanced — because they are seldom sufficiently acquainted at the outset with the proper expressions. Besides, many a printed passage will have to be explained in terms familiar to them.

122. How May an Appropriate Catechetical Language be Mastered? The reading or hearing of good catechists is more useful than an abundance of theoretical rules. Aug. Gruber, Alban Stolz, etc., are so many models that may profitably be imitated. Besides, a conscientious preparation of the lesson is indispensable. Jungmann writes: "When you have to give catechism prepare yourself as conscientiously as if you had to preach. Never neglect to write out the lesson completely, or at least to write out a complete schema to be thought over carefully: without these precautions you cannot expect results in the art of catechetical instruction; and you are certainly not fulfilling your duty." The catechist should also put to use the experience acquired in the schoolroom and profit by it to improve his sketches.

> In his instructions to his priests Gruber adverts repeatedly to that "dissatisfaction" of the catechist with the results attained, which "originates in a holy and laudable humility." The deacon Deogratias already gave vent to the same feeling. And the pious Count von Stolberg says: 'Whoever is readily satisfied with his written or oral lectures, may rest assured that they are superficial, that he himself lacks knowledge and feeling. . . . Yes, my friends, the deeper our knowledge of the faith; the more we realize the hidden meaning, the rich applications, the impenetrable wisdom and goodness of God manifested in the revelation of these truths and their appeal to holiness of life and heart, the more we become displeased with the words in which they are couched or conveyed to others; we fail to find the raiment worthy of setting off the great treasure we would fain present to our fellow Christians. Therefore never enter school or pulpit only half prepared! And after careful preparation do not rest content with what you have accomplished, but recognize that you should make continual progress."

Thorough preparation for catechization demands exertion, patience, and good will, and to a certain extent even more so than the sermon. For in the latter anticipated admiration and success prove to be a strong incentive; in catechization, however, there is nothing to flatter ambition. The catechist must be actuated above all by a great love for children; otherwise his interest will soon be on the wane. And we mean of course a supernatural love, not a natural partiality for the more intelligent or more attractive children.

We may well apply to catechization what Alban Stolz writes with regard to the prime requisite for popular, i.e., easily understood preaching. He requires in the first place "thorough, intimate knowledge of what one wishes to say"; in the second place, a love of his audience akin to the love of a mother for her children. A mother does not talk in the same way to her two year old and to her four year old child; to her six year old and her ten year old child, but in every case her language is adapted to that particular child's capacity. And the secret of this art is her love for her offspring. A similar but an infinitely nobler love prompted the Saviour in His manner of teaching; a similar love manifests itself even in the printed discourses of great preachers. It is this love which must animate the catechist.

123. A Danger to be guarded against when attempting to step down to the level of the child is this: the catechist aims at being readily understood, and hence gives the truth only in part, because the whole truth is not so easy to grasp. The last section of our thesis is directed against this manner of proceeding, which conveys incorrect notions to the children, and gives them erroneous ideas.

Sundry examples from Gruber will prove we are in the right. "When the catechist explains the notion of original sin by saying merely: Adam and Eve had to die because they had sinned; we also must all die; hence we say we have inherited their sin;—he has told nothing but what is true. Yet he makes it appear that we have only inherited the punishment and not the sin itself." Hence Gruber instructs even the smallest children in this wise: I must still tell you about a sad consequence of the sin of Adam and Eve. Their bad action has hurt all men who come into the world after them. . . . We come into the world, therefore, as sinners; and if God did not help us to become good, so that He may like us, we could not be saved.

"Or, when speaking of the mercy of God, the catechist says:

God forgives us when we beg for forgiveness, he has uttered the truth in simple words; yet an erroneous conception may result in so far as it appears that forgiveness may be obtained without true penance. . . . When the catechist explains the expression in the catechism: Faith is a virtue infused by God, by saying: God has made known His doctrine to us, God has given you parents and priests to instruct you; when you believe what they teach you in God's name, then God has infused faith into your soul, — he has spoken the truth, but he has altered the meaning given to the expression by the Church, for he has left out the interior assistance of God, the essential notion of the infusion of faith; he has fallen into Pelagianism. . . ."

124. The Practical Consequences which follow from these remarks about the danger of "easily understood, simple language," are chiefly:

(*a*) The catechist must possess a thorough knowledge of the faith. No one can expect to teach Christian Doctrine safely and correctly unless he be completely at home in it himself. Hence we realize even better why, as Bishop von Leonrod required, the catechist should be well grounded in dogma (No. 77, 1), "for without thorough dogmatical training he cannot acquit himself of his task. The bishops assembled in Freysing in 1850, in their deliberations on the catechism, expressed their regret that the difficulty of finding able preachers, and the poor results in catechization, were chiefly due to a lack of thorough dogmatical training of the young theologians; they declared that this evil could only be eradicated by a methodical study of theology, and the training of the clergy according to the rules and spirit of the Church. . . . If a well-trained theologian finds it difficult, at the outset of his catechetical career, to come down to the level of the children, this fault disappears after some practice, whilst the lack of dogmatical training is scarcely ever made up for in later life." And Bishop von Leonrod also points to the superficiality of homiletic and catechetical literature as the best proof that the bishops judged rightly.

(b) The second consequence is: every catechetical lesson demands thorough preparation. The above-named bishop recommends to catechists, "when preparing their lesson, to look over in their seminary textbooks, the tract it refers to." If careful preparation be required to become proficient in the use of simple catechetical language, the great need of thoroughness and accuracy requires this all the more; and if the latter are to be attained, even the very expressions of many a lesson will have to be put down beforehand: for to trust to the inspiration of the moment may easily lead to erroneous statements.

FIFTEENTH PRINCIPLE. — *With the lecture form the catechist should combine the question form. The latter has a twofold end in view: 1. To arouse the attention of the children and stimulate their intellectual activity; 2. To find out whether the children sufficiently understand and remember what has been said.*

125. Relation between Lecturing and Questioning.

— In the lecture form the teacher explains in coherent discourse, while the pupil listens; in the question form the teacher queries while the pupil answers. The catechist should endeavor to combine the two methods so as to obtain the best results. To effect this, he must know in what relation questioning and lecturing stand to each other.

Logically, and also in importance, the lecture form

takes precedence over the question form in catechization. "It takes precedence," but does not exclude, the question form. It takes precedence as being "more important": faith comes by hearing, not by questioning; hence lecturing, i.e., the statement of revealed truth, is an indispensable means to attain the end of catechization: to arouse and cultivate a lively faith. Questioning is but a condition, and an important one no doubt, which facilitates and secures the learning of the doctrine proposed.

It takes precedence "logically": the teacher must first expound the doctrine, and then test his pupils carefully by questioning. He should do so not after every word and sentence, but at definite intervals. The connection between lecturing and questioning appears more clearly from the following.

126. The Aim of Questioning in Catechization. — By questioning, the children should (a) be aroused to attention and intellectual activity. The child addressed is fairly compelled to pay attention, and the question directed at him stimulates him to personal exertion. Although we should avoid exaggerated recourse to the socratic method because of the positive character of Christian Doctrine (Nos. 36, 54), yet it is very useful, nay necessary, for it leads the children to deduce consequences from premises already known; it serves to emphasize a truth of the catechism, or a general doctrine in the corresponding biblical scene, or to apply a doctrine to a practical case in daily life.

Thus, e.g., from the story of the Fall the concept of sin in general may be thus deduced: disobedience against God = breaking a commandment of God. From the story of Dives the children can be led to deduce the doctrine of the immortality of the soul, the justice of God, the necessity of good works.

(b) The second aim in questioning is to find out whether the children have rightly grasped and understood what has been said. According to the answers he receives the catechist will either be enabled to pass on to other points or he will have to make his explanation still more distinct and lucid. Moreover, by questioning them the catechist ascertains whether the pupils remember what was said: "we know only as much as we remember."

The preacher does not have at his disposal this question form and its advantages. These can to a certain extent be supplied by rhetorical questions and the virtual dialog.

127. Some Practical Rules. — In questioning the catechist should (a) keep to a golden mean, asking neither too much nor too little. Novices at the work generally fail through lack of questioning. The rule should be not to devote too little of your time to explanatory and testing questions. If every child cannot be questioned during the course of each lesson, the catechist should nevertheless, in time, interrogate each child, passing over no one. When dealing with a large number of children he should refresh his memory with the help of written notes. He should especially avoid to question merely or most frequently the brightest children while neglecting the less generously endowed. Although one is naturally inclined to interrogate those from whom he may expect a correct answer, the unavoidable consequence would be that a majority of the class would feel they are neglected, thus losing interest in the catechism. And indeed it is the duller children who stand more particularly in need of our help. The more difficult questions may be reserved for the brighter ones, as this will stimulate their zeal.

(b) Questioning should not be left to chance, but should be carefully planned beforehand. Therefore lecturing and questioning should not be chaotically mixed so that it becomes impossible to distinguish whether you are reviewing, or expounding new matter: let a clear line be drawn between lecturing and questioning. This distinction may be carried further, and each lesson divided according to the above-mentioned stages: statement, explanation and proof, application and practice.

The doctrine to be treated is first explained, then recapitulated by means of suitable questions, before proceeding to a new head. The catechist may find it necessary to begin questioning after a small part of the doctrine has been explained; on the other side he may be compelled to deviate from his original plan when he reads on the faces of his children that they do not follow him.

(c) The questions should not be out of place, i.e., the children should not be interrogated about subjects which they have not yet studied. Let the catechist beware of taking for granted that he has explained in the lower grades what he has explained perhaps only in the higher classes. Unseasonable questions disconcert and discourage the children.

128. The Form of the Questions. — How should the questions be asked, and how should they be formulated? The general rule is that they should be addressed to all the children in common, to the whole class. Then, after all have had time to think, let one child only be called upon. In this wise the attention of all remains centered on the question, for no one knows who is going to be singled out to answer. Very seldom a child should be designated to answer before the query is put; and if this is done, another child, or the whole class may be appointed as judges of the answer.

The children may be allowed to indicate their ability to answer after the question has been put, but this must be done in a quiet and orderly manner. They should not be allowed to call out: "please, Father," or, "I know." The best way to break them of that bad habit is to refuse them the privilege of answering.

The question must be simple and definite; and the interrogative which points out the object referred to must be especially emphasized or put at the beginning of the question.

The question is simple when it does not ask several things at the same time, e.g., when and why do we keep Christmas; why and how should we pray. These and similar questions are faulty. The question is definite when it admits of only one correct answer. "What has a man got" is a very indefinite question.

As we have explained above (No. 54), the catechist should carefully avoid all questioning that may cast a doubt upon the doctrines of faith.

129. The Answers of the Children. — Let the catechist beware lest the children answer without being called upon, or lest they prompt one another. To maintain the necessary discipline he must be inexorable in this regard.

When called upon, let the child answer in a clear (but not a shrill), distinct, expressive voice, and in a complete sentence. With bashful children great difficulty is sometimes encountered, but frequent repetition of the answer will be beneficial.

When the answer is not given in the desired form it need not always be rejected in a pedantic manner. Then only when the child recites something which was to be literally memorized, should the catechist insist on great accuracy. When he receives no answer, or a wrong one, he should not be unnecessarily harsh in his remarks, for these, "like heavy footsteps in a freshly cultivated garden, crush the weak sprouts." Let him find out the reason and direct his course accordingly.

Perhaps the reason for an unsatisfactory answer is found in the question itself: if the latter was indefinite, too difficult, too long, the thing to do is to repeat it in a corrected form. . . . "Pay attention. I am going to ask you the question in another way." In dealing with smaller children, no answer is received quite often because words are lacking to formulate it; in that case they should be encouraged to give the answer in familiar language as used at home. But even when a reprehensible lack of attention or understanding is the cause of an incorrect answer, the child need not at once be censured: it is often possible to lead it to the right answer by fuller explanation, new questions and connection with what was not altogether wrong in the answer. And finally, when repeated efforts seem to be fruitless, let the catechist remember the words of St. Augustine: "When the catechumen is very dull, . . . he should be treated with sympathy; teach him the most necessary truths while passing quickly over the others; . . . instead of telling him much about God, recommend him to God in a special manner."

C. THE EXPLANATION

SIXTEENTH PRINCIPLE. — *The explanation is the most important part of catechization: hence the catechist should devote great care to it, applying the appropriate rules, in order to convey to the children a knowledge as thorough as possible of the religious truths.*

130. The Importance of Catechetical Explanation becomes evident from the fact that the intellectual powers of the children are not sufficiently developed to make, unaided, for right understanding. A child will accept without difficulty, and hold as true, whatever is presented to him; but for correct understanding, insight, and discrimination he stands in need of outside assistance. And haphazard explanations might easily give rise in the child mind to false notions, and thus the enemies of all religious education are furnished with new weapons.

In the sermon the preacher must be intent above all on solid demonstration, while in catechization the children, especially of the lower and intermediate grades, readily take for granted what they are told. Hence the requirement of our thesis is plain: that the catechist should concentrate his efforts on clear explanations, more so proportionately, than on argumentation and impression, although neither of these should be overlooked. The importance and the difficulties of explanation should be especially adverted to in connection with the catechism; Bible History and complementary instruction are easier of understanding.

Our thesis does not stand in need of further proof: it is self-evident, and recent experimental Didactics confirms it. We shall, however, go on to give some fundamental rules about "how" to proceed in the explanation.

131. Follow the Catechism strictly, and make sure that the children understand it thoroughly! Herein is expressed the principal aim of all catechetical instruction. Already the Fifth Principle has taught us that the correct understanding and permanent retention of the catechism are the main ends of catechetical instruction; here the catechist receives his first guidance in explanation. Hence the catechism and the oral explanation should not be treated as two disparate processes, but should go hand in hand: through the explanation the catechism should, as it were, be transmuted into their very life blood. Hence the catechist must necessarily connect his explanation with the catechism, even if he does not completely approve of the latter.

1. As a general rule, follow the order of the catechism. "As a general rule," for at times an exception is to be made, e.g., when the explanation of an important doctrine, such as that concerning the Church, should come at a time when the instruction is interrupted by sickness among the children or some other cause. Also, in order to make an explanation gain in distinctness, it may be well to neglect the usual order of the questions, putting together instead those that make for greater lucidity. Thus: when is contrition supernatural; when is contrition merely natural; the very contrast between the words "natural" and "supernatural" makes for clarity.

2. In your explanation remember that you should familiarize the children not only with that particular

doctrine, but also with the wording of the doctrine as given in the catechism. The explanation must also bear, therefore, on the words and phrases. Words more difficult of understanding, or more intricate grammatical constructions, must be fully explained.

132. Two More Rules to be Observed. — 1. First and foremost, explain the thing itself; then the word.

2. Do not couch your explanation in abstract terms, but start out from some concrete historical or Biblical fact. This concrete foundation of catechization which we have already required in connection with right "presentation," appears here as very desirable in connection with a good "explanation." The meaning of the two rules will stand out in clearer light when we treat both together. The explanation of the thing in the catechism means the explanation of the catechism truth; word-explanation is the explanation of its oral or written symbol, i.e., of the catechism text. The first rule sets forth a twofold requirement: first and foremost comes the explanation of the thing, i.e., it comes first in the order of time and also in importance, and therefore more care and effort must be devoted to the explanation of the thing.

No experienced catechist will deny that the latter is of paramount importance, since what he primarily strives after is to impart a thorough devout notion of revealed truth. Sometimes, however, criticism is leveled at the chronological and methodical sequence demanded by the second requirement, and it is argued that the children should not be led through the understanding of the text to that of the truth, but vice versa.

The following reasons militate in favor of our position:

(a) It is the more interesting and easier way for the children. More interesting, because by setting out with a story you at once arouse a lively interest which the dry catechism text can never call forth; and the rule holds always good: if you want men to love God, do not begin by boring them. Hence it follows also that it is the easier way to convey an understanding of the doctrine in question for the very reason that it is put forth in a clear-cut concrete form. And once the doctrine is substantially understood, the short text of the catechism will present no further difficulties for the children.

(b) The same conclusion follows from the position of the catechism as a manual of religion and the form in which, on that account, the text is cast. That the catechism is a manual of religion, no one doubts (Nos. 65–67); but it is not such in the sense that it is the one and wholly sufficient means prescribed by the bishop to teach the children Christian Doctrine. For in that case the catechism should be gotten up in a different form; its statements would not be so succinct, its language would be more childlike. The means and the way to bring the rich but condensed content of the catechism within the reach of the pupils is primarily the oral explanation of the catechist. It would be unreasonable, therefore, to try and impart a knowledge of doctrine by relying on the catechism only; the thorough comprehension of the text is rather the result of accurate explanation; and the explanation is accurate when it presents lucidly those concrete details which the catechism in its brevity cannot offer.

(c) St. Augustine proceeds in the same manner: through the relation of biblical facts the truths should be imparted to the catechumens. Other good catechists followed his example, e.g., Bossuet, Gruber. Nay, it is the method of the Saviour Himself. When asked who is our neighbor, he does not proceed to give a definition of the term, but relates the parable of the Good Samaritan: the answer to the question is thus made obvious.

The results of recent experimental didactics confirm completely this teaching method, always followed by the Church's greatest ministers. Although at times a different method was in vogue, this was entirely due to external influences; it will suffice to recall the rationalistic period and the fight waged against its deleterious policies by the champions of the Catholic restoration, such as Gruber, Overberg, etc.

(d) To all that we have said above concerning the avoidance of abstract formulas in the explanation should be added what we wrote before in the fourteenth thesis about perspicuity. One point we must especially call attention to: it is all-important to win the heart of the child from the outset, to awaken interest not merely to the extent of stimulating his attention, but also to enthuse it for the truth itself as bearing upon our daily life. And this can be done by a lucid, lively anecdote, preferably from Holy Writ, containing the doctrine in question. Then, by emphasizing the essential part of the story, the doctrine is formulated; finally the catechism text is read, explained, and its authority put in the right light. This is proceeding psychologically. Lively interest and deep feeling are a great help to knowledge and especially to the accurate comprehension of the doctrines of faith.

133. Complementary Remarks. — 1. It is evident that, since more time is required when following this method, the teacher should take into consideration the time at his disposal. As regards matters which the children already know thoroughly, it would be useless to explain them over again in the same manner.

2. How shall we find the appropriate Bible stories for every lesson? We should have recourse to Bible History first of all, as we have already amply proved (No. 120). Now, if the catechist's acquaintance with Bible material be rather limited, he may use a concordance to good advantage, especially one composed with reference to the catechism.

Father Vaughans's: The Divine Armory of Holy Scripture, very useful to preachers, could easily be arranged with regard to the catechism.

3. One example to illustrate our method: the explanation of contrition and its qualities.

What is contrition? Contrition is a hatred of sin and a true grief of the soul for having offended God, with a firm purpose of sinning no more. What kind of sorrow should we have for our sins? The sorrow we should have for our sins should be internal, supernatural, universal, and sovereign. What do you mean by saying that our sorrow should be interior, etc.? . . .

Instead of proceeding, as is often done, to read the text, explaining it word for word, and thus, through the understanding of the words, to convey to the child the understanding of the thing itself, it would be much better to follow the method recommended above and go about it in this wise:

Select one example, e.g., that of St. Peter: relate briefly, with warmth and conviction, how the Lord loved him above all others, and how nevertheless on the night of His Passion, Peter, from fear, so shamefully denied Him. Give a graphic description of the scene in the court of the High Priest: how the Saviour looks down upon Peter with eyes full of pity; how this look pierces Peter's heart, reveals to him his own shameful act, in contrast with the Master's love, and moves him to tears; how the memory of his ungrateful denial remains with him through life and spurs him on to faithfulness in the Master's service to the end. The story has gripped the hearts of the children, and review questions will prove it.

Now proceed to emphasize in this particular story the truths contained in the catechism text, the notion of contrition: Why does St. Peter shed tears? Because he is sorry in his heart; because in his soul he feels grief and aversion for what he himself has done. Notice now that when one feels this grief in the soul for the sins he has committed, he has contrition. This is what the catechism says: contrition is a true grief of the soul for having offended God.

In a similar manner one may explain the qualities of a good contrition, e.g., contrition must be interior: Peter said not a word, although he wept piteously. One does not have contrition by merely saying the act of contrition with the lips. But St. Peter deep down in his heart felt a great aversion for his act, and what would he not have given to bring about what he now desired so much: if only I had not done this!

While thus evolving the doctrine from the story, the catechist must keep the catechism text before him as a guide; it is not absolutely necessary that the children should already know it. To facilitate the explanation, the important words may be written on the blackboard. In conclusion the catechism text is read, and any explanation of the text that may be called for is added.

134. Synthesis or Analysis? — Two methods of catechism explanation are disputing the field at the present day: the so-called "old analytical" and the "new, synthetic or psychological" method. This terminology is rather misleading, and as we pointed out above (No. 112, 2), in accordance with the requirements of logic, what is called the "analytical method" should be called the "synthetic method," and vice versa. In the following remarks, in order to avoid all misunderstanding, whenever the expressions "analysis" and "synthesis" do not correspond with the Aristotelian terminology, they are put in quotation marks.

How do the followers of each method proceed? The exponent of the "analytical" method reads, or lets some one read, the catechism text, and dissects it: text analysis, resolving it into its component parts to explain them in succession; in conclusion he combines the parts into a whole.

EXAMPLE. The Church is the congregation of all the faithful. . . . After the catechist has read this answer, he sets out to explain what is meant by "the congregation of all the faithful"; by "who profess as the faith of Christ," etc. In conclusion he sums up his whole answer.

The followers of the "synthetic" method set out with an anecdote or a parable containing the truth in question. From it they abstract the elements of the doctrine, and by combining these in a final summing-up, the answer of the catechism is obtained.

Reverting to the above doctrine about the Church, the protagonist of the latter method may explain first its foundation on Pentecost, and its spread through the labors of the Apostles. He will advert especially to the preaching of the Gospel, the steadfast belief in God's word, the reception of the Sacraments; he will show how the faithful were of one mind, all subject to the

Apostles, and their chief, St. Peter. It becomes quite easy then to select the particular qualities which, when put together, practically give us the essentials of the catechism answer: the Church is the visible society of those who profess the same faith, partake of the same Sacraments, and obey the successor of St. Peter.

It may be noticed that this "synthesis" corresponds to what we have described above (Nos. 132–133) as the most appropriate form of explanation. But no unwarranted conclusions should be deduced from our recommendation of this method. Therefore,

1. The catechist should not use the "synthetic" method exclusively. When the children have sufficiently clear notions on a given subject, they may, and should, be taught to go from the general notion or principle, through conclusions, to the knowledge of the concrete.

2. Because "synthesis," rightly understood, proceeds psychologically, it cannot conflict with any psychological law, and more particularly not with the law that knowledge proceeds only gradually from an initial more superficial apprehension to a deeper understanding, so that cognition would remain incomplete without repeated consideration of the object. (Compare No. 105, 3.) Hence the "synthetic" method is in no way opposed to the "concentric" method. The former aims at a clear, distinct notion of the subject, i.e., its differentiation from other objects; it lays a good foundation for a deeper knowledge susceptible of progressive perfecting, particularly through recapitulation, in the successive grades.

3. In the "synthesis" everything must be avoided which might in any way minimize the authority of the

catechism. Hence it may be well to give the catechism text at the very outset; e.g., with the help of God's grace I am now going to explain to you the meaning of the answer: Contrition is a true grief of the soul, etc. . . ., so that in the future you may know how to make a good act of contrition.

There is nothing to prevent the catechist from making the children learn the text by heart beforehand, as long as it is not altogether unfamiliar to them (No. 143). Yet the text itself is not the easiest way to the understanding of the subject, nor should it be made the starting-point of the explanation.

Together with the use of the "synthetic" method, great care should be bestowed upon the explanation of the text. This can be done in the "summing-up" and also in the statement and explanation of the truth preceding it; the authority of the catechism text should also be pointed out explicitly.

135. Hold to the Right Course in your Explanation. — Do not make it too short or too long, and avoid digressions.

In order to keep to the right course, remember:

1. The aim of catechization, which is not to train young scientists, but faithful, deeply convinced Catholics. The catechist, therefore, need not communicate to the children whatever he knows himself.

2. Let the extent of the explanation be governed by the importance of the doctrine. All that we have said against mechanical uniformity should be especially kept in mind during the explanation (thirteenth thesis).

3. Adapt yourself to the intellectual capacity of the

children. You can be more succinct when dealing with older, more developed children. As soon as you notice that the doctrine has been grasped, go on to another point. Waste no time in explaining things that are self-evident.

136. Although Often Overlooked, an important help in leading the children to the understanding of Christian Doctrine is the practice of acts of faith. This praying of the act of faith strengthens the same, and to children also does the word of Christ apply: "If any man will do the will of Him he shall know of the doctrine, whether it be of God or whether I speak of myself." St. John, 7, 17. Moreover, for a full comprehension, in as far as this may be distinguished from conviction, the exercise of faith is of great importance. When the children are being instructed about sorrow for sin, and are at the same time made to pray the act of contrition, they thereby gain the best possible knowledge of it, for divine grace co-operates to make them realize inwardly what contrition is.

D. CATECHETICAL PROOFS

SEVENTEENTH PRINCIPLE. — *In order to ground the children's faith on a permanent foundation, the catechist should* 1. *adduce appropriate proofs for the religious doctrines;* 2. *He should also lead the children to make, with the grace of God, acts of faith, especially at the end of every lesson.*

137. Preliminary Remarks. — The full comprehension of a truth demands that we know on what basis it rests. Hence, a thorough explanation, besides giving the "how" of things, should also give the "why," i.e., the truth explained should also be proved. Much of what we have said thus far, especially when speaking of synthesis and analysis, may be applied to argumentation. It is well, however, to devote further consideration to it here, because in the domain of faith deep conviction is of such great import, and because, especially at the present day, so much is said and written about the proofs of faith.

A fundamental principle not to be lost sight of in this matter is that our conviction in matters of faith is due to three factors: 1. Insight into the motives of faith, i.e., the knowledge that the truth in question is revealed by God; 2. The free consent of the will accepting the truth on the authority of God; 3. The supernatural help of divine grace at all stages of the act of faith.

The first part of our thesis refers to the first of the above factors, whilst the latter part of the thesis is concerned with the other two.

138. A Proof is the means used to convince the mind of a truth, and therefore all proof must needs disclose the grounds of truth. What kind of conviction do we refer to when speaking of faith? In contrast with any conviction, no matter how acquired, it is a supernatural conviction giving us absolute certainty. And how can the latter be imparted? The catechist here faces the same problem as the preacher, who, basing himself on Holy Writ and dogmatic theology, answers: "Faith cometh by hearing, and hearing by the word of Christ." Rom. 10, 17. Supernatural belief can only come through the knowledge that something has been revealed by Christ, by God. Whatever may be advanced in confirmation of a truth outside of divine authority may be good and useful; it is altogether inadequate for producing an act of faith. The essential purpose of argumentation in matters of faith is therefore to show that a given truth belongs to the deposit of revelation; and while the Church is the guardian and organ of revelation, argumentation in the pulpit as in the catechism is the production, in favor of the doctrine in question, of the testimony of the Church as it is found in Holy Writ, the definitions of the Popes and Councils, the prayers, and the life of the whole Church. If the doctrine is explicitly testified to by these witnesses, even if only in figure or comparison, then we have direct proofs; when, in order to prove the doctrine, conclusions have to be drawn from these testimonies, we have indirect proofs.

Sometimes, with certain doctrines of faith, arguments are set forth which are not based on the living magisterium of the Church or on Holy Writ, but on human reason. In that case we have to deal, not with a proof of faith, but with a secondary argument which paves the way for faith, upholds it, shields it against attacks, but is in no way its adequate cause; nor can it be substituted for the essential, primary arguments.

Although proofs from reason are highly important at the present day, yet we must sound a decided warning against excessive insistence on secondary arguments, and the substitution of scientific theological disquisitions for the arguments proper to the catechist and preacher. Not infrequently we hear protests against an overestimation of apologetics, and the reason is found in the neglect of the primary proofs of faith. Due attention should be devoted to the latter because of their great importance. And it must be clear that argumentation does not consist in a chaotic piling-up or an obstreperous presentation of authoritative utterances; what is needed above all in the pulpit, as well as in catechization, is a thorough exposition of the meaning and the import of the text in question. When this method is used rightly, it brings out clearly the infinite distinction between divine and human authority, and one short divine utterance will carry more weight than many human reasons.

Gruber declares that the arguments and proofs of faith that are of practical value "are all found in the history of revelation and of the Church, and in the faith they enkindle in pure hearts. Our arguments are to be drawn from these sources and from the clear teaching of Christ, His Apostles and His Church, and more particularly from such testimonies as, because of their great simplicity, stand in no need of exegetical acumen to bring out their meaning. E.g., he who does not find the evident proof of our immortality in the divine economy of the Redemption, and in the clear utterances of Christ, will scarcely reach that conclusion from even the most thoroughgoing consideration of the soul's simplicity, unlimited perfectibility, etc."

139. It is Easier to prove a doctrine to children than it is to do so in the pulpit with adults. The proofs should be accommodated, however, to the age of the children.

1. With the youngest children the word of the bishop's messenger, the catechist, carries complete conviction. He only needs to explain the doctrine, and assure the children: this is what God has taught, and in His name I am teaching it to you. The innate reverence of children for the priest, their freedom from prejudice, suspicion, and doubt, and the influence of

divine grace, all combine to make long argumentation unnecessary.

2. As soon as the children begin to use the catechism, the book itself becomes for them the written testimony of the divinely sent diocesan shepherd, and as such it is in itself proof sufficient of the revealed doctrine. As their mental outlook widens, the more important proofs, the infallible testimonies of the Church, are adduced. But, be it remembered, these should be carefully selected, more with regard to their demonstrative value, than with regard to their number.

Direct testimonies should always be given preference. Among the indirect proofs that can be used to best advantage in the catechism are the "inductive proofs"; for "there is in them a peculiar attraction; they are clear, easily understood, and highly popular." It is obvious that the strongest proofs should be adduced in favor of the cardinal truths of Christian Doctrine; and the children should learn by heart the principal texts of Holy Writ, as also those embodying the decrees of Councils.

3. Finally, the maturer children, of the two highest grades, should, besides the essential proofs, be given also the secondary ones, to fortify them against the attacks of atheists and heretics, and shield them against lukewarmness in faith.

These arguments are of an apologetic character. When they leave school for good, the children should be familiar with the principal objections urged against their faith, and also their refutation. And in our day of unlimited intercommunication, even those children residing in entirely Catholic countries should not go without this instruction. It is a mistake to believe that violent outbursts against non-Catholics are best calculated to forestall loss of faith; by substantial and clear refutation of error only can this end be attained. Correct explanation and solid proof are the best safeguards. Moreover, it is not necessary to set apart special hours for this apologetical work, for the necessary proofs may easily be interwoven in the explanation of those doctrines calling for them.

. . . .

The following general remarks may also be kept in mind:

(*a*) Better one proof clearly stated, decisive, and comprehensible, than ten diffuse and inconclusive ones.

(*b*) The primary proofs are already at hand in the catechism and in the best printed explanations of the same. Unfortunately, the decisions of Councils and Popes, very valuable in this connection, are often lacking. The catechist will find ample scope for his zeal in supplying these as well as in the final adaptation of the secondary apologetical proofs.

An apologetical literature for young readers is largely one of the desiderata of the future. Good stories, showing religion in action, are perhaps best calculated to win their interest, while benefiting their minds.

Among the larger apologetical works which the catechist may consult with great profit to his instructions are: Christian Apologetics: Devivier-Messmer; Christian Apology, (3 vols): P. Schanz, D D.; The Catholic World View: V. Cathrein, S. J.

140. Making Frequent Acts of Faith, as we have already noted above (No. 136), greatly helps the understanding of Christian Doctrine. But the practice is especially to be recommended for strengthening religious conviction. The reason, as the Church teaches, and daily experience confirms, is found herein, that the assent of faith is determined not by the objective truth, but by an act of the free-will. Hence it does not suffice to convince the children that God has spoken, but they must be trained to accept the word of God unreservedly in all its fulness, so that they relish submitting themselves to God's guidance.

How to proceed in this matter may be learned from directions given by Hirscher, and from the example of St. Francis Xavier.

Hirscher advises: "Every time a truth has been explained to the children, make an act of faith with them. Conclude with the question: Do you believe this truth? The answer should be: Yes, I am convinced, I do believe. Then turn the question around and ask: What is it that you firmly believe? Explain it to me. And the answer should be succinctly given by the children. In these ever-recurring concrete acts of faith the word 'I believe' acquires gradually a fuller meaning, and the pupil is brought to an earnest realization of the truths it embraces."

St. Francis Xavier, in a letter of January 12, 1544, wrote from Cochin to his religious brethren in Rome: "On Sunday I gathered together in church men and women, boys and girls. They came with great joy, anxious to hear the word of God. Then, in their own language and in a distinct voice, I spoke before them the Sign of the Cross, the Our Father, the Hail Mary and the Creed, and let them all together recite it after me, which they readily did. Then I repeated the Creed alone, pausing after each article to ask whether they believed it fully and firmly. Crossing their hands over their heart they signified aloud and all together their earnest and firm faith. I have them repeat the Creed oftener than other prayers, teaching them that those who believe everything contained in it are called Christians.

"After the Creed I give them the Decalog, explaining to them that it contains the Christian rule of life, that those who live according to it are good Christians, sure of obtaining life everlasting, while those who transgress it are bad Christians, who will be condemned to everlasting punishment, unless they expiate their sins by penance. This thought greatly impresses the neophytes as well as the pagans; for it makes them realize the holiness of the Christian rule of life, and its consistency with itself and with reason.

"Besides, I say with them the important prayers, such as the Our Father and the Hail Mary. After it we repeat once more the Creed, adding to it the Our Father and Hail Mary with some appropriate invocation. Thus after the first article of the Creed they repeat after me: 'Jesus, Son of the living God, give us the grace firmly to believe this holy doctrine; we ask this of Thee by offering to Thee the prayer which Thou hast taught.' Then follows: 'Holy Mary, Mother of Jesus Christ Our Lord, obtain for us from thy Divine Son the grace to believe fully and firmly this first article of Christian Doctrine.'

"We follow this method for all the other articles. And I proceed in the same manner in teaching them the Ten Commandments. After we have recited in common the first Commandment reminding us of the love we owe to God, we continue: 'Jesus Christ, Son of the Living God, give us the grace to love Thee above all things;' and then we pray the Our Father to obtain this grace. Then we say: 'Holy Mary, Mother of Jesus Christ, obtain for us from thy Divine Son the grace faithfully to keep this first Commandment.' Then follows the Hail Mary. We proceed in the same manner for the following nine Commandments, adapting our invocation to each Commandment. I accustom them to ask fervently for this grace in their daily prayers, and from time to time I tell them that when they obtain it, they shall receive all else in richer measure than they themselves could desire."

Jungmann appends the following remark to this quotation for the benefit of his readers: "I am convinced, and you cannot deny, that the people of the coast, instructed in this manner, did make more progress in Christianity than they could have made had they been subjected to the tortures of the heuristic method."

The foregoing shows clearly the importance of divine grace in catechetical instruction. Hence, with the act of faith we should combine prayer to obtain the grace of the Holy Ghost, without which we cannot even pronounce the name of Jesus in becoming manner. Further on we shall develop more reasons why prayer must form an integral part of Christian Doctrine.

E. STAGE OF UTILIZATION
[CONFIRMATION, APPLICATION, PRACTICE]

(a) IMPRESSING THE TRUTH UPON THE MIND

EIGHTEENTH PRINCIPLE. — *The end of catechization requires that the children should know by heart at least the chief verities of the Christian religion. Hence the catechist should* 1. *Take care that the children memorize the catechism, and* 2. *He should provide for frequent recapitulations.*

141. Explanation of the Thesis. — The old proverb: we learn not for school but for life, finds its application especially in religious instruction. The ultimate aim of all religious instruction is a practical one: to ground and develop the Christian life. In other words, in catechetical instruction the children should learn the fundamental principles — the end and the way — that must regulate their every action, their feelings, words, and deeds, not only in infancy, but also in later life. Hence they should be so thoroughly familiarized with these doctrines that they become their abiding spiritual possession forever. There can be no question, then, of some sort of general, implicit knowledge, but they must have a clear and distinct explicit knowledge of the individual truths.

That at least the cardinal truths must be imparted to the children in this manner needs no further emphasizing, for already in the thirteenth thesis we have discriminated between religious truths according to their importance and their influence on the Christian life.

Our thesis is concerned with the means to attain this end: memorizing and reviewing. Let it be remarked at the very outset that these means are not the whole of catechetical instruction; and unfortunately there have been catechists who have turned religious instruction into a hateful memory task. This mistake must be avoided, but it does not alter the fact that memorizing and reviewing are absolutely necessary if the child is to be permanently benefited by religious instruction.

142. First Rule for Memorizing. — The catechist should insist that the catechism text be literally and correctly learned by heart. And this for very good reasons: the child should keep in mind the correct doctrine, for in religious matters much depends on accurate and definite expression, so that often the change of a single word alters the meaning of a sentence completely. And experience testifies that even when the literal expression has vanished from the memory, there remains the instinctive effort to conceive and express the religious truth correctly and clearly. Without memorizing, the doctrine will much more easily fade completely from the mind. It happens, of course, that even that which has been carefully memorized is forgotten; but in such cases it becomes an easy matter to refresh the memory. Memorizing, besides, makes for greater assiduity in learning. When the teacher is satisfied with any kind of an answer more or less faithful to the text, the brighter children at least will take no great pains, for they will experience no difficulty in finding an answer approximately correct; they rest content with it and make no ulterior effort. Hence the advantages for pedagogy in general of memorizing: it curbs the heedlessness of the child, the given text checking its wandering thoughts.

Finally, literal memorizing is not a hard task for any child, and an able catechist will know how to tone down whatever disagreeable features it may possess.

143. Other Rules which the catechist should keep steadfastly in mind, as they forestall abuses which might jeopardize completely the memorizing which is so indispensable from a pedagogical standpoint.

The second rule: never give the children too much to learn at once. Rather little, well done, than too much ill digested. The mental capacity of the children should also be taken into account: do not expect the same amount of work from all children indiscriminately. It may be well also, in order to stimulate their zeal, to point out a few questions which they are left free to memorize or not. Never forget that in this matter of memorizing, especially, it is easy to discourage the children, and to inoculate them with a thorough dislike for religious instruction.

Third rule: when selecting the matter to be memorized, ascertain beforehand that the children understand it.

We may distinguish a mechanical, a rational, and an artificial memorizing. Learning the words of a strange tongue is mechanical memorizing. In this case the attention is centered more on the words, signs, numbers, than on the thing itself; that which is to be impressed on the mind is repeated until it is fixed therein. Experienced teachers are justified in combating an extensive use of mechanical memorizing in any branch of study; on the other side, the total abolition of memory work is not to be countenanced.

"Not only rational memorizing, done in conjunction with reason, but also the mechanical memory, should be continually exercised. Mechanical memory, or the memory of word, number, and tone, is exercised by the learning of mottoes, formulas, numbers, stories, and songs. The children should never leave school without taking home with them some inspiring sayings." In the case of religious instruction mechanical memory may be exercised by the learning of prayers, hymns, and the clear-cut definitions of the catechism.

The word "mechanical," however, does not imply that this learning should be done altogether in an irrational manner, to the extent that the child does not understand anything of what it is learning. We have already noticed that in this kind of memory work attention is directed more, but not exclusively, to the outward signs, words, symbols, etc. It is impossible of course to circumscribe with mathematical accuracy the provinces of mechanical and rational memorizing. The latter, however, is especially concerned with the contents of the passage, the connection of ideas, in a word, with the substantial assimilation of it, in contrast with mere external mastering of a passage.

Artificial memorizing (mnemotechnic) is a valuable but always a subordinate adjunct in certain branches of the curriculum, e.g., history, geography.

We insist, then, that the children in the catechism class should learn nothing by heart which they do not understand. Yet it is not required that previous to their memorizing a passage, the same should be thoroughly grasped in all its details, for in that case the necessarily slow task of memorizing would consume too much time. From the many discussions on this question the following conclusions may be drawn:

(a) We must distinguish between the younger and the older children. During their last two or three years in school they are generally able to memorize the matter previous to its more extensive treatment in the classroom, since they have already acquired a certain amount of knowledge which enables them to learn by heart with some benefit. It may be well, generally, to read the matter impressively, or to have it read, adding the indispensable explanations.

(b) In the case of younger children, memorizing as a rule should be required only after the matter has been thoroughly explained. We speak here only of the catechism proper, and there is no valid reason why even the very youngest children should not be made to learn the prayers by heart from the moment they begin to have the use of reason.

(c) The teacher should always proceed, not in iron-bound fashion, but by adapting himself to every lesson and to the children themselves.

144. It is also the Duty of the Catechist, in so far as the teacher of the profane branches has not done this, practically to train the children in memorizing. This training must consist in this: that

1. He should teach the children how to study by heart: they should not read the lesson through mechanically a number of times, but divide it into paragraphs which they should ponder over for a little while before attempting to commit them to memory. Some exponents of experimental psychology claim that it is better to memorize the whole lesson at once rather than in parts. But they themselves are forced to limit their theory; for, practically, when we consider the majority of children, only the older ones will be able to do so: the energetic attention required for "global" memorizing is only found in exceptional cases even among children of the upper grades.

Furthermore, the children, when memorizing, should recite the paragraphs to themselves, aloud, with understanding and feeling. Evening time seems better suited for this task, for what is learned then is not supplanted by fresh impressions. Although one can learn quicker in the morning, the matter is not so easily retained. In any case, the children should frequently recite by themselves what they have acquired.

2. But also in school the catechist should exercise the children in memorizing. He can do this by asking them, individually or collectively, to read aloud, with understanding and feeling, a given passage, and then, the books being closed, requesting them to repeat it by heart.

145. What should the Children Learn by Heart? — First of all, the necessary prayers; then appropriate hymns and well-chosen mottoes or pithy sayings. In the catechism: at least the cardinal truths (compare No. 99 ff.); let the catechist demand an exact rendition of the definitions of important notions and of the fundamental formulas: faith, prayers, commandments, sacraments, works of mercy.

Bible History, generally speaking, is not literally learned by heart, but the child should render it in his own words. For, (a) the amount of matter to be memorized would be excessive; (b) moreover, Bible History is not taken textually from Holy Writ or from the authoritative declarations of the Church; (c) there is not time enough to explain Holy Writ as minutely as the catechism, and a literal memorizing of the text would not bring a corresponding benefit; (d) excessive insistence on memorizing would jeopardize the soul-inspiring and elevating influence of Holy Writ. A few passages, however, might be textually learned: the history of Creation, the Fall, the Annunciation, the Nativity, the sayings of Christ: experience teaches that children take especial delight in learning the latter, e.g., the sermon on the Mount. When making a selection of such passages, the catechist should keep in mind their demonstrative value for important doctrines of faith.

The zealous pastor should apply in his preaching and catechization the following advice of Bossuet with regard to the reading of Holy Writ: "Turn your attention to those beautiful passages which you understand, without worrying about the more difficult texts. In this manner the mind substantially assimilates the general contents of Holy Writ. For St. Augustine is right when he says that the obscure passages contain no verities different from those found in the easier ones. And the latter are, moreover, the most beautiful. If the education of a man still of an impressionable age were entrusted to me, and I were left free to do as I pleased, I would select a number of beautiful passages from the Bible and give him those to read repeatedly so that he might learn them by heart. And at any rate, any one acting upon this advice will familiarize himself with all that is noble in Holy Writ. The more difficult passages he can master later on."

146. The Value of Frequent Reviewing. — The second means toward the end we have in view is the frequent recapitulation of what has been already explained and learned. Peter Canisius was a great advocate of this practice. In the course of every instruction he asked his children to recite several parts of Christian Doctrine.

The "Speculum Catechismi" of Innsbruck (1588) thus sketches this review work: "When this repetition (i.e., a test review of the lesson appointed and explained the previous Sunday) is over, let two boys, who have been well trained and instructed for this purpose, stand up on two high chairs reserved for this exercise, and let them recite together, aloud, slowly, clearly, and distinctly, a chapter from the catechism. . . . The fifth chapter, while it is longer than the others, should be spread over two Sundays. And these two boys, if the other children receive nothing, should always, when they do well, receive their reward and honor."

It might be good policy to devote the last five minutes of every instruction to a short review of what has been learned already. The good results attained in one-class schools because of this frequent reviewing speak in favor of our oft-reiterated contention: rather decrease the amount of matter, and ground the children thoroughly and permanently in the doctrines taught them.

We must, however, warn just as emphatically against the practice of memorizing and reviewing for its own sake, so that it becomes the chief point attended to: as far as instruction in Christian Doctrine is concerned, explanation and understanding remain of paramount importance; on the educational side of catechization the faithful, earnest practice of what has been learned must never be lost sight of.

In order to avoid as much as possible the danger of mere catechism drills, the recapitulation should not be a mere review of the text but also of the matter, i.e., the explanation, the examples, and the application should all be included. Let the catechist also encourage the children explicitly to explain in their own words how they understand various doctrines, and how they would practise them. He may then, at the same time, by way of introduction or further explanation, add new elements, fresh examples, or comparisons. In this manner he will guard against mechanical repetition, while dispelling tediousness and avoiding narrow pedantism.

The "Speculum Catechismi" of Innsbruck describes this phase of the recapitulation process in a natural and clear manner: "After examining the children for at least fifteen minutes in the catechism lesson assigned for that day, the catechist begins his review, and, selecting different children, he asks them what they remember about the explanation of the catechism given on the previous Sunday. Let him make good use of the answers given by the children to explain and develop the matter more fully whenever necessary. The children who show progress should from time to time receive a reward, such as printed or painted pictures, rosaries, religious booklets, Agnus Dei, or other things of this kind. They will gladden the children's hearts and spur them on to renewed efforts."

147. Further Rules for Recapitulation. — According to a frequently quoted dictum, the review of the matter explained last should always take place at the beginning of the following lesson. However, we question the practical value of the rule, and at any rate the habit should never deviate into an iron-bound custom. In as far as it becomes necessary to connect the new lesson with the previous one, a few recapitulating questions will serve as a natural preparation for the coming explanation.

At the end of every lesson, and even after each important part of it, a short review seems in order. It is advisable to have the same also at the conclusion of every large division of the catechism. In former times there existed a predilection for a general review at the end of the school year in connection with some solemn distribution of premiums. This constituted an extensive test of the children's knowledge in matters of religion. The advisability of such an examination has to this day been a much-mooted question, to which we must return later. What we have said above about the fundamental catechism and the concentric method (No. 101 ff.) may be advantageously applied to the annual recapitulation and the general review of the catechism.

148. Tests in Religious Instruction. — Many teachers are opposed to examinations in religion, which constitute also a review, although not in the ordinary meaning of the word, because they make the study of religion compulsory, and to that extent hateful. The latter, however, can only be the case where the teaching betrays a lack of deep religious conviction or where the examinations are improperly conducted. In the case of well-trained Catholic children, examinations, especially those at the close of the year, are of great value. And the more earnest and thorough the examinations, the better the child will realize the great importance of religion.

On the other side, we need not deny that these examinations have their drawbacks. The child should be given to understand very clearly that the examination in religion has in view an end totally different from the one aimed at in other branches. In religion the main thing is not knowledge, but practice: a life in accordance with revealed truth. And of this no one is judge but God alone. Hence many a child, in the front ranks at examination time, may be relegated to the rear and far behind a child with poor marks, in the eyes of God. And it might be better not to mark in the report: Religion, but: Religious Instruction. From this the catechist may conclude that a brilliant examination on the part of his pupils is by no means a sign that he has done his work well. The examination has, not unfitly, been compared to a poisonous drug, which may effect a cure, but may also seriously disturb health, according as it is used properly or improperly.

149. Immanent Recapitulation is a term often met with in the new pedagogy. It consists in this, that, when treating a subject, other (logically or morally) correlated subjects, explained before, are reviewed at the same time. Thus, e.g., a Bible story emphasizing the Providence of God may give occasion to review the divine attributes; the doctrines of hell and purgatory may lead to a review of the doctrine of sin; a feast of the ecclesiastical year may bring about a review of the corresponding mystery of faith.

What is to be thought of this theory? What we have said above about "concentration" (No. 104), which is related to this "immanent repetition," may be applied in this case: its good points should be preserved. Nay, we contend that, to point out vividly the connection between theoretically correlated truths as well as their practical bearing on the religious life of the child, is a very effective means of strengthening their religious convictions. It is wrong and unpractical to make immanent repetition an exclusive rule. That it should have been advocated in a spirit of reaction against mechanical drilling, is easily understood; but it goes to extremes: without frequent and orderly reviewing it will be practically impossible to give the children a connected, thorough, and lasting knowledge of religion; whence, failure to attain the end of catechetical instruction.

(b) APPLICATION AND PRACTICE

NINETEENTH PRINCIPLE. — *In order to arouse and train the Christian conscience of the child, the catechist should: 1. Constantly apply all Christian teaching to the concrete occurrences of everyday life, i.e., he should draw from these doctrines practical consequences suited to the age of the children. Yet this is not sufficient to attain the end in view, but, 2. He should combine the former with the very practice of the duties following from the doctrine explained.*

150. The Expression "Application" has various meanings.

1. Sometimes it is used to designate the last stage of learning, which is also called its "utilization." The word "application" in this wider meaning comprises all functions of teaching and learning which are conducive to the right use of any rule acquired by study, and it includes, therefore, the "impressing," since the latter aims at establishing the rule so firmly in the mind that it is ever ready for effective use.

2. The second meaning of the word "application" is the one of which, e.g., there is question in the sermon, when the preacher, after stating the doctrine, points out concrete instances in which the general doctrine is, as it were, embodied or should be embodied.

3. Finally, "application" means, not something pointed out by teacher or preacher, but the carrying into effect of the doctrine by the scholar himself.

In the thesis now under consideration we use the word "application" in the second meaning; the third meaning of the word conveys what we call here "practice," which is not to be understood in a mechanical sense, but as synonymous with putting into effect (exercise of virtue = virtuous activity).

151. The Importance of the "Application," in the meaning just described, is plain from the wording of the thesis, when it lays special emphasis on training the religious conscience of the children. This seems indeed to belong to the second and highest aim of catechization: Christian training. And such is the case: the last stage in religious instruction, the practical use of what has been learned, naturally introduces us into the domain of heart and will training, and from a consideration of this higher viewpoint the method of instruction should receive its final perfectioning.

Because of the great importance of the application, the catechist ought to have a clear idea of what it consists in. A comparison with the profane branches, which must also have recourse to this application, may be useful here.

In language instruction, e.g., the rules of grammar and syntax are stated and explained; yet this is not sufficient. In order that the pupils may attain the required facility in the use of the rules, they must, by means of questions and exercises, be made to apply them frequently to many concrete cases. Thus the pupil is gradually trained to the right use of the rules, although he need no longer remember them explicitly.

In catechetical instruction we deal with the truths of faith, all of which, in a certain sense, are of a practical nature. The right carrying out of these supernatural truths and rules in real life demands more than the mere knowledge of them: they should constitute the norm in conformity with which the individual facts of real life are judged. The catechist should refer frequently to the concrete facts in which the doctrine is applied, so that the children may gradually learn to judge everything in accordance with supernatural rules. Thus, e.g., it would be scarcely sufficient to explain that sin is the only true evil; this truth must be applied to many individual cases: sickness, poverty, lack of food, bad fortune, unjust treatment on the part of others, even of superiors . . . all these are not real evils. But a deliberate lie, wilful distraction during prayer, disobedience, all these are true evils. The result of this application will be that the child accustoms himself not to look upon contrarieties as evils; but to dread real unhappiness from temptation; and the child will gradually apply this rule aright, even without referring reflectively to the general doctrine.

From the above it is sufficiently plain why we look upon the application as the necessary means to develop the Christian sense of faith or the Christian conscience. For conscience is the practical reason in as far as it applies the moral truths to individual cases; and the Christian conscience is but practical reason guided by faith, in as far as it applies the truths of the Christian religion to the individual life of the faithful. The sense of faith may be explained as the ability and promptness to judge everything in accordance with the rules of faith; it means therefore the same thing as "Christian conscience."

Presently we understand also why homiletics lays so much stress on practical applications in preaching.

Christians must as it were be led by the hand of their shepherd, and he must point out what is to be done and what is to be avoided. This is all the more true of the catechist in the presence of inexperienced children. And his reward will be all the greater if these applications are carefully attended to in catechetical instruction: in this way he lays the foundation of a conscientious life, and his task in general is lightened, for, through constant application to concrete cases, the whole Christian Doctrine is more readily grasped.

152. The Practice. — Let us go back once more to the example of language instruction: the general rules are applied to concrete cases in the answers to questions and the working of exercises. This application, which is no longer the work of the teacher, but a constant exercise on the part of the pupil, demands great exertion.

Thus also in catechization: the application of the doctrines must go hand in hand with personal practice on the part of the child. Yet it is very different from the practice usual in other school branches. For with the latter it always remains in the sphere of knowledge, although it is also related to the conative faculties, since it is called forth by an energizing act of the will and in turn reacts on the latter. In catechization however we deal with a practice which influences the will directly, disposing will and heart in such a manner that they oppose no obstacle to the clear judgment of conscience, and its execution. Only then will catechization train conscientious Christians in the fullest meaning of that term; for those only can be called by that name who not merely formulate correct judgments about the moral value of an action, but who live permanently in accordance with the dictates of conscience. Hence the complete training of the child's conscience requires that his heart and will be permanently bent to practise virtue and to shun sin. How is this end to be attained? It is quite obvious that even the best explanations and proofs must fall short, since directly they promote only knowledge. New means must be found, motives which shall directly rouse and influence the will. These means are treated exhaustively in the third part of this work.

153. Rules for the Application. — 1. The application should really be the carrying out in a particular case of the truths expounded, and it should not be a mere appendix to the explanation. Many an application, however valuable it may be in itself, does not deserve that name, because there is no connection between it and the truth of which it is supposed to be the application.

Example of a good application: when explaining God's omniscience, although the explanation has been begun with some illustrative narration, new historical facts must now be added, e.g.: the brothers of Joseph did evil; their own father was not aware of it, but did not another father witness their action? Who saw the sin of our first parents, the sin of Cain? When you commit sin in secret, who sees it? When you are in church, but your heart is far away from it, who knows it? When you are in sorrow, who is aware of it? Of whom should you therefore always think?

2. The application should refer more particularly to the present life of the children; but their later life should also be taken into consideration. If only the future were kept in view, the catechist would be gather-

ing materials for a building which he is never to start. Nor should the catechist fall into the opposite extreme. Especially are the older children to be instructed carefully in preparation for later life, with regard to the reception of the Sacraments, human respect, reading of bad books, mixed marriages, preparation for Christian marriage, etc. The first part of the rule is further explained in the ninth, the second part in the twelfth thesis.

3. Important applications should be reiterated on different occasions, of course with suitable changes in form, until conscience becomes very responsive to the doctrines in question.

Subjects calling for frequent practical applications are: prayer, purity, patience, self-renunciation (from the hour of rising in the morning and all through the day), work, honesty, social solidarity, beauty and joy of a life of grace, reverence and love for God, Jesus Christ, etc. References to purity can be made even outside of the lesson on the Sixth Commandment, e.g., when treating of God's omniscience, the scourging of Jesus, divine grace (the body is the temple of the Holy Ghost), the resurrection, hell, purgatory.

These repeated applications are especially effective if they are not separated by too long an interval of time, so that the former is still fresh in the memory, while the new one is made from a different standpoint.

4. While he should be zealous in these practical applications, the catechist must nevertheless use discretion in his selection of the same. For a mere piling-up of them might lead to a result opposite to the one aimed at: the deadening instead of the sharpening of the moral sense.

. . . .

The practical conclusion for the catechist, following from the above thesis, is, that without careful preparation in prayer, study, and observation of daily life he cannot hope to be equipped for his task. Never should he leave anything to chance.

PART III

CATECHETICAL EDUCATION (TRAINING OF THE HEART FOR A CHRISTIAN LIFE)

154.

PRELIMINARY Remarks. — Seconded by the general religious life of the parish, by the school in all its work, by the parental home and the good example of the people as a whole, catechization should train the children for a devout Christian life. Unfortunately the above-named helpful factors are often lacking completely or in part. In consequence the catechist is bound all the more to strive with all his might to imbue the youth with a Christian spirit by a conscientious preparation and a thoroughgoing exposition of Christian Doctrine. And what condition is of prime importance to attain this end? Since here we have to deal directly with the educational side of catechization, the personal qualities of the catechist come in for an even greater share of consideration than in the case of instruction. The true religious training of children is brought about, not so much by theoretical knowledge, as by the deeper qualities of mind and heart of the catechist. If he himself lives the life of faith, he will know no rest until he finds ways and means to train his pupils in a similar manner, and to make up for the shortcomings of others who have neglected their duty. The following exposé should prove helpful to the catechist in taking his bearings in matters educational, while acquainting him with the means to be used. It is also intended to secure him against erroneous views, which, although often refuted in theory and practise, continually crop out afresh and might prove harmful to the beginner.

We divide the matter into three chapters: the first gives the more general rules; the second enumerates the particular virtues which catechization should lead the children to practise; the third treats of some requirements for effective catechization, such as, e.g., school discipline. The latter must be kept in mind also in the instruction proper, but their bearing is more directly educational, and therefore we treat of them only in this third part.

It may not be amiss to recall in an introductory thesis the importance of the educational phase of catechization.

TWENTIETH PRINCIPLE. — *More necessary than instruction in Christian Doctrine and of greater importance is the catechist's duty to influence permanently the will of the children and to train their hearts for a Christian life.*

155. Explanation and Proof. — We are not of course detracting here in any way from what we said above about the importance of catechetical instruction. A solid training of the heart is impossible without a corresponding development of the mind. Sin cannot be banished from the soul unless error and darkness of the mind be dispelled. True love of God and His Holy Will is unthinkable without supernatural enlightenment. The children should see clearly what to do and what to avoid in order to please God. But if the catechist should conclude that his task is done when he has instructed his pupils, he is lamentably mistaken.

The proof of our thesis is based on this truth: the nobler the faculty to be developed, the more important it is to devote the greatest care to its development.

Now, the will, the heart of man, ranks higher than his intellect; all over, the upright man is held in higher esteem than the learned man. The same is true in the supernatural order. St. Bernard says that the value of a man is measured by his love. And he will be judged by God not according to the greater or lesser amount of religious knowledge he possesses, but according to the dispositions of his will and heart. Not the hearers of the word are justified before God (Rom., 2, 13; Math., 7, 21; James, 1, 22), but the doers of the law shall be justified. — Hence is seen the correctness of our thesis.

156. Authoritative Testimonies in Favor of Our Thesis are so numerous that it were superfluous to repeat them here. A few pertinent remarks shall be quoted however by way of warning against erroneous views not infrequently held by zealous catechists.

Thus it is a mistake to expect good results from an unlimited increase of knowledge, in religious as well as in profane matters. And especially in our own day, when even non-Catholic educationists inveigh strongly against an exaggerated intellectualism, no catechist could escape blame for falling into this very error. If the product of our modern schools is so deficient from an educational viewpoint, we owe it, according to F. W. Förster, to "that great delusion of the

18th century which we have not yet altogether shaken off, viz., the delusion that intellectual culture in itself means civilization, that morality necessarily goes hand in hand with intellectual progress. . . . Yet, any one familiar with the facts of real life realizes how limited is the training power of mere knowledge, — nay how this knowledge is injurious and leads to pedantry, if it be not made to subserve from the outset the building of character."

And Förster is not the first to pass this severe judgment on mere learning. The French physician Descuret wrote already in 1852: "The statistics of prisons and hospitals show that insanity, suicide and other crimes multiply apace with an increase in knowledge and so-called illuminism." And a German statistician, several decades ago, was forced to acknowledge that "among the peoples and classes which are more highly educated, there is a greater prevalence of suicide than among the less cultured classes. Those countries and places with a highly organized system of schools, show in general a higher frequency of suicide."

And in order to forestall a malicious interpretation of these testimonies as if putting a premium on ignorance, we quote further from Förster: "Truly logical thinking (without which no intellectual progress is possible), presupposes character, since character only shields the mind from the interference of external influences, personal interest and prejudice. When, therefore, training, not of the head but of the will and heart, is put forward as the highest aim of education, it is because thereby, and thereby only, true and not false culture is promoted."

Hirscher writes: "When you have stored the mind with doctrines of faith and morality, you have accomplished little indeed, unless at the same time you have aroused in your pupils a determined disposition to find joy in believing the truth and keeping the commandments. It is not one-sided knowledge that we should aim at, but the readiness to believe and practise what we learn. Nay, if the child firmly believed the fundamental truths of the Gospel, and treasured in his heart the feelings of a true Christian, it shall profit him more before God, if perhaps not before men, than if he were able to answer several hundred questions (often of little practical bearing) of the catechism, but lacked a vivid and active faith."

All experienced catechists and all writers on this subject are unanimous in declaring, also in regard to the instruction, that it is not quantity or novelty that matters, but thoroughness.

Jungmann, having noticed and deplored a frequent lack of zeal in religious instruction, declares: "It would be a mistake, — and this is not the first time I give vent to this conviction — it would be a mistake if you were to believe that the real cause and the deep root of an ever-spreading unbelief and its dread consequences is, in presence of the development of natural sciences, the lack of a corresponding increase of religious knowledge, the want of theoretical familiarity with those proofs by means of which science is accustomed to establish and justify the doctrines of Christianity. I do not mean to say that ignorance in religious matters is not at least partly responsible for this evil; but it is more especially due to perversity of the will and corruption of the supernatural moral life. *Corde creditur ad justitiam:* the faith that sanctifies man resides in the heart, not in the head or the understanding; and it is also in the heart that atheism is born and develops: for first it falls away from the love of God into sin; then from sin into impiety, from impiety into unbelief. It is related that one day Chateaubriand called together in his salon all the great writers of Paris. 'Gentlemen,' he said to them, 'I take the liberty of asking you a question: answer me on your honor and conscience. Would not all of you have the courage to be Catholics if you had the courage to be chaste?'" All was silence; some grinned, but not one answered: no.

What is the conclusion? That the teaching of the word of God in general, but more particularly in the case of children, must above all things strive to keep the young hearts free from sin, and to foster in them the love of God; that the aim of catechization is far from being attained when the children sufficiently understand and remember the contents of the catechism, but that it is of much greater importance and necessity that the priest also train the hearts of the children to earnest piety and fashion them in the mold of a true Christian life. If this is overlooked, you beget "hearers of the law," but not "doers" of the same. Yet not the former, but the latter only are justified before God (Rom. 2, 13); you train Christians who cry: Lord, Lord; yet to such the Kingdom of heaven has not been promised, but only to those who do the will of the Father who is in heaven (Math. 7, 21).

May the number of those catechists decrease unto extinction of whom Alban Stolz writes: "They merely take the heads of the children into consideration, making them learn by heart and recite at examination time. The instruction moves on in general sentences and is scarcely or not at all applied to daily life; their heart and will are left as cold and unmoved by these daily intellectual drills as by arithmetical figures. Hence it comes that frequently the worst rascals give the best answers in catechism. Nay often it is not a question of understanding, but of mere reproduction from memory. Many children give the correct answer of the catechism without grasping it at all, just as the altar boy glibly recites his Confiteor and strikes his breast. Thus arid instruction often ends in making religion itself an unsufferable bore. Hence also, that so few pupils in our schools acquire the right Catholic instinct, because the teacher lacks zeal, or ability, or both."

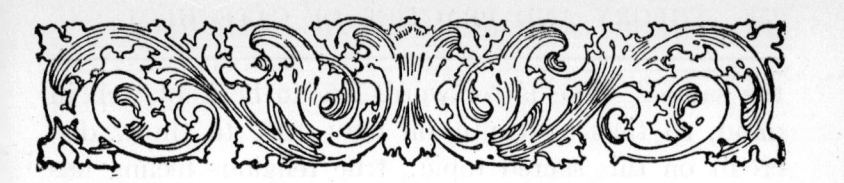

CHAPTER I

GENERAL MEANS FOR TRAINING THE HEART

WE cannot pass in review all educational means, but only those that are useful in catechization, in the oral intercourse between teacher and pupil. We shall chiefly consider:
1. The unction in catechization;
2. The use of the right motives required by this unction;
3. The exercise or practice of the virtues.

We treat the last-named means only from a general directive standpoint. The more important particular virtues are again taken up partly in the second, partly in the third chapter, and also in Special Catechetics.

§ I. UNCTION IN CATECHIZATION

TWENTY-FIRST PRINCIPLE. — *Catechization should be full of unction, i.e., it should appeal to the religious emotions of the children, and thus influence their hearts actively and decisively.*

157. Explanation. — To make clear what is meant by "unction" we may borrow the definition which is given of it in homiletics: "Unction is that affective quality which should characterize the preaching of God's word; spiritual discourses are replete with unction when they react deeply on the heart and call forth religious emotions that permanently influence the same." The latter words are to be kept well in mind, so that no confusion may arise to throw discredit on this sacred topic: true religious feeling has nothing in common with those impulses which are but simulation, hollow semblance, or unruly excitement, idle vanity, unreasoned zeal, and instability. God is not found in such effervescent transports, for His Kingdom is "justice and peace and joy in the Holy Ghost." Rom. 14, 17. Gruber's catechetical works are splendid models of warm religious feeling well worthy of imitation.

This is not the place to explain at length what is to be understood by feeling, emotional activity, etc., and why the Christian religion may rightly make an appeal to the affective side of man. But to avoid all misunderstanding in this matter, as if we stood for a vague sentimental religion, which has done so much harm already, we give the definition of emotion, and its seat, conscience. An emotion is a harmonious activity of both appetitive faculties, the higher (spiritual) and the lower (sensuous) in presence of the suprasensible goodness or evil of a thing. Conscience, as the immediate principle of the psychical processus in question, is the combined (spiritual and sensuous) appetitive power in man, in so far as it becomes naturally active in presence of moral good or ill. This conception of conscience is the very opposite of a subjectively and objectively vague stimulation of the emotions: for, as we understand it, emotion is objectively related to the true good, and subjectively, even including reflex emotions or feelings in the restricted sense, it makes for complete harmony between the spiritual and sensuous man.

How is this unction brought about? Three factors concur in its production: the grace of the Holy Ghost, a catechist deeply imbued with religious feelings, and the stimulating power inherent in the religious doctrines themselves. Of course, deep religious feeling also depends upon clear comprehension and strong conviction; but on these we have sufficiently insisted already. And it is important to keep in mind the above three factors in order to prevent the catechism lesson from degenerating into a mere instruction. They will help us in discovering the means the catechist should use in order to give unction to his words.

158. (A) The First Means: Prayer. — The custom, often emphasized by an explicit prescription of the diocesan authorities, to begin and end the catechism lesson with prayer, is a conclusion following from a fundamental truth: that the author of our whole supernatural life as well as of every supernatural act is the Holy Ghost. Hence the catechist should begin by imploring His divine assistance, not only in his own prayers, but also by making catechization itself a religious exercise. The method of St. Francis Xavier (No. 140) cannot be followed too closely, and the underlying principle at least should never be lost sight of by the catechist: it is the plain truth that children no more than adults can make an act of faith, nor a resolve to keep the commandments — much less carry out the same — unless by humble prayer they implore divine grace.

In the Rituale Salisburgense of 1740, under the caption: What the catechist should do in the beginning of the lesson, we read: "First of all he should recommend to God in private prayer the lesson he is about to begin as something on which depends the salvation of many precious souls fashioned after His image, and redeemed by the precious Blood of Jesus Christ. He should invoke divine grace and help that he may perform his task to the honor of God and the edification of the Catholic Church, as St. Paul says: 'Neither he that planteth is anything nor he that watereth; but God that giveth the increase.' The prayer at the beginning of the lesson may be preceded by a hymn, such as: Come Holy Ghost, or a Christmas hymn at Christmas time, or another suitable hymn at Easter, etc. The catechist himself should say the Lord's Prayer, the Hail Mary, the Apostles' Creed, while the children kneel down. He should remain in his place, facing the children, make the Sign of the Cross, and begin in distinct and clear voice: In the Name of the Father and of the Son, etc. . . . At the end of the lesson the children should all kneel down and join their hands; while the catechist stands facing them, he makes the Sign of the Cross, recites the Ten Commandments, the Precepts of the Church, and the Four Last Things; then he dismisses them under God's protection." In this manner the religious instruction becomes what it should be: an hour of edification. A pious atmosphere pervades the whole, and the solemn prayer at the beginning and at the end of the instruction will undoubtedly leave a permanent impress upon the hearts of the children. — Go and do likewise.

159. (B) The Enthusiasm of the Catechist himself. — The prime requisite to influence the heart of the young is that the catechist himself first of all should have taken the truth to heart and become enthused for it. When the priest personally remains cold in the presence of the truths and facts of faith, his instructions are dry and unattractive; let his heart be gripped by enthusiasm for the ideals of religion, and this inward fire will soon break forth and set aglow the hearts of the children. Spontaneously and at the right moment he will rise to true pathos, i.e., he will give appropriate expression to his own feelings and work powerfully on the impressionable consciences of the young. The short admonition: my child, remain virtuous, or: dear children, never offend our dear Lord, when uttered with deep feeling and love, will produce a stronger and more lasting effect than a long cold summing-up of arguments or a mere declamatory and unnatural appeal to their emotions.

When the catechist is thus moved by faith he is also in a position to give expression to that virtual pathos which consists in the appropriate exposition of those phases of Christian Doctrine which are best calculated to appeal to the heart. Only a soul fired with deep religious devotion is able to call forth the latent powers of Christian Doctrine and to bring them to full fruition in the hearts of his hearers. And here we have already touched upon the third factor of which more is to be said later on (No. 160).

No doubt, "when catechizing children, there is no call for that pathetic oratorical presentation of the subject which is very appropriate in the sermon. Yet, if the catechist is to stir the hearts of the children, he should have recourse to a vivid and warm exposition, infusing into his words in a natural manner that religious fervor by which he himself is animated." Hirscher writes anent this subject: "If any religious truth or fact is to make a deep impression upon the heart of the child, it must first of all have fired the catechist himself; it must have deeply moved his own soul. That side of it which has aroused the liveliest emotions within his breast, he will propose to his pupils. And it will be effective since it is given in a manner that has proved to be effective. Add to this the power of example. One can hardly expect great fervor on the part of the pupils when they see their own leader unmoved. Instinctively they doubt the reality of something treated in perfunctory fashion. Let the catechist be deeply moved, and his emotion is transfused into them: they strive naturally (especially when they love the catechist), to represent to themselves, and to arouse in their souls, the emotions revealed in the voice, features, and expression of the teacher. Let the catechist be deeply stirred, and loved: then the very language that gives expression to your thoughts, your whole exterior bearing, will co-operate in your effort to influence the heart; you will experience no difficulty in finding the appropriate words to express your meaning. You will thus translate your own deep experience, and at the same time set your pupils' hearts aglow. Evoking a vision you will exclaim: Oh, I see the damned rise up against their seducers; you will give vent to your feelings in a fervent appeal: Oh, if you thought of this one thing all the time; you will express your sorrow: Indeed, none who dishonors his parents can succeed; the comminatory words will rise to your lips: Let him be accursed who scandalizes the innocent; or again, you will excite in your pupils feelings and desires befitting the subject, by exhortation, question, wish, warning, expostulation, etc." Some expressions and examples which Hirscher adduces further, might appear to be pathetic to excess. It is wrong to let the appeal to the emotions degenerate into mere sentimentalism; on the other side, a cold, excessively dry exposition is also to be avoided.

160. (C) Presentation of Motives. — Already at the end of Part II we noted that, outside of explanation and proof, catechization stands in need of other helps, viz., moving and driving powers, motives. Having defined unction as the permanent supernatural influencing of the hearers' conscience, it becomes clear that for this purpose the presentation and development of motives is best adapted.

Gruber complains: "There are found catechists who waste their time analyzing religious verities to their minutest details, proving their truth by scientific or popular arguments, pointing out their applicability in various occurrences of human life. But with all their punctiliousness they often forget to set forth their inherent power to counteract all incentives to sensuality, their compelling influence in arousing love for the things of eternity, their ability to lift our souls from earth to heaven, — thus indeed training men in the spirit of divine revelation.

"Because of this vital oversight, religious instruction becomes arid and a mere matter of the intellect; or it degenerates into stringent commands to do this or that, their sternness unrelieved by the consoling thought that an everlasting reward is the prize of their fulfilment."

A catechist endowed with that prime requisite, personal fervor (No. 159), will not find it difficult to set in motion, even in childish hearts, the incentives to Christian life contained in divine truth. Because of its importance, we go into this matter at greater length in the following thesis. But we must first answer the question:

161. What Religious Emotions should be Cultivated?
— 1. First of all cultivate in the children a disposition of soul which makes faith light and attractive for them, i.e., a joyful inclination of the heart to submit in everything to God's will. And this applies not only to the doctrines of the Creed, but also to all revealed truths embodying a moral obligation.

2. When explaining truths which directly express a moral precept, it is not sufficient to teach the children what the precept commands or forbids, what means should be used to keep it; endeavor besides to arouse in their hearts love and willingness to keep it, aversion and fear of transgressing the same.

An example from Hirscher: "The second commandment is: Thou shalt not take the name of the Lord thy God in vain. Its meaning is: you shall do nothing whatever opposed to the honor due to God; or, positively expressed: you shall have great reverence for the majesty of the Lord your God. What is most necessary from our present standpoint, in explaining this commandment, is to inculcate a deep fear of God and an awesome respect for Him, a fear and respect such as effectually to prevent the idle and blasphemous use of God's name in telling a lie, in murmuring against His Providence or His decrees, in breaking a vow.

"It is a sad but undeniable fact that in daily life the name of God is used incredibly often in an idle, thoughtless manner to confirm something of no importance, or even the untruth; that it is profaned equally often by blasphemous language. Why? Because there is no fear of God whatever, no reverence for His majesty. These sentiments should be implanted in the children; they should be vivid realities to them in everyday life. The priest should bring home to them the infinite greatness and majesty of God, His spotless sanctity and justice, His infinite power, His Omnipresence; and on the other side, the littleness of man, his absolute and complete dependence upon the assistance of his Creator.

"By taking to heart these facts the children will grow in fear and holy awe; they will feel deeply the greatness of the guilt which stains their souls in the commission of the above sins, and hence come to shun even the smallest desecration of God's name. Besides, they should make the firm resolution to exhibit this reverence towards God in their prayers, their conversation, their behavior, on every occasion. If the catechization on the second commandment does not dwell on all these points with warmth and emphasis, if it does not arouse in the children corresponding emotions and through them a deep and holy fear of everything which in any way detracts from the majesty of God, then the priest need not expect that sins against the second commandment will be avoided or abhorred, or even understood and realized. His word has failed to enlighten and to stir; the child's mind has developed but his heart is left untouched and untrained."

3. **When explaining a truth which does not directly contain any precept, e.g., the attributes of God, the catechist needs to prepare himself carefully in order to know what feelings he should endeavor to awaken.** The difficulty is not so much to find a practical appli-

cation, but rather to limit one's self so that the abundance of practical applications does not confuse the pupils. The better catechisms give valuable directions in this regard. But they prove insufficient if the priest himself as a spiritual man has not experienced the power of God's truth.

An example to show how an abundance of applications is always at hand, is taken from Hirscher. When explaining God's justice, address the children in the following manner: dread greatly to fall into the hands of the just God, especially when in mortal sin. Never envy the happiness of sinners, but realize that the happiness in which they live blindly, constitutes their greatest misfortune. Look upon undeserved suffering not as a punishment, but as a divinely ordained means for our improvement and perseverance in virtue; accept just punishment in humble submission, recognizing that it is righteous and conducive to our sanctification. Never lose heart at sight of the suffering and evil in the world; encourage those who are unjustly persecuted, pointing out to them that their redemption is at hand. Zealously practise works of charity, for the greater the labor and patience, the greater the reward (II Cor. 9, 6). Do not lightly consider yourselves as just, for but one is judge; and not he who justifies himself is therefore justified. Do not put off repentance, relying on God's forbearance, for who knows when His outraged justice may put an end to His patience. At the sight of all the violence, oppression, and evil in the world, seek consolation, joy, and strength in the conviction that an all-powerful Judge and Rewarder lives and reigns (2 Tim. 4, 8; Apoc. 7, 17; James 1, 12).

§ II. USE OF THE RIGHT MOTIVES

TWENTY-SECOND PRINCIPLE. — *The motives which the catechist should invoke to influence the heart are not the natural, but the supernatural, revealed motives; they are more particularly: the mercy and love of God for us (the Incarnation), His infinite majesty, His justice. However, all motivation should in the end arouse and foster in the children a great love of God.*

162. The Importance of this Thesis becomes clear when we realize that the upbuilding of a Christian life in the children depends largely upon the use of the right motives.

The true value of human activity, of human life and character, is gaged by the motives which inspire it. The science of ethics establishes the morality of an action from the threefold consideration of its object, circumstances, end. The last-named however is the most important: a good end makes an action, good in itself, still better; an action indifferent and aimless in itself becomes meritorious in the sight of God if performed with a good intention. An evil end however vitiates the best action. The same object, the same good, is called "motive" in so far as it impels men to act (*in ordine intentionis*), and it is called "end" in so far as it is attained by his activity (*in ordine executionis*). Hence the truth of the axiom: as are the motives that actuate him so is the man; as are his motives, so is his character.

He who is actuated by motives of pride, is a proud man; he who seeks sensual satisfactions, is a sensualist. Whoever is actuated by natural motives only, remains a natural man; a truly Christian character seeks inspiration in motives supplied by faith. What Christ said of evil actions: "From within, out of the heart of men proceed evil thoughts, adulteries, fornications, murders, thefts, etc." (Mark 7, 21) applies equally to virtuous actions: not the external performance or omission, but the deeper internal tendencies of the heart, its aims and motives, these supply the true measure of a man's moral worth.

It is therefore of paramount importance that the heart of the child, since it is to be guided through life by the true Christian spirit, should be supplied with the right motives.

163. These Right Motives, as we said above, are those drawn from revelation: the love of God as made manifest in the work of our redemption; His greatness which demands our unconditional submission, etc. The goods and evils which faith makes known to us should be presented to the child by the catechist in order to incline him towards virtue and fill him with aversion for sin.

For, (*a*) with that end in view divine revelation has been vouchsafed to us. It was not given us merely for the greater illumination of our understanding, but above all for the uplifting and complete conversion of our hearts. Justification before God consists in a life modeled upon faith: the just live by faith. And this means nothing else but to strive after those goods and to shun those evils which faith indicates as true goods and real evils, i.e., to draw the motives of our actions and omissions from the supernatural order.

(*b*) Moreover, those motives only are strong enough to steel the heart to do right even when caprice, aversion, disappointment, opposition and difficulties, pain and impending temporal misfortune would deter us from virtue. Supernatural motives fire the soul unto self-sacrifice and heroism.

(*c*) Finally the same conclusion follows from the very object of catechization: it must strive to rouse "religious" feelings, and the latter can proceed only from supernatural motives.

164. Two Fallacies, of a naturalistic character, regarding the above norm have been thoroughly exposed already by Gruber. The first consists in an excessive insistence on the "utility" motive: when one endeavors to cultivate morality in the children by pointing out to them with marked predilection the temporal benefits or evils consequent upon a given action, the result will be that he trains egotistic and astute politicians, men who will not shrink from duplicity and injustice if these can be turned to their personal advantage.

Gruber repeatedly deprecates the method of many catechists who imagine that, as the supernatural eternal consequences of our actions are beyond the grasp of children, they should preferably call attention to the proximate results, amongst which the natural temporal effects take first place, such as sickness, disgrace, punishment. But such persons (a) degrade children to the level of their own carnal minds; they fail to understand what a pure child heart strongly grasps; they overlook entirely how in this manner they undermine the true religious morality of the child, turn away his impressionable heart from God and center it on a debasing selfishness. While such teachers are themselves chiefly concerned about the temporal consequences of their actions, while they are actuated only by a desire for health, wealth, honor, and pleasure, they do not in the least realize how susceptible is the soul of the sinless child to the beautiful thought: God loves me; and how little such a child is impressed by considerations of money and honor. Such teachers, in whose hearts sensual considerations preponderate, give little thought to consequences of import for eternity; hence they imagine that an innocent child is unmoved by eternal rewards and punishments.

(b) It is erroneous, moreover, to think that the eternal consequences of our actions are far removed. Death is uncertain: daily experience tells us that not only aged people die, but also strong men and young children. This ought to make us clearly realize that eternity lies close to us. A truly religious man sees himself daily at the door of the other world, and only our imagination endeavors to relegate it into the dim future. Hence I will certainly make a stronger impression on the ordinary virtuous child caught in the commission of a serious fault, by saying to him: Child, if God had let you die at this moment, what would have happened to you? I will make a stronger impression on him than I could expect to make in this manner on a gray-haired, hardened sinner. And if it must indeed be granted that the things of eternity are ordinarily far removed from our thoughts, then the eye of the mind should be trained assiduously to look upon them with a clearer vision, even as the bodily eye, when affected by short-sightedness, is improved by being trained to look at distant objects.

(c) Besides, it is clear that when the heart of the young catechumen is trained to love God and our neighbor, it is safeguarded against deadening egotism.

(d) Add to this that the calculations of worldlings often miscarry. For the unruly impulse of evil desires upsets them to such an extent that as far as the consequences of their actions are concerned, they do not attain the intended result; but in an excess of passion they do things the deplorable effects of which they may have much cause to regret. No, Christians should not steal, lie, be impure, in order to avoid prison, corporal punishment, disgrace in the eyes of men, painful sickness, or early death; they should not work and save to accumulate treasures and escape want. They should avoid evil actions and perform good deeds because God desires it, because thus they please Him; because on their account He will love them. Each duty must be presented to the children as a commandment of God: of a God who loves us, and because of this love demands unconditional obedience from us. And the various parts of a duty, as analyzed by reason, should be presented as flowing from the command of God, i.e., as necessarily required by God through this commandment. Thus all precepts that regulate our life and action are derived from God, and ultimately lead back to Him, who is the fundamental motive of their observance.

165. We may Add another Example from Gruber, to show the right and the wrong way of proceeding.

It should be remarked however that Gruber was dealing with the concrete evils of rationalistic catechization; his intention was not to exclude each and every natural motive from catechization, but to combat excessive insistence on the natural at the expense of the supernatural.

Teaching the children their duties towards their parents, Gruber writes, is often done in this wise: "You were a small child unable to help yourself; you were as helpless as your smaller brother or sister is now; you have grown up, and yet you are unable to provide yourself with bread, clothing, and home: you have no money to buy all these. Your mother has taken care of you, borne you about, helped you as she does your smaller brother. Even now your father and mother work for you and give you a share of what they earn: they feed, clothe, assist you continually. See how they love you, how much you receive from them, and how you should love them in return, make life agreeable for them, and delight in dwelling with them. . . . You give them joy by always doing what they desire, by performing at once and willingly what they command, by being obedient to them. And what they command you is for the best, for they know what is good for you. . . . A father told his child: Do not touch that knife! The child took it, however, and cut himself. A mother said: Child, don't eat that fruit, it is not yet ripe. The child did eat, became sick, suffered great pain, and died. If those children had listened, all this would not have happened: your parents know what is good or dangerous for you. . . . Since your parents do so much for you, you should look upon them as your superiors, and honor them; pray fervently to God that He may give them long life and enable them to take good care of you. When you are grown up, and your parents have become old, you should treat them as they have treated you: return their manifold kindnesses in a grateful spirit. . . . Remember, child, that God expects this of you, for He it was who commanded you to honor your parents, etc. . . ." Where, Gruber asks, is true morality to be found in this kind of instruction? What place is made to supernatural love? If at the end the commandment of God and the example of Christ are recalled, they can make but little impression when every previous appeal was based upon egotistical selfish motives!

How different the instruction on this commandment when it is based from the outset on the authority of God and His revelation! And how different the results, if the catechist in treating of the Decalog, would, after the explanation of the three first commandments relating to God, proceed to the explanation of the remaining seven, concerning man, in this wise: "Amongst all persons those to whom we owe most after God are our parents. Hence the fourth commandment runs: thou shalt honor thy father and thy mother. You see, children, our loving Father in heaven who has made you, has also provided you with whatever you need and has given you a father and mother who take His place and apportion to you your share of the things God has allotted to you. You can see them and should behave towards them as you should behave towards God whom you cannot see. God has made you, but he Has commanded your parents to take care of you as long as you are small. Your father and mother do this from love of God and you, and in obedience to God. Hence you must love them in return as taking the place of God; you must rejoice that God has given them to you; you must be a source of satisfaction to them, and thus you also merit God's approval since they take His place. When you grieve your parents, you grieve God, and incur His displeasure. What they command you, you must do for it is God's will. You must do everything that God commands, and do it well, quickly, and willingly, because God expects this of you. In the same way you must do everything that your parents command, as if God Himself commanded it: for your parents command you in God's place. You must honor your parents and look upon them as God's representatives; you must pray for them because God gave them to you and they do so much for you. You should listen to them even after you have grown up; and you will please God very much when, after your parents have become old, you continue to honor them and to assist them until their death. Because the parents are God's representatives He blesses those who honor them, punishes those who despise them and grieve them." . . . Then for the edification and admonition of the children, relate the stories of Joseph and Jacob, of David and Absalom. The example of Jesus should be held up for their imitation: God Himself was obedient to His mother and foster-father, and even in the midst of His awful sufferings on the cross thought of Mary.

In this way the whole instruction takes God as its starting-point and leads back to Him; thus the children are taught a pure, unselfish morality, and all danger from motives of temporal gain is obviated. In connection with these examples from Gruber it may be remarked that the catechist, considering the frequent quarrels upsetting whole families, should carefully instruct the children on how to bear the faults of their parents. Förster develops this point at length in his "Jugendlehre."

166. Another Mistake consists in this that the catechist, instead of basing his teaching on divine love, appeals preferably to "the sense of duty and personal conviction" of his audience. Why is this wrong? Should not the children be trained to esteem duty and conviction?

Answer: These expressions may indeed be understood in a perfectly correct meaning, viz., to act according to conscience. But then the question recurs: why should we follow the dictates of conscience? The only adequate answer is: because our conscience manifests God's will to us. It would be contradictory to assert: I must follow my conscience, unless its dictates be those of a power superior to me. If they were merely my own, I could never be under compulsion to them, since no one can at the same time and in the same reality command and obey. It is totally false therefore to substitute "duty," "personal conviction," "categorical imperative" for the command of

God. The attempt has been made, although it was not of Christian origin, and in practice (whether intentionally or not matters little here) it has led to contempt for divine authority and the undermining of Christian morality. We cannot lay too much stress on the will of God and His divine commands manifested to us in manifold ways, as motives for our moral actions. We may discourse most impressively on duty, conviction, conscience, but the blunt truth remains: there is no duty without God's binding command, no conviction unless it agree with God's unerring truthfulness, no conscience unless it be the voice of God.

It is not within our province to dilate further on moral "autonomy" or "heteronomy." It may not be out of place, however, to quote from Willmann the following striking characterization of autonomous morality: Illuminism held fast to the maxim that "whatever is useful is good." "Law" and "duty" were avoided since they impose limitations on the dear "ego." Yet the utilitarian maxim was inadequate since it had no unifying power. Assistance was needed. "Kant came gladly to the rescue with his doctrine: what I command to myself is good; let every one do what the categorical imperative dictates; his liberty is the source of law and duty. . . . In this way it became once more possible to discourse on law and duty since they stood no longer so pitiably aloof. While they were formerly limitations of the autonomous subject, they now became its satellites. The curtailing of the individual will contained in the maxim: do what you impose on yourself, was less important; the main point was that the subject should act freely, and thus he was bound to discover the form of the commandment. To be able to act up to the full measure of his own capacity like Alcibiades, and to be at the same time an upholder of the law like Aristides, nay a legislator like Solon, — this was the prospect offered by Kantian morality, and who could refuse to be thankful for it?"

Kant often takes opportunity to illustrate his theories by striking examples. Thus in the second part of the "Critique of Practical Reason" he alludes to "the history of a reasonable man whom his enemies try to coerce into making common cause with the accusers of an innocent person, who is besides without any influence (as was the case with Anne Boleyn, accused by Henry VIII). . . ." Willmann remarks on this head: "The mention of Henry VIII shows whom Kant had in mind, viz., the chancellor of England, Thomas More. But Kant was careful not to mention the sources from which this true hero of virtue drew his moral strength. What stopped More was the divine command not to bear false witness, together with the authority of the Church and the example of her martyrs. But autonomism can know nothing of such a motive to abstain from sinning — what withholds me, must be external to myself and consequently determine my will heteronomously, — to say nothing of the determination to avoid evil on religious grounds together with the holy firmness entirely based upon them. When Kant desires to present true morality, he must quietly borrow from the Church; and it is one more example of how an impoverished generation appropriates the fruit from the gardens of its predecessors which no longer belong to it."

167. In how far may the Motive of Temporal Benefit be Invoked? — When it is asked: shall we never mention to children the temporal benefits accruing from the practice of virtue or the evil consequent upon sin, we answer:

1. These natural motives may be adduced, not exclusively or principally, but as secondary factors.

2. When made use of in this wise, they ought to be treated as revelation demands, i.e., temporal happiness or unhappiness as consequences of virtue and vice are indeed rewards and punishments ordained by God's love and justice; yet they are but partial and preliminary to the full retribution of eternity. Our

shortsightedness makes us view many things as punishments or hardships, while in the plan of Providence they are salutary means of amendment. Unless catechization advert to this, it will train servants of God willing indeed to do something for Him, but merely with a view to earthly rewards. When their hopes are not fulfilled, but reverses and suffering press upon them, they feel disappointed, revolt perhaps against Providence, and suffer shipwreck of their faith.

168. The Chief Motives assigned in our thesis are: the mercy and love of God as manifested more especially in the Incarnation and Redemption; God's greatness and majesty compelling our unconditional submission and profoundest reverence; and lastly, His perfect justice.

The latter attribute begets in the souls of men fear and hope. The fear of the Lord, called the beginning of wisdom, nay wisdom itself (Job, 28, 28) by the Holy Ghost, must be deeply rooted in the heart; otherwise the external and internal enemies of the soul gain the upper hand. — Yet the catechist must not forget that fear and hope, if absolutely required, are subordinate motives in the Christian's life struggle; they are indispensable, but must go hand in hand with higher motives: willing obedience to God, deep reverence for His infinite majesty, and warm love in return for His great condescension. Leaving aside the fact that these latter motives are nobler and more worthy of Christians, they should be cultivated because of the real character of Christian perfection which is based not on fear but on love of God. Fear is but the first stage on the road to perfection. And lastly, it were a mistake to suppose the children unable to grasp the higher motives.

You would greatly err, Jungmann told his hearers, in believing that fear has under all circumstances, especially in dealing with children, a greater effect than obedience and love. Nursery maids and ignorant female teachers often act under the impression that everything children should be taught to avoid must be presented to them as mortal sin, and that the prospect of Hell must be held up before them for every transgression. But a pure and stainless heart that has not yet lost by any grievous sin the baptismal grace infused by the Holy Ghost, is more surely and permanently influenced by a feeling of reverence for the greatness and holiness of the omnipresent God, by a prompting to obey His authority, by gratefulness and love to which the remembrance of countless proofs of kindness and mercy irresistibly impel it, than by any effort to avoid personal evil and even eternal damnation. Good children become more readily and lastingly pious, shun all wilful transgression of divine commands, when, in consequence of their catechetical training the voice of their heart tells them at the critical moment: I must do this, it is the will of God; or, this is not allowed; or, how could I do this evil act and sin against my God, — than if they were constantly reminded of God's justice and eternal punishment.

169. Love of God the Ultimate Aim of all Motivation. — The catechist who does not endeavor with all his might to arouse and cultivate in the hearts of the children the love of God, which includes also the love of our neighbor, overlooks not only an important, but the essential point of Christian revelation. The catechist's whole activity and more immediately his motivation must influence the child to this one end. For what is the ultimate aim of all divine revelation? According to St. Augustine all catechization must aim at making the catechumens understand and feel how much God loves us and desires in return to be loved by us. And he proves it in this manner: the center of all revelation is the Incarnation. And why did it take place? To awaken us from our indifference, so that, while before we were slow in loving Him, we should now at least be more prompt in returning His love. Hence, since the Old Testament points constantly to the Incarnate Son of God, who is the central figure of the New, it is also true that charity is the end of all revelation. If you keep well in mind that charity is the ultimate end towards which all your teaching should tend, then instruct by means of appropriate examples and in such a manner that he to whom you speak, through hearing believe, by belief progress to hope and from hope to charity.

In these words of St. Augustine, says Gruber, lies so much wisdom that our ordinary catechization appears to me as mere bungling, from which we must needs rise to the spirit that animated catechetical instruction in the first ages of Christianity.

170. How to Proceed in order to excite love of God the catechist may learn from God Himself: God has loved us first that we may love Him in return. Thus the catechist must always put the love of God for us in the right light: "Of all the dealings of God which we narrate let us give the causes and reasons, referring them to that end, viz., love, of which he who acts or speaks should never lose sight." (St. Augustine.) God's wisdom could find no better way to the heart of men than love. When the catechist thoroughly understands how to bring home to the children this great love of God, he may rest assured of success. "For nothing incites more to love than the feeling that we are loved in return; and that heart is cold indeed that not only does not give its love freely, but is even unwilling to return it." Thus writes St. Augustine, and that he is right, is proved by experience. It is enough e.g., to recall the influence of the mere enumeration of God's mercies as found in the final meditation of the Exercises of St. Ignatius.

Space is lacking to give at length the excellent remarks of St. Augustine on this subject of divine love. We recommend, therefore, the reading and study of the saint's treatise: On the Instruction of the Ignorant.

171. The Greatest Obstacle to Divine Love, and to all supernatural life in general, is confessedly the pride of the human heart. To the experienced eye of St. Augustine it appeared highly important to call the attention of the catechist explicitly to this obstacle: ". . . Nothing is so opposed to charity as envy and the mother of envy is pride." The root of all sin, in the last analysis, is pride and the history of sin is the history of human pride. Whatever is opposed to sin, and the love of God is in direct opposition to it, bears the mark of humility. Hence, He who triumphed over sin and restored the kingdom of love, was humility personified: "The same Lord Jesus Christ, the God-man, is a proof of God's love for us and at the same time an example of humility in our midst, in order that our own great disorder might be cured by an even more powerful antidote. A proud man is a great evil; but a humble God is a still greater mercy." (St. Augustine.) Consequently, when the zealous efforts of the catechist to awaken the love of God in the hearts of the children prove fruitless, let him investigate whether this obstacle is not in the way. Yet, the catechist should not wait until this evil openly manifests itself; but realizing the deplorable fact that in every human mind is found the germ of self-conceit, he should strive at an early date to build up humility in the hearts of his charges; constantly recalling to their minds the example of the abnegation and humiliation of the Saviour will help to make the children realize the love of God for us.

This carries us back to the motive introduced in the first place: the fear of the Lord. Love should always reign supreme, but in our present state fear and love must go hand in hand. True love is at the same time humbly fearful; the true Christian rejoices at the infinite mercy and love of God, but never forgets His exacting justice.

172. Two False Conceptions of Divine Love. — Thus far we have dwelt with great emphasis on the fear as well as the love of God. If both motives and their mutual relation were always given due consideration, many erroneous opinions concerning the chief commandment of love could never have originated.

One error had its source in the slight consideration given the justice of God, and the fear of God consequent upon it. About a century ago this error was widespread, and even many a sentimental tendency of the present day prepares the ground anew for its revival. Not a few speak of the "dear Lord" as a "Father who has made the world to let it run its course in peace; as long as we do His will in certain matters, He will provide for us an even better world in the future." Beda Weber thus characterizes this tendency: "Its God is a debonair oriental potentate; his beard bedewed with tears of emotion, he carries a green reed for a shepherd's staff which can hurt no one." In fine, when the justice of God is belittled, and only His goodness and love are taken into account, then a sickly sentimentality takes the place of the love of God for us, and the true and sound love of man for God and his neighbor. The catechist must ward off this danger from his charges.

In connection herewith Jungmann gives the following advice, which needs to be correctly understood: he refers to the misleading tendency which exhibits a special predilection for the expression "the dear Lord," and he adds: "I believe it is to this expression that the false tendency referred to owes more particularly its widespread popularity. Hence I feel fully justified in advising you to avoid completely this pietistic sentimentality and never to have recourse to it when expounding God's word in catechization or sermon. It is certainly not calculated to impress the children with that much-needed reverence for the Lord of Hosts, often so alien to the frivolous minds of men, when they find the priest making constant use of the expression with which they are wont to address their 'dear uncle,' 'dear aunt,' 'dear Fanny,' 'dear Johnny.' As long as sin is so widespread, as long as the name of God instead of being used with reverence, is pronounced a million times in an idle and frivolous manner, is used in a thousand expressions to curse and blaspheme, we must forcibly admit that God's awe-inspiring majesty has not been brought home to such souls. He who has arrived at a deep knowledge of God will never use His name in vain."

Hirscher draws a more comprehensive conclusion from these observations, but I am fully convinced that he will agree with me when I say that the expression "the dear Lord" is detrimental to a true knowledge of God, and is calculated to further the vain use of His Holy Name. And in Holy Writ, in the Fathers, in the language of the Church, you will search in vain for expressions of this kind: yet, there and nowhere else should we look for models to copy in our teaching.

173. Continuation. — An opposite error is an extreme rigoristic conception of divine love, as originated by Jansenism. The latter taught that perfect love of God — and this is what our thesis maintains must be the ultimate aim of catechization — should in no way be influenced by considerations of our own welfare; it should not be based therefore on gratitude, on regard for the blessings received from God, but it must exclusively be concerned with God Himself. Is this right?

Any one at all acquainted with the manner in which Holy Writ encourages us to love God and to forsake the ways of sin, notices at once that this rigoristic conception is carried to excess.

"Is this the return thou makest to the Lord, oh foolish and senseless people? Is not He thy father that hath possessed thee and created thee? . . . As the eagle enticing her young to fly, and hovering over them he spread his wings, and hath taken him and carried him on his shoulders. . . . He set him upon high land: that he might eat the fruits of the field, that he might suck honey out of the rock, and oil out of the hardest stone, butter of the herd and milk of the sheep with the fat of lambs . . ." (Deut. 32, 6 ff.). The remembrance of these benefits should lead Israel back to God. And the New Testament also, when it exhorts us to love God, constantly reminds us of His benefits, especially the Incarnation and Redemption. And the words of St. John: "Let us therefore love God, because God hath first loved us" (I John 4, 19), beautifully sum up these exhortations and their motivation.

And indeed, the remembrance of God's favors is the surest road to perfect love of God. For God's charity is best revealed in His infinite benignity; whoever reflects on it, feels drawn spontaneously to love the giver. Only a heart steeped in selfishness could stop at God's benefits and forget the dispenser of them. As soon however as we rise from the contemplation of the gift to that of the giver, there is no longer an incomplete but a complete love, which is the term of all Christian striving.

Hence it follows further that children are easily brought to a perfect love of God. For they depend entirely on the help and assistance of their parents, and hence they are deeply devoted to them. When they are brought to understand that this parental kindness is but a feeble reflection of God's love, they are easily drawn to give Him their whole heart. Hence it may be concluded further that all attempts aimed at destroying the family also tend to uproot the love of God in future generations.

A few considerations from Bossuet to help in exciting perfect contrition are given here, to make them readily accessible on account of their practical importance. "In order to excite ourselves to hatred and contrition for sin, we may reflect that God is just and inflexible, and that mortal sin is a fearful evil since it deserves the eternal punishment of hell. We may further consider that the mercy of God is infinite, that He is our Creator to Whom we owe everything, who loves us more than the kindest father loves his children; that the Son of God has become man for us, that for our sake He became a child poor and subject to all the discomforts of this life; that He took all possible suffering upon Himself in order to redeem us; that the sins which we intend to confess are the cause of His death. If any one had caused the death of his father, he would deplore the misdeed his whole life long. Jesus Christ, however, is more to us than a father, and He has given His life for us. This motive for contrition, viz., love, is the best of all motives, and contrition perfected by love has the power, when at the same time we have the desire to receive the Sacrament of penance, to replace us at once into the state of sanctifying grace." And Jungmann adds: "This is the true Catholic doctrine of perfect contrition; and for that reason it is practical, easily understood, and within the reach of every Christian." And Bossuet wrote thus thirteen years before the errors of Quietism about unselfish love were condemned in Rome. It is indeed almost beyond belief that for a century and a half after that condemnation the right conception of this doctrine was so often distorted and supplanted by erroneous quietistic ideas: nay, how the latter could ever find followers, instead of the plain clear truth.

. . . .

From all that we have thus far said about right motives, it follows clearly that the catechist is expected to have mastered the divine doctrine in all its purity and to have experienced its power in his own heart. And he himself must approach the treasures of revelation with a pure and humble soul, so that he may become the fitting channel through which the light and warmth of divine wisdom flow into the heart of the child in all their purity and vigor.

§ III. THE PRACTICE OF VIRTUE IN GENERAL

TWENTY-THIRD PRINCIPLE. — *The catechist should take care that the children accustom themselves to a Christian life by the constant practice of virtue. An especially frequent opportunity for its exercise is found in ever-recurring temptations: let the catechist train the children for the battle against the visible and invisible enemies of the Christian life.*

174. What this Practice Consists in we have indicated already when concluding our exposition of the teaching method (No. 152). It is not merely an exercise of the mind, but a training of the will and the heart. Although the vivid presentation of right motives and telling examples may lead us to expect good results with moral certainty in the case of normal children, yet the teacher should pay due attention to the ultimate effects of instruction and motivation: the emotions of the heart and the activities of the will, to direct them, frequently to renew and strengthen them, so that under his guiding hand they may grow into habitual tendencies of the heart and dispositions of the will.

And at any rate, the little that the catechist can do towards stabilitating the children in virtue under present school conditions, is altogether insufficient. When the parental home and the school do not work in harmony with other agencies, the catechist can only be partially successful in his task. For as a rule the heart of the child is much more susceptible to those influences that play upon him during by far the greater part of his days and hours than to the influences of two or three catechism lessons a week. The catechist should then be all the more alert in making the most of the scant opportunities at his disposal for the practical training of the children in virtue. And that such opportunities are at hand, shall shortly appear.

175. This Practice should bear especially on what has been called for short the "religious exercises," i.e., the practices of piety and devotion in private prayer as well as in public worship, in the reception of the Sacraments, in a devout life before God. In the following chapter and also in Special Catechetics we shall have more to say on this subject. Further opportunities of practising various virtues are afforded by obedience in school, zeal and application, love of order, truthfulness, reverence towards superiors, politeness, helpfulness, brotherly love. Already in school the children can be trained in the external practice of these virtues. In the case of other virtues, however, such as temperance, charity, etc., the catechist will have to rest content with exhorting his pupils to interior acts of virtue, to firm resolutions and to perseverance.

Temptations, whose influence on the Christian life is often overlooked, present frequent opportunities and create an urgent need for the exercise of virtue. We mention them here in a general way in connection with the practice of virtue because they are not confined to a small province of the spiritual life, but must be considered as the negative side of the whole Christian life. If they are not yet very much in evidence in children, these must nevertheless be trained to combat them. The second part of our thesis is concerned with them.

176. The Means and Ways for the practice of virtue are: reciting the acts of virtue during the instruction, as we have repeatedly recommended (Nos. 136–140); exhorting the children to do the same privately while not neglecting the external practices of virtue; watching out for these practices for which school life offers an opportunity; appropriate praise for good behavior and reproof for transgressions. The best means to overcome temptations shall be treated separately. But the living example is far more efficacious than all other means. Institutions of learning animated by the right spirit work wonders without visible effort. Hence let the catechist do his utmost to provide the children with the best possible surroundings. It is taken for granted that they should not discover the slightest moral blemish in his character, i.e., he must not only be free from grossly immoral actions and habits, but the children should not even notice the smallest discrepancy between the high moral doctrine he propounds and his personal life, for even this greatly impairs his usefulness as an educator.

The "Hints for Beginners" collected by Förster in his work: "School and Character" may well be taken to heart by every teacher. Förster concedes that "the most potent factor for discipline is the teacher's own self-control. . . . It is rightly said: only example educates, and personal self-education is the strongest example even when, apparently, it remains unnoticed. Already from the very first day the children observe our greater composure, concentration of will, more definite enunciation. A well-known teacher of hygiene in Germany fasts several times a month in order to enhance and preserve his suggestive will-power by this practice of self-denial. Let the teacher set out by turning to account the opportunities of the schoolroom to grow into self-discipline."

177. Temptations. — Various intellectual tendencies of the present day manifest a peculiar weakness for slurring over the existence of sin and all inclination thereto. Yet the truth is otherwise: the positive virtues directly tending towards perfection are naturally the crown of the Christian life, but this reward is only for him who has learned to fight evil and to extirpate it in its roots as far as possible, viz., by overcoming temptations and the germs from which they proceed. The catechist must never forget, although he must guard against an excess of pessimism in this regard, that external and internal enemies threaten the virtue even of children, and that, as they grow older, these temptations become stronger and more frequent. Hence the child should be trained as a prudent and courageous soldier.

Due regard for this side of the spiritual life will preserve the catechist from many illusions and from expecting on the part of the children a perfection impossible of attainment. His catechization, while not so lofty, will gain in solidity; his motivation, while free from exaggeration, will have a more lasting influence; what he inculcates in the hearts of the young, will weather the storms of later life.

Before attempting to combat temptations it is necessary to have a correct idea of the rôle temptations play in the Christian life. The theory and practice of the Christian life, or asceticism, enlightens us in this regard. Temptations are (*a*) a danger, or rather the danger for the Christian life; when it has suffered any hurt from slight lapses or venial sins, or even shipwreck through mortal sin, temptation has always been at the root of every fall. Temptations are moreover (*b*) a test of virtue and Christian strength, revealing to man the condition of his soul. And finally, (*c*) when manfully resisted, they become a source of power and perseverance in virtue. Hence it is easy to see why God allows them.

178. Arming the Children against Spiritual Dangers. — It is the catechist's duty to prepare the children against those unavoidable pitfalls presented by temptation, i.e., he must so equip them that they learn to turn those assaults to advantage for progress in virtue. To a certain extent the child should be protected against temptation by shielding him in every possible way from danger. Yet, this is insufficient. He must be taught besides to fight his own battles and to triumph over those obstacles which he cannot possibly avoid.

1. Hence the catechist should dwell particularly on those doctrines which (*a*) enlighten us about the enemies of the Christian life and their assaults, viz., the invisible evil spirits animated by hatred of God and everything made after His image; also the visible enemies of the soul, viz., the world and its allurements, the children of the world whose example and enticements constitute a grave danger especially for young hearts. The children must be taught above all that man's own evil inclinations are his worst enemies.

The catechist should moreover point out (*b*) the means to be used in this struggle against evil: watchfulness, prayer, confidence in God; vigilance and precaution against one's self and against external dangers (examination of conscience); fervent prayer in time of temptation; courage and confidence because Christ has triumphed over Satan and He never allows any one to perish who struggles valiantly under the standard of the Cross.

(*c*) Well calculated to inspire resignation and to increase confidence is the doctrine about God's will allowing temptations to come over us to test our loyalty, to purify and strengthen us. When Christians are not duly instructed on this subject, they often when tempted come to murmur against God, and not seldom give up the struggle completely and succumb.

2. The catechist should not confine himself to mere

theoretical recommendations, but should strive to influence the hearts of the children and lead them to personal exertion. The doctrines just quoted afford opportunity for the exercise and strengthening of the will; negatively, by inspiring a deep hatred for the enemies of salvation, fear of giving in to temptation, salutary diffidence of our own strength, precautionary self-denial even in matters not sinful; positively, by the practice of various virtues: prayer, the resolution to be constantly on the alert and to be firmly and quickly on our guard at the first sign of danger; eliciting acts of boundless confidence in God even in long protracted and difficult struggles, etc.

In general the catechist may take for granted that the child heart readily clings to all that is good and noble. Experience testifies that the child is naturally averse to evil and that it must be perverted almost forcibly before it finds pleasure in sin. The catechist should take advantage of those favorable dispositions due to sanctifying grace. And he should begin this task early, before the contact with sin renders his efforts vain. Pius X has shown us how to bring this about: by leading the children as early as possible to Christ in the Holy Eucharist.

3. How far beyond this the catechist may go, either on the occasion of special occurrences in school life, or by constant methodical influence over his pupils, depends largely on the individual character of the children, the school conditions in general, the authority of the catechist himself, and his position towards the parents. The greatest prudence should guide all his steps, and before he determines on taking some sweep-

ing measure, e.g., the exclusion from the school of a corrupt child because he is a danger for his companions or in order to abate even greater evils, he must be certain of securing good results through this action; for in school life also corruption and evil have outwitted at times morality and discipline.

What Peter Canisius relates of one of his teachers could apply as a general rule only in boarding schools, and with our present school conditions a catechist could only partly try the experiment. The account, however, remains interesting: hence we give an extract of the prayer which to the end of his days the saint repeated in thanksgiving for such a teacher: "You have given me (in Cologne) a real father in the person of Nicholas Eschius, a priest of extraordinary piety (Canisius came to Cologne to study at the end of 1535 or the beginning of 1536, when he was fifteen years old).... Bless the Lord, O my soul, and do not forget the goodness of him who gave me such a teacher, daily exhorting me to piety, constantly intent on my soul and my eternal salvation. With him as a guide I began slowly to turn away from myself in order to please Thee the better, O my God, Whom I still knew and feared so little in those early years. His counsel, habits, and example revealed a new life to me. With his help I repressed the inconsidered movements and vain ardors of youth; happy in his presence, I dispensed easily with other needs and diversions. None that I know of was dearer or closer to me, and I deferred to his judgment in all that a father could desire of a son. And not only did I frequently and completely open my soul to him in confession, but even before I went to sleep at night I exposed to him in familiar conversation (such was my confidence in him) the falls, sins, and shortcomings of my soul, so as to give him an account, as to a judge, of my errings and of my whole day, and to receive a penance in expiation of my sins if he so willed."

And the following prayer of the same guide of souls is worthy of remembrance: "Open, O Lord, the eyes of those blind and unreasonable parents and educators, that they may cease to be blind and evil leaders who can only guide the blind and untrained youth to eternal perdition. May they realize how great a risk they run in their false feeling of security, together with the children confided to their care. May they come to see that youth is inclined to evil, falls easily into sin, and can be led along the path of virtue only by painstaking exertion."

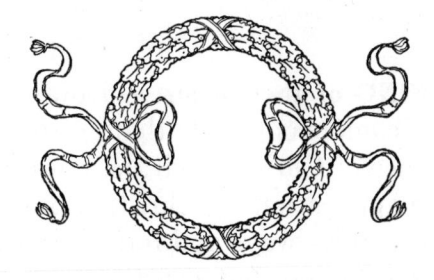

CHAPTER II

THE MOST IMPORTANT VIRTUES

Twenty-Fourth Principle. — *The catechist should endeavor to train the children especially to piety and self-abnegation in earnest and sustained work, according to the motto:* ora et labora, *pray and work.*

179.

MEANING of the Thesis. — However numerous the component parts that go to make up the edifice of Christian virtue, however manifold the applications of Christian morality to real life, yet these various ways and forces are not a motley mass without cohesion, but constitute an harmonious and organic whole. Hence while the catechist lays stress on the upbuilding of particular virtues, he should not lose sight of their interconnection, and the correlation of the secondary with the fundamental virtues; otherwise his teaching is bound to result in confusion and will lack virility.

In the above formulation of our thesis we have laid stress only on the two primordial virtues which occupy a prominent place in education, while they can also be practised constantly in catechization. They give rise spontaneously to particular virtues of great import, as shall appear from the following.

"Train the children in piety and earnest work," is the motto that contains the two chief laws of education; and Christian teachers at least are at one in admitting that it expresses the final aim of all education. For the latter consists in preparing the child to serve God as perfectly as possible by the harmonious exercise of all its powers as a member of God's family. In order then to serve God the child must know His holy will, embrace it lovingly, and execute it in its entirety. Piety consists in knowing and loving God's will, in making it our own will in all things; to execute it is to strive with all our might, by earnest sustained endeavor or labor, to accomplish it.

The consideration of the two fundamental laws of Christian asceticism: prayer and self-denial, leads to the same conclusion. Prayer obtains for us God's grace; self-denial clears away the obstacles preventing the accomplishment of God's holy will. Prayer, and piety in a somewhat wider meaning, are one and the same thing. Self-denial, however, in order not to lead us astray, must be practised in the first place in those cases where its omission would entail neglect of duty, especially of those duties required by our state of life.

We shall enumerate first those virtues comprised under the general appellation of "piety," including at the same time the obstacles, sins, and passions opposed to them. Then we shall give some general directions concerning application to work.

Three other virtues: obedience, truthfulness, purity, deserve special mention, since at the present day they are in greater danger than ever, and constitute the indispensable foundation of all educational work. The virtue of purity we have treated in a special booklet [1]; our following thesis therefore is concerned only with truthfulness and obedience, thus concluding the chapter on particular virtues, although it might profitably be enlarged. It is unavoidable that in this chapter we should also touch upon different points which con-

[1] Educating to Purity, translated by Fr. Vander Donck, Fr. Pustet & Co., 1912.

cern not only the catechist, but also others engaged in educational work, more especially the parents. But since under present conditions the catechist's influence in the school is rather limited, he must fall back all the more on the co-operation of others who have a share in the education of the child, and he must assist them as far as possible in the fulfilment of their task. Hence the following hints about the duties of parents may not be deemed superfluous.

180. Piety, in our thesis, is to be understood in its wider meaning, as including all duties of gratefulness, love, and reverence towards God. Hence it embraces the divine virtues of faith, hope, and charity, and the virtue of religion in the restricted sense.

This latter, which for the greater part coincides with the spirit of prayer, is to be treated of more exhaustively in Special Catechetics. The theological virtues we have explained at length (Faith: Nos. 161–162; Hope: Nos. 108, 171–172; Charity: Nos. 168–173). The following complementary remarks are added here for a better understanding of the influences at work outside of catechization, which can nevertheless be impressed into service.

1. In general, the child should learn to look upon faith, (*a*) as a great grace, to prize it accordingly, and (*b*) to live in conformity with its supernatural principles; (*c*) since the latter find their concrete expression in the life of Jesus Christ, the child should learn to gaze upon Him constantly in order to imitate Him; (*d*) lastly, the child should be trained to submit in all things to the doctrines and prescriptions of the Church as the divinely ordained teacher of faith.

Hope must be cultivated in every Christian heart, since without firm confidence in God no one is able to fulfil regularly and faithfully the duties of his state of life, to triumph over the difficulties which Divine Providence permits, to overcome human respect, pusillanimity, superstitious means of success. And as soon as man comes in contact with life's hardships, divine hope should be enkindled in his heart, — and this is not seldom the case with young children.

All the catechist's efforts should tend towards awakening and fostering divine love, since it is the chief commandment of the whole Christian law. And it should be an active charity, not a spurious, sentimental love losing itself in idle dreams.

2. In order to cultivate real piety, the following particulars should be kept in mind: (*a*) the admission of the child to participation in the supernatural life through baptism; its early administration, the imposition of a Christian name, care in the selection of nurses; prayer for the child, early instruction of the child in prayer: all these are important duties incumbent upon parents, and of which the catechist should not fail to remind them. Even if he is not the parents' pastor, he should nevertheless, at every favorable opportunity, call their attention to these matters, since the success of subsequent religious training depends to a large extent on the earlier instruction imparted to the child.

(*b*) The teaching about God begun in the parental home must be completed by the catechist.

(*c*) The same applies to assistance at divine service and participation in the general life of the Church, and (*d*) to the preparation for the first and frequent reception of the Sacraments.

181. Obstacles to Piety. — The growth of true piety is hindered by sin and passion; and these must be repressed at an early date. True, in the first years of childhood the commission of formal sin is not possible, since the child lacks a full comprehension of the nature of sin; but it is equally true that even young children do and say things that are wrong, although not sinful for lack of understanding. Whence these "material sins"? They have their origin in the germs of inordinate passion. If we allow these to develop freely, they will have waxed so strong by the time the child reaches the age of reason, that they are not only a prolific source of temptations and danger, but frequently also the cause of deplorable moral lapses. Already under the parental roof the work of curbing the passions should begin. And as we pointed out above (No. 179), earnest, orderly work will prove of great assistance in this regard.

Before enlarging on the latter point, it may be helpful to put down a few of the faults oftenest met with even in young children. Obstinateness, to which the mother never should give in, and which the teacher later on must counteract by strict insistence on discipline and unconditional obedience.

Fits of anger on the part of the child should never provoke the teacher to anger. The best policy is to leave the child alone till he has calmed down; only then can he expect to have any influence over him. The causes of his anger are often an index to the child's character. When the anger is directed against unworthy behavior in church, or other disorders, it is a good sign, and needs only to be trained and kept within bounds. When anger gives itself vent in quarreling and blaspheming, the catechist should earnestly reprimand the culprit, warn him (cursing brings a curse on the house) and lead him to practise the opposite virtues (say the doxology on hearing blasphemous language).

Against Sulkiness, which is to be met with at all ages, Alban Stolz gives the following remedy: pay no attention to the sulky child, and smilingly turn your back to him until his little lordship, like a beetle that has been touched and feigns death, gets in motion of himself again. This intentional neglect of the morose young person makes him realize best of all that nothing is to be gained by such behavior. In case of odd, capricious conduct, investigate whether it is caused by sickness; then try to train the child to patience by pointing at the example of the Crucified Saviour, instead of spoiling him by misplaced pity. Whoever realizes how capriciousness is frequently the cause of much trouble in later life, — often a capricious woman upsets a whole family — will not pass lightly over this seemingly unimportant outgrowth of self-love.

Envy must be energetically combated. Holy Writ presents us with many motives: the hatred of Satan for man, Cain, Herod, the Pharisees. Of course the teacher should be careful not to give rise to this feeling by his own ill-considered partiality to some, or vice versa, by treating all absolutely alike, when some, more deserving, have a just claim to be rewarded. Always give to each one according to his deserts, for so does God's Providence proceed. Only then can you effectively repress all outcroppings of envy.

Vanity and Pride will hardly take root in the heart if the catechist keeps in mind what has been said above (Nos. 168–172) about the fear of God and the example of the Saviour's humility, and when at the same time the spirit of obedience is inculcated in the right manner.

182. We have already Defined Work as the exercise of the human faculties in the accomplishment of God's will. In this wider acceptation prayer, self-correction, the practice of charity, may all be regarded as work. A more restricted definition of work may thus be given: "a conscious exercise of the human faculties for the purpose of producing good." "Conscious": mere vegetative activity can be called work only in a general sense; thus, e.g., the heart, the lungs, work. "Human faculties": bodily and spiritual faculties work together; yet now one, now the other activity preponderates. "Good": material, mental or spiritual, for the worker and for other men. If the word "culture" be understood to mean a certain complexus of material mental and spiritual accomplishments, we may say that the aim of all work is the creation and advancement of culture.

Although labor is contrasted with mere enjoyment, yet recreation rightly understood is not a hindrance to work, but a necessary complement of it. Both body and mind need relaxation and pleasure after long protracted effort. The body finds it in rest and sleep; the mind in congenial recreation.

183. Some Rules: Love of Work. — The pupil should be trained to appreciate and to love work, and gradually he should be familiarized with the reasons for it, viz., work is a duty incumbent upon every one to a greater or less extent, and is imposed by natural and divine law. Labor is ennobling, since it is an image of the ever active God. Even the pagans admitted that mental labor enhances man's dignity. Bodily labor has been ennobled by the example of Christ and His praise of the poor who are mostly engaged in it, and also by the example of the Apostles and other Saints. Finally labor is a source of blessings and happiness because it gratifies spiritual and bodily needs, brings joy into our life (tedium and melancholy generally originate in laziness or desultory occupations which have nothing in common with earnest labor); it restrains sinful inclinations and unites men in the bonds of true, i.e., active love; in short, labor prevents individual and social misery, it fosters individual and social life and happiness. Yet, all this notwithstanding, work in our present existence remains a trial entailing great effort. In order to make it less irksome its noble and elevating aspect should be clearly brought out. When presented in this light it cannot fail to appeal to the better side of our enthusiastic youth. Moreover the correct presentation of the Christian view of labor is one of the most pressing duties of the pastor as well as of the catechist because of the current errors on the subject.

184. Second Rule: Familiarization with Work. — The child should be taught not only to put a high value upon work, but should be encouraged early to earnest and constant application. Childish activity finds an outlet first of all in play: it might be made to bear the character of light work. At an early age real bodily exertion is to be added to play: the child should learn to help himself; the parents need not gratify his slightest whims, but he ought to render them small services. In the school the children must be familiarized with mental work earnestly and steadily prosecuted, yet carefully adapted to their abilities and powers. Nothing, not even the desire to have the children shine in examinations, should be made a pretext for overburdening them. A certain variety in the work and timely interruption by periods of rest are daily more insisted upon by modern pedagogy. The introduction of manual work and half hour study periods, at least in the lower grades, tend to correct the mistakes caused by the excessive demands of the newer pedagogy.

185. Third Rule: Orderly Work. — The child must be trained to habits of orderly work.

1. He should learn to have order (*a*) with regard to the object of his work. The well-known rule: first what is necessary, then what is useful, and only afterwards what is agreeable, is derived from the very nature of work: it should be an exercise of the faculties in accordance with the divine will, viz., a real service of God. And the divine will, being supreme order, never puts the less important before the necessary. And evidently, among all labor the exertion required for our soul's salvation comes in the first place, and no one is dispensed from applying himself above all things to this primary duty.

The above already includes (*b*) the right appreciation, hence the correct subordination of the ends of work. The worker must have an end in view, otherwise he is a busy loafer. The true end of work is the production of good: work is judged from the character of its product. Spiritual goods are of their very nature superior to material goods; supernatural goods rank above all natural ones. Christianity only demands that this gradation be kept in mind. It does not countenance placing an excessive value upon purely material and intellectual exertion such as is expressed in the motto: success is the measure of a man's worth. Yet it is a wilful perversion of the truth to say that the Church is the enemy of any, especially of intellectual labor.

Leo XIII in his Encyclical of 1893 on the Rosary thus expatiates on this truth: "There are many who fancy that by fixing our mind on eternity, we must needs lose sight of our earthy dwelling place. . . . Yet nothing is more reprehensible or more devoid of truth. For the things we hope for are not such as to preoccupy the mind of man to the extent that he becomes indifferent to the things of the present. . . . For God is the author of both the natural and the supernatural. He does not intend that the one should stand in opposition to the other and be in constant warfare with it, but that they should live on friendly terms, to the end that, with the help of both we may better attain that eternal happiness for which we have been destined."

Finally, order prescribes also (c) the kind and manner of work, demanding good judgment in the selection even of free work, dividing all work in an intelligent manner, providing for the necessary recreation, so that the task may be completed without undue strain, which is generally followed by exhaustion and disgust.

2. How can the child be trained to a sense of order? He should be taught (a) to have order in material things (in his clothes, toys, school material). The early neglect of these small matters has not unfrequently been regretted in later life. The child must learn to respect everything he handles and to be neat in all his belongings. He must also learn early (b) to order his various activities. This will bring about a well-regulated day, and he should deviate from this order for good reasons only, not as caprice dictates. This applies particularly to exercises of piety, the neglect of which produces weak and fickle minds. Nothing so effectually puts to naught the tirades of some philosophers against all hard and fast rules as the hard experiential fact that licentious freedom leads to dis-

order and self-loathing. A well-ordered and definite method of proceeding in all things begets joy and love of work.

(c) Naturally the school's efforts to train the child in habits of order are bound to be frustrated unless the parents set the good example at home; hence both should co-operate that this end may be attained.

186. Fourth Rule: Recreation. — The child must be allowed to enjoy the necessary recreation and be accustomed to take it as an expression of the divine will. God's will is that (a) sinful recreation, forbidden pleasures be avoided; (b) that no excesses be indulged in. "Let us be careful, when we relax our minds, lest we destroy all harmony and break up the concert of good works." (St. Ambrose.) Recreation and play should never transgress the bounds of morality; they should never lessen, but increase the desire for the resumption of serious work. Recreation should keep in mind the rule: (c) let it agree with the persons (different for children, for those advanced in years, for boys and girls), the time (during Holy Week it should not become a noisome frolic), the place, and other circumstances. Youth should not be allowed to indulge in anything that implies a breach of good manners. On the other side teach the young to be forbearing with regard to the faults of others; not to become excited, but to be patient in the presence of rude and ill-mannered people.—It may be remarked here that levity is out of place in the exposition of a religious theme; although jokes may flow gracefully from the lips of a profane orator, the preacher should not make an effort to introduce them.

The belief that bodily exertion following immediately upon close mental application is sufficient relaxation, is erroneous, for mental labor also fatigues the body. Recess time, therefore, should not be taken up with difficult gymnastic exercises, but should preferably be given over to easy free movement or play.

. . . .

What we have said thus far about work shows plainly why in the beginning (No. 179) and in the formulation of the thesis itself we could truly assert that self-denial and earnest work are to a great extent one and the same thing. If the children are trained to habits of work in accordance with the above principles, it will be found to be the most practical education, free from illusions and admirably suited to combat self-indulgence and all evil inclinations of the heart.

TWENTY–FIFTH PRINCIPLE. — *The catechist should strive very particularly to develop in the children the virtues of obedience, truthfulness, and chastity.*

Although, as we have remarked already (No. 179), we shall not treat the virtue of chastity here, as it has been exhaustively dealt with in a special booklet, we include it in our thesis to remind the catechist of the great importance of this virtue.

1. OBEDIENCE

187. Its Importance. — "Obedience is an essential requisite in every school and must be demanded as something self-evident; hence it is plain also that the catechist should command or forbid only where there is ground for his interference." (Hirscher.) The importance of obedience springs from:

1. Its pedagogical necessity. The reprimands of

the teacher are of no avail when the pupil does not receive them in a spirit of willing obedience. A naturalistic pedagogy, modeled after Rousseau, and doing away with the terms "command" and "obey," cannot look for any educational results, or, notwithstanding all its protests, it is bound nevertheless to have recourse to disciplinary measures.

2. Obedience is still of greater importance when we consider the child's end in life: he will never serve God or submit to human laws unless he learn early to practise the virtue of obedience.

3. And this is all the more true at the present day when attacks upon authority are of such common occurrence. Not only are these attacks directed against those who are charged in the first place with the upholding of public authority, but relentless war is waged against anything which, in the heart of man, reveals itself as a barrier, against all moral and divine law as such.

An unbiased witness, of no small authority in matters pedagogical, contends that "scarcely at any period of history has there been such a complete and open disregard of moral authority as at the present day, among the leaders of public opinion. Ridicule is heaped upon all time-honored laws and conventions, not only in the press, but also in the conversation of many young men and women of good breeding. The shibboleth that each and every one is entitled to his full share of 'life' rules them all, and barely hides a refined or a gross sensuality. . . . A certain becoming all-inclusive philanthropy together with the utmost tolerance will make up the moral ideal of the future. . . . This is not a new theory, indeed, but formerly it was held only in secret and its protagonists did not make bold to force it upon the public. We may say, however, without exaggeration that at no time was there such a concerted effort to undermine authority in every domain as there is at the present day. Even the French Revolution, although marked by greater violence than the Reformation, returned to the old beaten path in everything outside of the field of politics. Presently, however, men are especially intent on emancipating themselves in the domain of morals." (Dr. W. Münch, Professor at the Berlin University).

188. Means of Training in the Virtue of Obedience. — The catechist should keep clearly in mind the distinction between obedience as the aim of education, and obedience as an educational means. Only then will he be enabled to use to advantage the various educational helps that foster the virtue of obedience. These helps are: to accustom the children from their tenderest years to do the will of their parents and teachers. With the awakening of reason they should be told the motive for their obedience. The main reason is the will of God manifested in the enactments of constituted authority. "Therefore he that resisteth the power, resisteth the ordinance of God." Rom., 13, 2. "Be ye subject therefore to every human creature for God's sake, whether it be to a king . . . or to governors." I Petri, 2, 13–18. Only an obedience based on the wisdom and will of God is becoming to man, will rule him through life, and preserve him from servility or pharisaism. The obedience of Christ unto the death of the Cross, the blessing of God vouchsafed to all those who are obedient, etc., are all motives which can be invoked only by Christian faith.

Förster, answering the tirades often launched against the Catholic conception of authority, writes: "It should not be forgotten that the heroic epoch of obedience, the Middle Ages, attained its remarkable results in the restraint of self-will only because the religious conception of obedience based on faith was held in the highest esteem. To ground obedience on a religious foundation is but to conciliate it with individual life, to point out its importance for spiritual good and spiritual growth. Look upon the features of the personages figuring in the masterpieces of the Middle Ages from the standpoint of the pedagogy of obedience: theirs is not a mere external subjection; no, their external submission is the symbol of the interior resignation of the personal self, of its complete surrender, of unlimited spontaneity. . . ."

As the child grows, he should gradually be allowed some freedom, i.e., the restraints of obedience should be slowly relaxed, not indeed to his moral undoing, but in order that he may come to walk by himself the path of virtue, and follow of his own volition the road marked out by the laws of constituted authority. For character in this sense is the aim of education. Unless he learn to rely on himself, the child will remain a lifelong weakling, the prey of every leader or tempter; or he will become embittered against the irrational education of which he has been the victim, or against all order and authority.

This gradual emancipation of the pupils consists in restricting the number of commands: the order is oftener put in the form of a wish, desire, proposal, or request, while the reasons for orders given are made plain. This can be taken up at an early age, especially if the child ask for it, and with the understanding that it shall not foster any desire of fault-finding or wilfulness. And one point should always be emphasized: the Christian obeys not merely because the command is reasonable, but he obeys most readily because it is reasonable and ennobling to obey God. The Christian does not submit his will to a creature, but to the all-powerful and all-wise God. — Every young person has a particular right to freedom in the choice of a state of life. He should receive and take to heart the advice of parents and teachers, but these cannot force any state of life upon him. They should carefully test his abilities and inclinations and in accordance therewith furnish him a befitting education and training in those years during which he is still wanting in mature judgment.

189. Frequent Mistakes are made by teachers in connection with the child's training by and in obedience. Some parents fondle and spoil their children; this ill-considered kindness soon leads the children to lord it over their parents who thus bitterly expiate their misplaced affection. Other parents fail to be consistent in carrying out an order once given. Some go to the other extreme and find delight — due to lack of judgment or to caprice — in giving petty orders all the time. Some teachers are nothing short of real despots, and treat their pupils as defenseless slaves, instead of bestowing upon them the loving care they deserve as children of God. Open and persistent rebelliousness on the child's part need not always be ascribed to malice, but may point to mistakes on the teacher's side, which he should endeavor to remedy at once. A change to another good family or to a good educational institution may prove beneficial. If the child remains passionate, the teacher must bear his soul in patience and be satisfied with incomplete results, or he may be forced to have recourse to greater severity.

. . . .

It remains true that training in and by obedience is not always an easy task. If however we are to overcome all difficulties, even those raised by autonomous morality, this can only be done by obedience conceived after the Christian pattern. Förster's book: School and Character abundantly upholds this contention.

Let every catechist and teacher familiarize himself by meditation, study, and personal exertion with the spirit of Christian obedience, and he will find it fairly easy to avoid the many pitfalls, some of which have been indicated above. He will not be deceived by the specious arguments directed against the "pedagogy of obedience," but instead consider this virtue as the indispensable, God-given remedy against many evils of the day.

2. Truthfulness

190. Nature and Importance of Truthfulness. — This virtue may be treated from a twofold standpoint, according as we refer to the agreement of the word with the interior deliberate thoughts, or the agreement of the external actions with the interior deliberate convictions. This word "deliberate" should not be overlooked; for involuntary feelings are not to be taken into account. As a rule the term "truthfulness" combines both meanings and denotes a permanent habit of sincerity in word and action. Opposed to it are: mendacity (habit of lying, or untruthfulness in word) and insincerity (habit of deception, pharisaism, intrigue, untruthfulness in deed).

Truthfulness, equally with obedience, is a necessary requisite in educational work. For how could the teacher come to a full knowledge of the child and its needs if the latter were lacking in sincerity? And in later life sincerity becomes indispensable for peaceful and happy social intercourse. When lying and deception, distrust and intrigue have the upper hand, social life becomes unbearable. In fine, untruthfulness corrupts character and makes man insincere towards God; hence Holy Writ testifies so frequently to the aversion of God for the liar.

An experienced teacher need not take a tragic view of every untruthfulness he may find the child guilty of; for the latter — and not unfrequently even the adult — does scarcely realize fully the importance of this virtue. Nevertheless the catechist will find the above-mentioned reasons peremptory enough to make him put forth his best efforts in training the children to love of truth and aversion for lying and misrepresentation. This also helps to strengthen other virtues, and thus many a vice is prevented from gaining access to the heart.

191. Dangers to Truthfulness. — A thorough training in truthfulness demands a knowledge of the dangers that beset it. The greatest danger is bad example, especially when it comes from adults, or from the teacher himself. And the latter happens not unfrequently, e.g., when promises or threats are not carried out; when the child is deceived in some manner in order to derive pleasure from his discomfiture; when he is misled by captious questions; when the child is almost driven to lying (e.g., to give the teacher false reasons for missing school); when lying and dissimulation are indulged in the child's presence (this is sometimes the case in disrupted families where the mother deceives the father, while not unfrequently also it is the outgrowth of our modern politeness, e.g., it happens often that as soon as a caller has left the house he is mercilessly criticized whilst during his presence he was treated with extreme courtesy). Also the insincerity of companions may become a great danger, and as Förster remarks, it not seldom gives rise in our schools to "social lying." The child has a natural desire to shine in the presence of his companions; hence he may come to boast, or to hide, to falsify or to deny facts that might expose him to ridicule or contempt. Here we see again the element of danger which group-life introduces into the school, a danger manifesting itself also in the domain of untruthfulness.

Another danger is extreme severity on the teacher's part, especially in administering punishment.

Förster writes in this connection: "Let the teacher ask himself the question in class: What are the lies that are told in school and for what reason? And he will be truly astounded at the abundance of ready-to-hand opportunities for lies which school experience will reveal to him. And then he must needs realize that the school offers ample occasion for the perversion of the sense of truthfulness, — unless this corruption be counteracted by something different from threats, which lead only to more lies and have never yet prevented one. The worst temptations befalling a child originate in the régime of fear which still rules our schools, doing incalculable moral and bodily harm. And when a lie has been exposed, inquisitorial means are resorted to, disgrace and punishment follow; what ought to be done instead is to bring our whole school-discipline before an inquisitorial tribunal, and set out, by means of quiet talks, to help our children in acquiring the moral strength they need so much in the struggle against lying."

Förster's description of the deleterious influence of school-lies need not be generalized too extensively; yet the facts of experience warn us not to demand overmuch of the child, and to use loving care lest his weak virtue be exposed to too great temptations. Even in matters of directly religious import all excessive severity is to be avoided so that dissimulation and religious hypocrisy be not fostered.

192. Sources of Untruthfulness. — Besides these and other dangers there are in the child itself many sources or germs of a spirit of untruthfulness. Recent pedagogs have rightly distinguished the fantastic — at times carried to a pathological extreme — the heroical, and the egotistic lie. The study of the causes of insincerity will prove very helpful to the catechist in the use of the appropriate correctives. Whoever is cognizant of the vivid activity of childish imaginations; their restless desire for play, which often finds an outlet in conversation; of the general inability even of adults to perceive correctly and to express accurately what has but recently been seen or heard, will be able to distinguish between inaccuracy and insincerity and instead of interfering intempestively, he will endeavor to teach the child carefulness in observation and expression. It is quite evident that a "heroical" lie, i.e., one proceeding from noble motives, must be judged in a different light from the base egotistical lie.

193. Helpful Means. — Besides the means already mentioned to cultivate sincerity, we may call attention to the following: in accordance with their age the children should be thoroughly familiarized with the full significance of truthfulness, the evil and hatefulness of lying. The best motives that may be adduced are the presence of an all-knowing God and of our guardian angel. We may confidently build on the germs of sincerity deposited in the unsullied child heart; when cultivated in the right manner they may be developed into heroism. As a general rule the outward appearance of sincerity is to be slightly more mistrusted in girls than in boys.

When punishing, it is well to tell the children, and to hold to that principle, that a fault confessed in a manly way is judged less severely than one for which we try to escape punishment by lying. Moreover, no deception can circumvent God's justice. And in all punishment, but in this case especially, avoid anything that might reflect upon the child's sense of honor or destroy it, for in that case a result opposite to the one intended is sure to follow.

In the interest of real sincerity Förster condemns all discipline based on policy, and points out the connection between general insincerity, and dishonorable action and conversation often all too manifest in higher school classes in Germany and Switzerland. And it is very characteristic that, in administrative circles, a régime which tends to destroy personality, at the same time weakens the sense of truthfulness.

Good example, presented to the children in stories, and especially in real life, contributes powerfully towards strengthening their love of truth; and conversely bad example fosters a spirit of insincerity. And since even the greatest watchfulness is not always able to prevent all danger from bad example — under present school conditions this is well-nigh impossible — let the catechist use all possible means to develop in the child a strong Christian character that fears God only, cares nothing for human respect, and spurns the whole world when it drifts from the path of justice.

And a few such children in a classroom may, under the skilful guidance of the teacher and catechist, be brought to influence the "public opinion of the class" and to dominate the untruthful element, — a very good educational policy.

CHAPTER III

NECESSARY REQUIREMENTS FOR SUCCESS IN CATECHIZATION

AS we saw before (No. 154) these requirements also apply to instruction, but their preponderant influence in education leads us to treat of them here. The most important points are condensed in the following

TWENTY–SIXTH THESIS. — *Three requirements are of special importance for catechization: 1. The catechist must know how to maintain discipline; 2. As far as possible he should make catechization agreeable and easy; 3. Above all he must gain the hearts of the children.*

1. DISCIPLINE

194. What is Discipline and what does it Aim at? — Discipline: what is the meaning of the term? When we say: in this schoolroom there is discipline we mean that the general behavior of the pupils is such that the instruction proceeds without interruption and is attended by the desired results. Often the word discipline connotes the prevention of open disorder. It is preferable however to go deeper into the essence of discipline and to include therefore in the definition whatever is calculated to secure permanence of exterior order. To secure discipline in this sense, order must be kept not merely because of a given command or from fear of punishment, but through a spontaneous and willing submission of the children themselves. Hence Förster defines school discipline as "the sum-total of measures by means of which the ethical conditions of uninterrupted and exact schoolwork are secured." In general therefore disciplinary measures should aim at training the children to the voluntary keeping of the necessary order.

To go into details, in order to secure good discipline it is required 1. That regular school attendance and timely arrival of the children obtain (the free time elapsing before lessons are started and also all recess time demand the supervision of the teacher, not of a pupil); 2. That quiet and order be observed from the beginning of the lesson: hence do away with whatever on the school desks or within sight of the children has no relation with the catechism lesson, and might distract their attention; only the catechism and Bible History manual should be allowed to remain, and those preferably with their back turned towards the pupil; 3. So that order and quiet may reign during the lesson, let the posture of the children, whether sitting or standing, be erect and straight, yet not stiff and unchanged for a long time; the hands generally should be held on top of the desk; fatigue may be forestalled by timely variations in the instruction (prayer, singing, liturgical topics, see No. 199); the seats should be so arranged that the teacher from his place can see all the children at one glance; he should never for any considerable length of time have his back turned toward them, e.g., when writing on the blackboard; he should not walk up and down between the seats or devote himself to a few pupils to such an extent that he is prevented from giving his attention to others. The turbulent or restless children should not be close together, but be so placed that they may constantly be seen and prevented from disturbing the others. Noise, talking, prompting, should be severely forbidden. Those children who are requested to answer should not disturb the others by jerky, loud, or faulty enunciation. (No. 129.) To these external conditions should be added attention (No. 195, 2), zeal (No. 195, 3), and willing obedience. Or rather, external order will flow spontaneously from these inner sources. 4. School discipline also extends to the correct behavior of the children after the lesson; this is usually provided for when the secular teachers are required to look to a certain extent after the children on their return home.

195. Means to Preserve Discipline. — 1. The general behavior of the catechist himself inside and outside of the school has a great influence upon the children: his countenance and bearing, his speech and dress, all about him should bear silent witness to his character, as that of a man who knows how to order all things right and is not given to eccentricities of any sort. And mere external semblance does not suffice; only the deepest interior conviction can make for permanent results. The small, yet exasperating annoyances of school life afford ample opportunity for the exercise of self-mastery. The catechist should never become unduly excited. Even when he has to reprove, let him remain self-possessed and use only carefully chosen expressions. It is entirely out of place for him to have recourse to satirical or scoffing language or to nicknames; noisy speech on the teacher's part and too frequent threats do not help to foster discipline.

The words of the American pedagog Hughes are worth taking to heart: he who loses self-control, soon loses all control over others. Förster adds: "An irascible and excited teacher does not fulfil the chief end of his high and representative position: he is not the personification of majestic authority but of that very disorder and uncontrollable unrest which he wishes to prevent. Despite all his disciplinary efforts he is not a model of orderly activity. . . . Only when I have entirely freed myself from the faults of others, can I free them from theirs. This quiet and composed bearing of the teacher depends entirely on his guarding himself against excessive scolding and noisy disciplinary admonitions. . . . These latter means soon lose their efficiency; they are not in accordance with the profession of the teacher, since, so to speak, they make him party to a noise-competition, and drag him down to the level of the children, to whom he gradually becomes more an object of laughter than of fear. On the contrary, the greater the uproar, the more composed the speech of the teacher ought to be."

2. A second means to uphold discipline is the teaching ability of the catechist. When, in deep study and fervent prayer, he has thoroughly assimilated the Christian Doctrine and learned to put it before the children in attractive form and with warm conviction, he will easily secure, without much exhortation, the needed attention; and with it go quiet and order. The catechist can gage his teaching ability from the attention of the children. What should he therefore keep especially in mind?

(a) He must strive with all his might to facilitate attention. The rules given in the second part of this treatise, especially those concerning perspicuity, will prove helpful. The catechist should endeavor to make every pupil feel that what is said, is addressed to him personally, thus increasing his interest in it. However, this constant attention will prove to be quite a strain on the child, which can be kept up only by an unflagging effort of the will. Hence, besides using objective and other means, he should (*b*) at times put forward various weighty religious motives to enforce attention, while severely reproving and punishing more serious offenses against it.

Hirscher recommends also the following to foster attention among pupils: "Much disorder can be prevented by observing a definite order on entering and leaving; an efficient arrangement of the seats affording the catechist a full view of all the children; holding the body erect when sitting down." Pupils especially inattentive and disorderly "should be placed in such a manner as to be always in close proximity to the catechist. They should be questioned more frequently than the others, taken by surprise, when they are seen to be distracted, with an interrogation. At the first sign of trouble, a sharp look of warning, a short pause to inquire whether they need anything; this being of no avail, recourse must be had prudently but with a gradually increasing severity to public reprimands, threats, punishment. But more effective than all this as a rule, is a private friendly talk with the culprit, and discreet praise when he has succeeded in mastering his disorderly propensities." Influence brought to bear privately on the pupil will have to be taken into consideration more so now than in Hirscher's time.

3. Finally, any catechist desirous of maintaining good order in his class must be familiar with the fundamental theories of education and apply them. And only a continual study of pedagogical questions together with much observation and personal investigation will fit him for this task.

Directly related to the preservation of discipline is

the art and manner in which the catechist manages
orders and rules, keeps the children's zeal at white
heat, apportions praise and blame, reward and punishment.

(*a*) How orders should be given and obedience
exacted is easy to conclude from the rules which have
just been laid down (*sub* 1) concerning the quiet
bearing of the catechist, and they have been summarized
in the above (twenty-fifth) thesis on training in obedience: on one side, authority in general and the
authority of the catechist in particular should not be
in any way minimized; on the other side, every educator should exercise his authority in such a manner
that the pupils shoulder joyfully the yoke of obedience,
so that, when released from the supervision of the
school, they have acquired the habit of respecting all
rightful authority from deep inner conviction.

A few extracts from a work by L. Wiese: "German Letters on
English Education," may prove of interest here: "The great
freedom and indulgence shown towards the young in England is
permissible in that country, because, however self-conscious and
independent, they exhibit a surprising regard for authority. It
affords one great satisfaction to discover and follow up this characteristic trait amongst almost all classes; for the combination
of two seemingly opposed tendencies is observed equally in family
circle and school, in church and State. . . . They firmly believe
that the individual mind can only reach its full development by
submission to a more experienced and cultured mind, in a word,
by obedience. . . . The law there is held in higher esteem, in
public life and by the youth, than anywhere; the children learn
early that schooling in obedience leads to freedom."

(*b*) The application of the children should never be
allowed to flag, since otherwise no efficient instruction

is possible, nor can any satisfactory educational results be looked for. The ultimate consequence would be: disgust with the school and its work, followed by disorder and bad behavior. What we have said above concerning the training in orderly work (Nos. 182–186) shows the necessity of diligence and at the same time gives the rules for its cultivation. A good sign that it has become a permanent habit is when it shows itself in the form of willing and persevering application to duty.

In this connection Hirscher writes: "In order to instil into his pupils the spirit of zealous, joyful and persevering endeavor, the catechist must insist not only on punctual memorizing and thorough understanding of the lesson assigned; but he should also keep a watchful eye on the assiduity of the children in general. He should see to it that the teachers always keep the children at some useful work (this of course is only possible in schools where the priest has complete supervision over the whole school); he should find out whether and to what extent they perform their tasks, reprimanding the laggards and encouraging the industrious pupils as much as possible. He should endeavor to make them realize that their application to work is a matter of conscience, a duty they owe to themselves and to God, whilst laziness shows lack of moral earnestness, is dishonorable and marks the beginning of all evil. . . . The surest way to bring dull children to work, to make the lazy diligent, the careless attentive to their duty, is, never to pass over a task that was neglected or slovenly done; make the child finish it with due care: one quickly finds the means to do right what no one tolerates otherwise. . . . Of course, special circumstances, such as sickness, age, domestic surroundings, personal dispositions of the children should always be taken into account."

(c) Discipline often suffers because the important pedagogical helps: praise and blame, reward and punishment are not tactfully used.

196. Reward and Punishment. — It is erroneous to say that neither man's nor the child's free will should be influenced by promised rewards or threatened punishment. Yet it remains true that the use of these educational helps calls for much discrimination. The catechist in common with every educator ought to realize

1. What to reward or to punish. Since reward and punishment are intended to strengthen the moral stamina of the pupil, it becomes evident that not only should good discipline be rewarded and every violation of it punished, but the whole moral character of the child may be an object of reward or punishment (and to this extent the paragraph on reward and punishment does not exclusively belong to the chapter on Discipline). And moreover only morally meritorious actions and moral wrongs should be rewarded or punished, and not a naturally retentive memory, bodily abilities, unintentional faults, hard hearing, stammering.

2. Another requirement is: punishment should be the exception and meted out reluctantly. Praise and reward may be bestowed with greater generosity, so that the catechist may not leave the impression that he is hard to please. Yet he must guard against excess, for otherwise he will defeat his own end, or foster vanity and misguided emulation.

3. What means of reward and punishment are at the catechist's disposal? A look of satisfaction, a word of approbation, a good report, a little office of honor which may consist in allowing the pupil to help in class (bringing in the pictures), a small useful present

(picture, book), having him show the pictures to the whole class. On the other side, a look of disapprobation, a sign of disapproval, interruption of the lesson, warning, censure, earnest scolding, threatening greater punishment: these should be sufficient under ordinary circumstances.

Extraordinary punishment (inflicted for grave, wilful, repeated breaches of discipline, obstinate laziness, malicious lying) may consist in: standing up in the seat or outside of it (never send the child out in the hall), placing him in a separate seat (a special dunces' bench is not to be recommended), staying in after school hours under supervision (not during meal time, or the parents should be notified).

What is to be said about corporal punishment? Even when it is allowed by law, the catechist should not have recourse to it, but should call the attention of the teacher and parents to the matter. In most countries the law only allows that parents be notified of the necessity of corporal punishment. The catechist should endeavor to forestall the need of it. The penalty inflicted should never be merely punitive but corrective and directive. It may to very good advantage be followed by a kind exhortation to do better.

The following remarks are worthy of notice as a warning against frequent punishment. "In the church peace and order reign supreme; human passions calm down, and even the evil-minded feel in a better mood. Should not the moral spirit work a similar result in the school?" Let the catechist remember and put into practice the rule that his instruction should be full of unction, and he need have no fear of being frequently called upon to punish.

Förster is fundamentally opposed to corporal punishment in the school. In the catechism class this should be the invariable rule. L. Wiese, quoted above, remarks in the following manner on the practice of corporal punishment in vogue in the higher English schools: "To form a correct judgment in this matter we must remember that this form of punishment is lawful and of long standing. . . . Public opinion sees in it nothing contumelious; I have been assured that this punishment is inflicted without passion and both parties may remain on good terms; and the use of the rod has a salutary effect because it is not easily forgotten. It would become unbearable, however, if it were to wound the pupils' self-respect. But the latter is safeguarded as the culprit is made to realize that the moral equilibrium disturbed by his transgression must be re-established by punishment."

4. A self-evident requirement is that justice be observed in reward and punishment. Rewarding should never degenerate into partiality towards certain children, and punishment should never be inflicted in a fit of anger, or proceed from an evil temper: the epoch of school tyranny must never be allowed to return.

Closely related to the question of reward and punishment is the question:

197. Is the Spirit of Emulation a Legitimate Educational Means? — It if be true, as prominent educationists of the present day have claimed, that the sense of honor of children should be tactfully cultivated, it is easily seen that it may be made to play an important rôle in furthering the aims of education.

Perhaps the word "emulation" is only ambiguous because in ordinary conversation it denotes an inordinate desire for recognition; at the same time it cannot be denied that sometimes mistakes have been made by those educationists against whom the objection has been raised of cultivating personal ambition to excess.

But these men themselves must be held responsible for their mistakes, which cannot justly be fastened upon an educational system as a whole. Thoroughly Christian training has always opposed the spirit of self-glorification and self-seeking, of vanity and egotism, and yet has succeeded in putting to good use natural emulative zeal. Gruber explains the matter thus: "It is a well-known fact that many children show great application in the catechism class, while others are slow and indifferent, and consequently make little progress. Often, to make them more industrious, the former are praised and rewarded; the latter are aroused to greater activity by reprimand and punishment, or at times also by praise and reward. This procedure cannot be unreservedly approved. Indeed, only those who perceive no difference between religious instruction and profane learning may have recourse to such means. But any one realizing fully that religious instruction is a divine office, concerned with the salvation of immortal souls, must make very careful use of praise and blame, punishment and reward, in order not to defeat the end of religious instruction while endeavoring to further instruction itself. As the teaching of all Christian Doctrine centers about God, our relations towards Him and the duties following therefrom, the children, when being praised, should be taught at the same time to refer this praise to God whom they have pleased by their endeavors. Add besides that God expects them to fulfil faithfully the duties they have been instructed in, and all the more strictly so as they know them more thoroughly. They should be warned not to pride themselves on their knowledge or proficiency, as if these were due to their own unaided efforts, but to view them in all humility as a grace and gift of God. The reward should be bestowed as a sign of God's satisfaction, and with a reminder of the eternal reward which is given not to those who know, but to those who practise what they know. When reprimanding the laggards to arouse them to greater endeavors, let them feel that they have incurred not so much the disapprobation of the catechist as the displeasure of God. When punishment is meted out to the persistently careless ones, let them realize that it is another expression of God's displeasure, whose offended justice must be satisfied. Only when used in this spirit can praise and blame, reward and punishment become efficient means of religious training."

2. Ease and Charm of Catechization

198. Negative Precautions. — Homiletics rightly demands that the preacher make his discourse easy and attractive for his audience; this is all the more true of catechization. The teacher however should look upon this twofold requirement not as an end in itself, but as a very useful means to attain the real end: religious knowledge and an edifying life. "Delectation perfects the operation, because the agent, pleased at his action, takes a greater interest in it, and performs it with greater diligence"; these words of St. Thomas constitute the foundation for the requirement we have laid down, that the catechist should, as far as possible, make his lessons easy and attractive. The qualifying clause "as far as possible" forestalls the danger that in an endeavor to make his lessons attractive, the catechist may forget the serious side of his work and substitute childish play for earnest endeavor.

In order to make catechization easy and attractive, he should avoid whatever makes it unnecessarily hard and difficult. Sailer writes on this subject: "A capable teacher eliminates from the instruction, as far as possible, all disagreeable features. For, recalling the difficulties they met with, the children conceive an aversion for religion, identifying as they do religion with instruction in it, and the instruction with the disagreeable impressions. This aversion may proceed from:

"1. Prolonged sessions; 2. Cold, unclean rooms; 3. Peevish or stern countenance of the teacher; 4. His noisy blustering manner; 5. The sneers or beatings resorted to, to pound the truth into the children; 6. The fact that the subject-matter of the lesson as explained by the teacher offers nothing of interest to the children; 7. The method used, insisting only and everlastingly on memorizing; 8. The use of terms unfamiliar to the children."

A more detailed elucidation of this catalog is uncalled for here, as the various points have been explained above, or are to be treated later on. But we shall quote a passage from St. Augustine, which because of the seeming unimportance of its object shows all the more clearly the Saint's great love for souls.

"It also happens frequently that the person under instruction displays great interest at the outset, but soon tires of staying and listening: he is seen to yawn, and involuntarily shows that he is thinking of leaving. In such cases either try to arouse his interest anew by your discourse . . . or assist him by inviting him to sit down. Moreover, it will doubtless be better to have him always sit down from the outset of the instruction. In certain dioceses across the sea (in Rome and Milan) it is customary not only for the preacher himself to sit down, but also for all those present. This custom is very praiseworthy, for weaker persons are thus saved the needless fatigue resulting from long standing, which will cause them either to cease paying attention to the discourse, or to leave the church. And yet it is by far not as detrimental when, in a large crowd, one already a member of the Christian community leaves the church to gather new strength, as it would be in case one who is still preparing for baptism acted thus. The former will not tell the reason for his leaving since he is ashamed. And yet it is often impossible for him to stay if he is not to collapse from fatigue. I say this from personal experience: once I had to instruct a man from the country in the rudiments of faith and the very thing I have been describing happened to him. That fact has taught me always to keep this point well in mind. And after all is it not a sign of unjustifiable pride when men who are our brothers or whom we should help to become our brothers, and who on this account have an even greater claim on our loving foresight; when we, I say, do not allow such people to sit down in preference to ourselves, while the woman in the Gospel (Luke 10, 39) listened, sitting, to the word of Christ whom the angels surround? When the sermon is to be short, or when the place offers no sitting accommodations, the auditors may remain standing, supposing however that there are not many of them, and that they are not neophytes still to be received into the Church. For while instructing even only one, or two or three who have applied for admission among the faithful, it is never advisable to let them stand up. In case the instruction has been started that way, as soon as you notice that the auditor is tired, then by all means allow him to sit down, or even better, invite him to do so. . . . Moreover, in such cases let him feel that the instruction is soon coming to a close, and do indeed terminate it somewhat earlier."

199. Among the Positive Means must be enumerated anything that tends to make the instruction more perspicuous, allowing the children to grasp it more easily. "However, the trick sometimes resorted to of announcing to the children that you are going to tell them something really nice which it is profitable for them to know, becomes a hollow ineffectual stock phrase if used too frequently. For generally it is followed by a very ordinary story from a reader or a commonplace question regarding ordinary topics. And in the end the teacher can really point to none of those important or beautiful things announced with such great flourish. Much more effective in arousing attention than this pompous introduction to beautiful and salutary things to come is a simple reminder that, in God's presence, we are again to speak of Him; then say a prayer, taking care that the children recite it with devotion and attention." (Jungmann.) Another means is to introduce variety into the lesson. A prolonged effort of the same faculty produces fatigue and restlessness. Instruction, therefore, should alternate with an appeal to the emotions or with practical resolutions, with the recitation of prayers, mottoes, catechism lessons, or mutual questioning by the children, — taking care in the latter case not to excite any jealousy, — singing, drilling in devotional practices. All these means prove helpful in forestalling weariness of body and mind. We have already explained them at length in the second part of this treatise.

3. Winsomeness of the Catechist

200. First Requirement: Piety. — "Rhetoricians are mistaken when they imagine that the personality of the orator contributes nothing to the success of his discourse: indeed, it is upon his personality that success primarily, nay almost entirely, depends." This assertion of Aristotle concerning the profane orator may, if rightly understood, be applied to the teaching of the priest. When he enjoys the complete confidence of his audience and has gained their hearts, he cannot fail of success; and this holds equally true of the catechist's relation to the children. "The Church," thus writes Alban Stolz, "knows from daily experience that no one can be brought more willingly to the acceptance of the Christian faith and the love of God than children. But to accomplish this the personality and the ways of the priest are of such importance in their eyes, that their love or dislike of religion is largely determined by them."

The first requisite, therefore, if the children are to follow trustingly the leadership of the catechist, is, that he should constantly endeavor to be what the children expect him to be from his position and his teaching. And what do they expect him to be? In the child's eye "the priest is a superior, saintly being; as long as painful occurrences do not disillusion him, it remains for him a plain, self-evident truth that the priest is and practises what he teaches." Hence it is not only right, but the catechist is also in conscience bound to the sacred duty of bringing his heart and manner of life in complete harmony with the doctrine he teaches the children. Any scandal given by a religious teacher remains stamped indelibly upon their minds, and renders his teaching ineffective. When, on the contrary, he is a man of deep and true piety, his very presence exercises a salutary influence, making disciplinary measures largely unnecessary.

"If, generally speaking, example is more potent than words, this is especially true with children, who, so to speak, hear more with their eyes than with their ears. Instruction fits the mind with knowledge, but example engraves permanent impressions upon the child's plastic soul. The unobtrusive presence of a truly and deeply devout priest does more to hold the children in check than noisy remarks from a catechist unworthy of their consideration. Adults and experienced Christians are better able to account for a sacerdotal life not in accordance with priestly teaching, and the harm done is perhaps not so great. But children judge of things as they see them. Exhortations which are but empty verbiage on the catechist's part, find no echo in the child's heart, and are more of a drawback than a help, for thus children are led all the more surely to that despicable and otherwise already so common vice of hypocrisy."

201. Second Requirement: Love of the Children. — It was through His infinite love that God found a way to man's heart. The catechist also, therefore, besides piety and other requisites, must possess a deep love of children.

L. Roth thus sums up the teaching of St. Augustine on this subject: "The catechist stands in great need of that charity which is diffused in our hearts by the Holy Ghost and makes him a child among children; a charity which begets life in others, suffers with them, strengthens them, fears to offend them, stoops down to some and reaches up to others, is kind to some and severe to others, but unfriendly to none and maternal to all. It is submissive to God's will, seeks not its own glory, but the eternal salvation of souls; it is ingeniously patient, compassionate with the backward, and is more intent on praying to God for them than in speaking of God to them; it does not so much speak of itself as it lets God speak by its mouth; although praised by men, it puts its confidence not in itself but in God before whom ascend the prayers of captives, and who sees our humiliation and travail and forgives all our sins."

In the qualifications just quoted are given as many marks differentiating true from false charity. Another practical mark is: true charity is never partial. While mere natural affection is tainted by self-love, is inclined to prefer those children favored by natural advantages, alertness, comeliness, ingratiating manners, true affection however, begotten from love of God, devotes itself preferably to the weaker, neglected, perhaps repulsive children, in an endeavor to break through the seemingly only rough envelope, and to open the soul to the influx of divine grace.

It may not be superfluous to point out two very simple means that may be used to advantage by the catechist to gain the confidence of the pupils. "The first means is to address the children in a friendly manner when meeting them on the street or any other place, asking them where they go or come from, how they are, etc. The children feel flattered, go home, tell their parents about it, who in their turn are pleased.

"A second means is to familiarize yourself with the Christian name of the children, using it when addressing them or questioning them. Children feel honored when addressed by their first name, and the parents are proud to see that they are remembered in this special manner."

Another remark may here be added, but need not be rigoristically understood: "The catechist appears before the children as the representative of God to announce His truth, descended from heaven and leading to it. With this dignity, which should be apparent in his whole demeanor, it is hard to reconcile the use, on the catechist's part, of nicknames such as children employ amongst themselves, when calling upon them for an answer. While several children in the class may have the same name, the catechist might adopt the custom of calling them both by their first and second names: this more dignified way makes them realize that they are no longer on the street. It is not impossible to act in a childlike manner without descending to childishness."

202. Third Requisite: Cheerfulness of the Catechist. — This is a capital means to gain the hearts of the children, and make catechization attractive. A stern, forbidding countenance, a catechist exercising his office in a peevish manner, repels the children, acts on them like frost on a tender plant. And evidently there can be no question here of a merely external joviality, which would be out of place. The cheerfulness here spoken of must be the outward manifestation of the inward happiness that fills the soul.

How great an importance St. Augustine attached to this disposition appears from the fact that in his short treatise on The Catechization of the Ignorant he handles this topic exhaustively. He enumerates the principal obstacles that prevent the catechist from finding joy in his work, but make it a burden to him; he points out the remedies, and indicates how cheerfulness may be recovered. Since the work is addressed to a zealous and devoted man, the saint is chiefly concerned with those difficulties which are likely to beset as fervent a teacher as the deacon Deogratias. Much of it however is valuable for every catechist, and deserves his careful attention.

203. Obstacles and Aids to Cheerfulness. — 1. The first case treated by St. Augustine is: the auditor does not catch our meaning, and we are forced to come down from our intellectual height and dwell at length on expressions of a simple nature.

The remedy is to look upon Him who, although God, condescended to us, becoming, according to St. Paul, like a little child in our midst, or, as a nurse cherishing her children (2 Cor. 5, 13; 1 Thess. 2, 7). It is sweeter for a mother to hand little crumbs to her babe than to sit down herself to a copious meal. Moreover, by coming down to the level of the little ones, we give the best proof of self-abnegation and true love.

2. When becoming dispirited because forced to repeat indefinitely things that are perfectly known to us "let us approach the little ones in a spirit of brotherly, fatherly, motherly love, and when our hearts thus beat in unison with theirs, we will view things under a new aspect. . . . Has it not happened to us that, while showing the beauties of city or country to a stranger, — sights which we ourselves have often glanced upon indifferently, — we derived unwonted pleasure from their enjoyment of these novel scenes? The dearer those persons are to us, the greater our own satisfaction." And all this comes true in the highest degree when divine doctrines and examples are concerned, whose unfolding leads from the death of error to the life of faith.

Gruber writes thus anent this subject: "Believe me (your own experience will confirm it in the course of time), when imparting the most familiar and elementary notions to the catechumens with true love and to their inner satisfaction, you will often discover some aspect of these elementary truths which has never occurred to you before: by teaching we learn, yet, only when teaching is a work of love. When instructing others in a cold, formal manner, because we have a task to perform, we neither teach nor learn; the catechumens fail to grasp even the plainest truths, and we ourselves discover no new, fruitful, or beautiful side to them."

3. Other reasons adduced by St. Augustine for this distaste sometimes experienced in catechization, are: the discovery by the catechist that he has made a mistake, or has been wrongly understood; lack of interest on the children's part during the instruction; interruption of an occupation that has grown dear to us from long habit, in order to go and give catechism; brooding over some scandal discovered in the neighborhood; grief over our own sins. Especially worthy of notice is the treatment of the last two points in the fourteenth chapter.

When scandal has been given, the only course to pursue is: to redouble your zeal, and to rejoice that at least with the catechumens you have an opportunity to work for God's glory.

> Gruber comments in the following manner on St. Augustine's words: "When sadness fills your heart at sight of the selfishness of men, of the cold indifference of so many towards the good and the eternal, towards God and virtue, the mad endeavor of others to break away from God; and this gloomy view overwhelms you just at the moment when you are called upon to give catechetical instruction; oh, then let this painful feeling be transmuted into joy at the thought that there are still men who are desirous of knowing divine truth; at the thought that you are going to address a number of children who have not yet been ensnared by the spirit of the world, whose hearts are still receptive to the love of God and our neighbor. Your brooding over this widespread corruption is not from a pure source when it leads to discouragement: the loftier your motives of anxiety for the present condition of men, the stronger and more exalted will be your zeal for the virtuous training of the young generation."

When however the spirits of the catechist are depressed because of personal shortcomings and mistakes, he should not rest content with quoting the Psalmist: an afflicted spirit is a sacrifice to God; but he should realize that the imparting of religious instruction is eminently a work of mercy of which it is said in Holy Writ: "Water quencheth a flaming fire, and alms resisteth sins." Eccli. 3, 33.

4. Since St. Augustine limits himself to such troubles, and their causes, upsetting the catechist's equanimity, as may come even to the best teachers, his treatment is obviously not exhaustive. Gruber therefore adds the following comment: "Only the catechist who does not take deeply to heart the doctrines of faith, and is not filled with a burning desire for saving souls, falls into melancholy brooding. And indeed how could he succeed in firing the souls of his pupils with zealous enthusiasm for those priceless treasures which he himself scarcely values aright?" Equally objectionable is that "pride of mind which shows such a decided preference for the higher speculations of reason that it limits itself to these exclusively" and looks down upon the children and the common people with contemptuous pity. Another evil is the inclination to worldly things. "To one the supervision of the work on his earthly farm is more important, as bringing him returns in money, than the cultivation of the field of youthful souls. To another it is a real bore to have to look after the spiritual training of children in musty schoolrooms when he would prefer to indulge his own sensual pleasures. To another it is a drudgery to instruct children, since the work brings him no monetary remuneration of any kind."

Finally the lack of preparation prevents one from

finding real enjoyment in catechetical work: the faulty answers on the part of the children emphasize the conclusion that little success need be expected from such instruction, which drags barely along, and offers nothing to catechist and children alike but disappointment.

N.B. 1. From what has been said about catechetical cheerfulness, its obstacles and remedies, it is abundantly clear that a reverent cheerfulness is referred to. It is scarcely necessary to insist that "the teacher of children, however amiable, lovable and cheerful, need never be a jester. Be condescending but never familiar; be childlike with the children but never childish, for otherwise you soon lose all dignity."

2. In the beginning of this third part we remarked that success in education depends more upon the catechist's qualities of mind and heart than upon acquaintance with theoretical directions. In the course of our exposition this same truth came often to the fore. We close this part by a renewed appeal to the heart of the young catechist: let him become enthusiastic over his work, for, says St. John Chrysostom, "he who is apt at training the hearts of children surpasses by far the best painter, the best sculptor, indeed any artist or scientist."

PART IV
SPECIAL CATECHETICS

204.

SUMMARY. — Practical considerations led us, in the second and the third parts, to touch upon many topics that properly belonged in "Special Catechetics." Thus in our treatment of the aims of catechetical instruction; of the various stages of learning (presentation, explanation, proof, application); in the section treating of the training in obedience, truthfulness.

The remaining questions we shall treat in the following order:

In the first chapter: how to proceed in the catechism lesson, or the arrangement of a catechetical instruction. Although we are not in sympathy with anything savoring of a mechanical method, yet we firmly believe that a well-defined plan should form the basis of every lesson, and we shall proceed to explain what is required in this regard.

In the second chapter we explain the most important practices of piety: prayer, the three divine virtues, contrition, reception of the Sacraments. As this part is essentially concerned with details, we shall have little farther occasion to state fundamental principles of general application. Only in the first chapter can this be done.

CHAPTER I

HOW TO PROCEED IN INDIVIDUAL LESSONS

§ I. CATECHIZATION IN GENERAL

TWENTY-SEVENTH PRINCIPLE. — *Each lesson should constitute a methodical unit, i.e., should revolve around one theme, which the children should grasp clearly and distinctly; moreover, at the beginning of each lesson the children should be in the right disposition, namely, they should be imbued with a desire for the truth to be explained.*

205.

EXPLANATION and Demonstration. — 1. The first part of the thesis is applicable to all spiritual discourses. It would be a mistake to treat two topics in one sermon, e.g., truthfulness in confession, and love of our enemies. It would be equally wrong to disregard unity in the catechetical lesson without necessity. Let the catechist appear before the children with but one topic to treat. The comprehension of the doctrine propounded demands this unity, and makes it possible besides to exercise a more lasting influence on the heart.

Whoever has taken pains to appear regularly before his class with one topic, systematically expounded, with its own conclusions and practical applications, has realized what great benefit the pupils derive from a treatment complete in itself. . . . Unity is light, and power also. The latter assertion is to be understood in this way that the application following each particular lesson, impresses the child far more deeply than if it were adduced only after the explanation of other doctrines has been wedged in between. Moreover, by thus rounding out each lesson, the exhortation becomes shorter, and this is also an advantage, since long-protracted exhortations are distasteful to the child.

Biblical catechization, generally speaking, adapts itself easily to this unity in treatment. In the catechism proper however it is just as easily and frequently lost sight of: the teacher goes on to explain a few questions, as many as the time at his disposal allows, and has no regard for the unity or lack of it in the matter thus expounded. The protagonists of the Munich method deserve credit for their endeavors to bring about a change in this regard.

We do not contend however that only ONE question of the catechism should make the subject of ONE lesson. Often it is advisable that, in connection with the exhaustive and thorough treatment of some one question of the catechism, others be touched upon that are related to it, but need not be given the same extensive treatment. Nay it is possible to treat two different topics during the same lesson, e.g., oaths, and vows. Yet they should be sharply differentiated, and explained, not together, but one after the other. In that case the lesson comprises two catechizations. Conversely, it may happen at times that the treatment of one topic is spread over two consecutive lessons. A methodical unit is determined, not by time, but by internal reasons.

2. The second part of the thesis demands that the one topic be presented to the children in such a way that from the outset they grasp it clearly and dis-

tinctly. And in an analogous manner the preacher, especially in dogmatical sermons, should from the outset so define his object and aim that the hearers get a clear notion of what they are to be taught. The reason is that from the very beginning their attention and interest must be focused on the subject to be treated; this they cannot do unless they know what the discourse is about.

3. This rule of course does not prevent one from stating the subject in an attractive and captivating manner. On the contrary, such a course is perfectly in accordance with the requirement expressed in the third part of our thesis. As the introduction to the sermon should put the audience in the right frame of mind, so also in catechism the interest of the children must be aroused from the beginning, and a corresponding desire awakened for the instruction. This preparation of the auditors may be compared to the plowing of a field, which takes place before the seeding. When the child is really desirous of hearing God's word, he will listen more attentively and readily, and consequently with greater profit. And this rule is confirmed by the example of Our Lord on various occasions: His talk with the Samaritan woman, with Nicodemus, with His Apostles after His first apparition to them on Easter. This preparation may be effected by prayer, or an appropriate hymn at the beginning of the lesson; then recall what has preceded, connecting it with the present lesson, the subject of which should then be stated in the right way (No. 206, 3).

Jungmann and Gruber explain in this wise the importance of this disposition of the heart for catechization: "In the very beginning of the larger sketch of catechetical instruction included by St. Augustine in his treatise On the Catechization of the Ignorant, he utters some very deep truths: the rest of God after the Creation on the seventh day, the endless rest of the future life, man falling away from God and finding again the rest he has lost through faith in the Incarnate Son of God. In this short, yet very comprehensive survey comprising the leading ideas of the whole economy of salvation, the saint wishes to grip the heart of his catechumens yearning after God, and make them anxious for a fuller explanation of the whole; thus the catechumen rather guesses than sees what important doctrines about God he is to be taught more in detail and desires all the more to know them, as they foreshadow the ardently wished-for rest in God. St. Augustine's manner of proceeding was psychologically more correct than that of many present-day catechists. He first gains the heart of the catechumen. Giving him to understand the vanity of earthly things, he arouses in him a desire for the eternal God, and then proposes to him the doctrine: rest in God is found by belief in His Word made flesh. The catechumen grasps this proposition, and listens to its explanation with tense attention and growing interest.

It is true, a doctrine like the above, so rich in content, can scarcely be proposed to our small children, and St. Augustine himself would not address them in this manner; but the principle he goes by is nevertheless applicable to them if rightly understood. False wisdom pays little heed to the saint's manner of proceeding. Instead of going straight to the child's heart by an appeal to the innate feeling that "we owe due reverence to God, the Lord of all," and making this the starting-point for the development of the other doctrines about God and the means of salvation He has vouchsafed us, many a catechist delights in adducing comparisons from well-known objects, deducing therefrom conclusions meant to enlighten the intellect, and thus he endeavors to give a piecemeal knowledge of God and His existence. Is this the appropriate way? Do the sundry impressions of an object, or the total impression of the whole, work most powerfully on man? And can we expect to arouse the mind to activity when no feeling of interest has previously been awakened?"

§ 2. THE CATECHISM LESSON

206. The Arrangement of the Catechism Lesson will naturally embrace the following elements:

1. Preparation: prayer or song; then connect the present lesson with what the children have previously learned and thoroughly grasped.

A recapitulation for the sake of connecting the present lesson with the previous one need not be confounded with a review of the matter for the purpose of testing the children's knowledge. The former is intended to familiarize the pupil with the ideas of the new lesson and to awaken in them the right dispositions. E.g., when the lesson deals with the consequences of mortal sin, some questions may profitably be asked concerning the nature of mortal sin as previously explained.

Many didacticians insist that this preparatory review should never be omitted. It is perhaps better to say: a succinct review of what has already been studied no doubt facilitates the comprehension of new doctrines; hence it should often be resorted to in the explanation. Whether it should always take place at the outset of the lesson depends largely on whether it helps in preparing the hearts of the children for the new lesson. If the latter result can be better attained by a few words of encouragement, or by the simple statement of the doctrine, then this preparation will suffice, if only to save time.

2. Another component part of the lesson is the indication of the aim or the announcement of the subject. This must never be done in vague terms, e.g., today we are going to speak of the Church. Make your statement very definite: today, with God's assistance,

I am going to explain to you what the Holy Catholic Church is (definition of the Church); or: how the Catholic Church is holy (second mark of the Church). — It may be well to write the subject of the lesson on the blackboard: e.g., the resurrection of the body.

3. Then follows the presentation of the doctrine. Let this be done as far as possible by means of an event from Bible History or from the lives of saints, by a comparison, description or parable, in short, in a concrete way. If you use a story already well known, it should not be slurred over hurriedly. Prolixity, that loses itself in a maze of details, must be avoided; but whatever is required for the illustration of a doctrine should be presented with completeness, attractiveness, perspicuity. "Completeness" means the efficient presentation of those details in which the doctrine in question is embodied.

As a rule one story will be sufficient for a plain statement of the doctrine, and after giving it ask the children to repeat it.

4. The doctrine having been stated, an easily grasped explanation of it should follow. The explanation makes plain the notion of the doctrine, and also the terms in which it is expressed. How the explanation may best be given: by seizing upon the essential characteristics of the object, marking them on the blackboard, pointing out their connections with other doctrines, has been sufficiently made clear in Part II, No. 131 ff.

Let the catechist be mindful not to slight either the explanation of the matter or that of the text, elucidating the concepts as to their content and their bearing, connecting them for this purpose with doctrines already familiar to the child; e.g., when explaining the Holy Eucharist he may refer to its connection with sanctifying grace, the resurrection of the body, chastity. And he should be especially mindful to point out clearly and vividly how all doctrines and all supernatural life center in Christ (Nos. 116, 169).

5. The demonstration, whose importance we must here also recall to mind (Nos. 137–140), may follow upon the explanation of the matter or the text. When the doctrine has been clearly stated, the primary proofs will generally be easy. Thus, e.g., when the explanation of the Holy Eucharist has been preceded by the recital of what took place at the Last Supper, it is sufficient for all proof, to refer to the words of the institution as spoken by Jesus Christ.

6. The conclusion of the lesson is found in the practical application (Nos. 150–153).

7. Where in the lesson shall room be found for what we have said above about unction and motivation? And is the practical application to be relegated to the end of the lesson? We answer: whatever is intended to appeal to the heart and will should pervade the whole lesson, not in a chaotic manner but according as opportunity offers.

207. Abridgments and Complements. — The arrangement just given will prove useful for the first treatment of at least the most important doctrines of the catechism. When however the same doctrine comes to be treated for the second or third time, it may be better to proceed in a more concise manner, at least if the doctrine is not to be gone deeper into than was the case the first time.

If we recommend the above arrangement it is not with the intention that no deviation from it be allowed. Already the necessary questioning necessitates some changes. This questioning may be done: after the presentation, after the explanation of the text, after the demonstration, at the application. In general however the catechist, while following a predetermined order in his lesson, should ever remember that it is but a means towards an end: arouse lively faith in the children's hearts. Hence, following a rule should not degenerate into a dry-as-dust mechanical procedure. Finally we repeat once more that a well rounded out lesson may be gone through twice in one hour, or the matter may be distributed over two successive periods.

We have already said before that there is no compelling reason why reviews held for testing the children's knowledge should always find place at the outset of the lesson. For the rest whatever need be kept in mind about reviewing is found in Part III, Nos. 146–149.

§ 3. BIBLICAL CATECHIZATION

208. It should be Planned in Practically the same Way as the Catechism Lesson (see Nos. 79–83; 98–99). — The children should be given a general outline of the whole divine revelation; yet biblical instruction should never be confined to a mere historical exposition. "As in the catechism lesson, so also in Bible History the chief aim must be to acquaint the children with religious and moral truths in a tangible manner, to arouse their hearts and minds to act upon the dictates of faith. Hence the moral and dogmatical lessons contained in each chapter should be pointed out for the child's benefit, and applied to his life."

1. When announcing the subject, do so in concrete terms. It is better to say: I am going to tell you how Christ made Lazarus rise from the dead, than to say: I am going to tell you about the resurrection of Lazarus. At the same time it is well to advert to the practical aim of the lesson, by adding: in order that you may understand that Christ is all-powerful and may adore Him as the Son of God.

2. The narration of the story itself should follow as closely as possible the text of the book; let it be animated, free, plain and not too hurried. In the eyes of the children the catechist can read the effect which his recital produces. Let the narrative also form a whole, so that the children get a clear general idea of the complete event. Very long stories, such as that of Joseph in Egypt, must naturally be divided up.

3. Short explanations may be interwoven in the narrative in order to facilitate the understanding of the biblical event. Here and there it may be necessary to give a succinct introduction concerning the time, place, customs, etc. In order to understand the explanation of Joseph's dreams, one must have some knowledge of Egypt, the inundations of the Nile, the fertility of the country, etc.

The annunciation of the nativity of John the Baptist presupposes a knowledge of some Jewish institutions and the Temple of Jerusalem. In any case all such explanations should be given before any questioning or reviewing is attempted.

In general the catechist should bear in mind that the child is altogether unfamiliar with many of the objects mentioned in Holy Writ. Due attention should also be paid to the explanation of words and sentences in the Bible History manual, although the instruction need not be turned into a grammar lesson.

4. The narration and the explanation are followed by the recapitulation, in this manner: the catechist narrates a paragraph as much as possible in the same terms as previously, and at once questions the children, so that they may repeat it after him. Here also explanations may be added if it should appear from the answers of the children that they are required. Some picture, if at hand, may be exhibited to them and explained.

5. When the whole story has thus been reviewed, the constituent parts of the revealed doctrine which are incorporated in the biblical event, are brought out in relief, and this is best done by using the terms of the catechism, so that the result be a thorough knowledge of divine truth. This part of biblical catechization corresponds to the concept-elaboration or the explanation of the matter, in the catechism lesson.

The principal aim of this explanation, according to Bishop Knecht, must be: "To point out the connection between almost every lesson of the Old and the New Testament, on one side, and dogma and morals, the worship and the institutions of the Church on the other side. The teacher of Bible History should consider this latter his most important work; for the explanation gives him the means to increase and deepen the religious knowledge of his pupils, and to strengthen their religious convictions. Hence he should use the Bible lessons to illustrate and prove religious-ethical truths. And bearing in mind the needs of the times, he must more particularly devote special attention to those facts and texts which have a demonstrative value for the fundamental doctrines of the divinity of Christ, the divine origin of the Church, and the infallibility of the Pope."

6. In the last words of this quotation is shown how demonstration may be incorporated into Bible History. In order to acquaint our Catholic youth with the best apologetical arguments, due attention should be paid in the higher grades to a thorough setting forth of the whole history of Revelation centering in Christ; His doctrines and miracles not yet touched upon should now be mentioned; short proofs of the veracity and credibility of Holy Writ should be given, etc.

7. The conclusion, here as above, consists in the practical application of what has been explained.

CHAPTER II

PIOUS PRACTICES

§ 1. PRAYER

209.

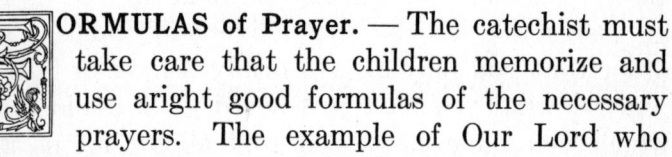

FORMULAS of Prayer. — The catechist must take care that the children memorize and use aright good formulas of the necessary prayers. The example of Our Lord who taught His Apostles a definite formula of prayer, is the best argument in favor of this requirement. Moreover, public prayer in common would be impossible without definite formulas. Hence three things are to be taken into consideration:

1. The children must be given good formulas of prayer. Such are in the first place: the Sign of the Cross, The Lord's Prayer, the Hail Mary, the Creed, formulas for the acts of faith, hope, charity and contrition, the good intention, the Angelus, morning and evening prayers, the Rosary. The child should memorize those prayers which he is to use in later life; besides also some — not too many — rhymed prayers may be recommended for the very youngest. Most catechisms, besides these necessary prayers, contain a selection of others; prayer books may also be pressed into service.

Many catechists know from experience that many children start school without having acquired at home any knowledge of the obligatory prayers; or, at best they are able to recite some mutilated formulas. Hence another reason for bestowing great care on the teaching of those prayers.

2. Let the formulas be rehearsed often so that they may be impressed upon the minds of even the least gifted. For this purpose they may be repeated again and again by individual children, or by the whole class. This may frequently be done in the midst of an instruction on the most divergent topics, e.g., in order that you may always firmly believe or faithfully practise what you have just heard, — or avoid the sins which you have just been told about, let us attentively pray the Our Father, the Hail Mary, the prayer to the Guardian Angel. In the same manner the acts of faith, hope, love and contrition may be interwoven in the instruction. This gives unction to the teaching, provides variety, promotes attention, and helps to impress more thoroughly the importance of prayer (compare No. 140: the practice of St. Francis Xavier). And of course, the children should be exhorted to use the prayers learned, at home or in church, whenever occasion offers, in danger and especially in temptation.

3. The children should be accustomed to say their prayers in a dignified manner, as becomes the reverence due to God: not hurriedly nor yet too slowly, without mutilating words or sentences, but in a clear, tempered, yet not a drowsy voice; provide for pauses at well-defined places. A reverential attitude in prayer on the part of the children promotes devotion in the whole congregation, and may become a potent factor

in improving or even reforming prayer in the parish, if the priest goes at it diligently and intelligently. At times, a slight reduction in the quantity will improve the quality of congregational prayer.

In order to secure reverent enunciation in the formulas of prayer, the catechist must watch, exhort, teach, set the good example. Deeply felt interior reverence is the most important factor. By pointing out the origin of the Our Father, Hail Mary, etc., you can cultivate more easily due reverence for the words of the prayer.

210. Prayer in Common. — The best manner of prayer in common is the one generally used when saying the Rosary: one or more say part of the prayer, and the others continue it. The same applies to the saying of Litanies. Especially ill-suited for children is the way of saying a prayer piecemeal, and having it repeated in that manner by the pupils: the children fail to grasp the meaning, and pay no attention. The best thing to do in that case is to divide the prayer so that the various parts have a complete meaning. Best of all is to have those prayers said by all together, after indicating clearly what is to be said: children may easily be trained with a little practice to learn and recite by heart some familiar prayers, when the necessary pauses have been pointed out beforehand.

211. The External Part of Devotion. — However much has been said and written against external manifestations of interior piety, we are bound to hold that interior and exterior piety must coalesce into a harmonious whole; that the whole man, his body also, must reverence His maker; that, with normal upright men, the interior dispositions influence the exterior conduct, and that, vice versa, external behavior reacts on the disposition of the heart. All ranting against exterior manifestations of piety may be answered by the query: what charges would not be brought against the Catholic Church on humanitarian and pedagogical grounds if she were to allow interior prayer only, and forbid all manifestation of that which stirs the soul to its very depth?

The catechist therefore should pay due regard to the dignified external behavior of the children while at their devotions, and should accustom them: always to make the Sign of the Cross attentively and in an edifying manner; never to let their eyes wander around during prayer, but to fix them on the altar or a picture, or to pray with eyes downcast or closed; to take care that the whole attitude of the body, whether kneeling, standing or sitting, be always reverent and earnest. Rigorism however is to be avoided: when the service is long, children should not be expected to remain kneeling all the time, or to remain absolutely motionless. Neither is it reasonable to demand that during prayer the hands be always folded on the breast. During short prayers this may be done, since it is a beautiful position; in the case of longer devotions, e.g., processions, etc., a certain amount of freedom must be allowed, if only for the reason that in later life this stricter attitude cannot be enforced. It is in no wise contrary to reverence to join the hands while praying, or to rest them on the seat ahead. — Tell the children: as long as you are healthy, do not say your morning or evening prayers in bed.

The means to attain this dignified behavior are: practice, e.g., how to genuflect; watching the children and patiently exhorting them to do right; insistent inculcating of the reasons for external reverence towards God. Of great influence is the example of adults, especially of the teacher himself. Let the priest also carefully select those who serve at the altar, for their example is far-reaching in its effects. The priest himself must of course set the example in every respect, and avoid even the appearance of irreverence in presence of the Blessed Sacrament.

212. Interior Devotion. — While it is the catechist's duty to train the children to a dignified demeanor during prayer, he should be equally careful to prevent their devotion degenerating into a perfunctory mechanical task: let them learn to pray with their whole heart and soul.

"Catechists of former times as well as many of the present day are largely responsible for the prevalent spiritless manner of praying. They have paid far too little attention to training in this matter. They have not applied themselves to teaching children how to pray when they first started to attend school, i.e., they have failed to instil the real spirit of prayer, when inculcating its formulas. There are flowers that bloom only in early spring; if they fail at that time, they seldom bloom later on. Devotion is such a flower. The Holy Ghost has planted it in the soul at baptism; but as soon as the sun of faith spreads its rays over the young heart, it must be tended and cultivated. To complain about indifferent mothers is of little avail: we must take things as they are, and as a matter of fact many parents are convinced they have done all that is required when they send their children to school. If the children do not learn there how to pray, do not learn it early and regularly, many will never learn it, others only late, after being taught in the school of adversity." (Mey.)

When the priest himself is a man of prayer, it will not prove a difficult task to teach the children how to pray with their whole heart and soul. By following the directions here given, he may confidently look for good results.

1. The meaning and contents of each prayer should be thoroughly explained to the children. This thorough explanation cannot be imparted by going through it once; this needs to be done frequently; when elucidating the most diverse doctrines it will often be necessary to point out the great importance of prayer, for the right conduct of life. What manifold applications can be made, e.g., of every petition of the Our Father?

That difficulties will be met with, is obvious. It is not easy to make young children grasp the meaning of the formulas. Now and then a complete explanation may have to be postponed until later. Yet not every little difficulty should be considered from the outset as insuperable. "The Holy Ghost, the teacher of prayer, dwells in the children; they are His temples; He aids their infirmity (Rom. 8, 26). And with regard to the Our Father, St. Gregory expresses a beautiful thought in these words: 'The Lord's Prayer is a stream through which an elephant may swim, and in which a lamb may bathe.'"

2. While good prayer is not identical with complete understanding of the same, but is above all a movement of the heart, the catechist must try to arouse the children to a vivid realization of their needs, so that the words spoken by the lips proceed indeed from the heart's depth. When for instance the sixth petition

of the Lord's Prayer: Lead us not into temptation, is recited attentively, howbeit without the co-operation of the heart, i.e., when the heart does not feel a vivid desire for what the words express, there is no prayer. In order to arouse this desire, the children should be instructed about the power of the internal and external enemies of salvation, about human frailty and God's all-powerful help. Then the petition, uttered spontaneously by the lips, comes indeed from the heart. — What we have said in the Third Part about unction and motives, finds its application here.

It must not be concluded from the above that a prayer whose recitation is not accompanied by any deep feeling is altogether worthless. For, in the first place, we know that true devotion, holy and meritorious resolutions, may be present without any sensible desires. Moreover, in public prayer, and generally speaking in oral prayer, it may suffice that the heart be occupied in one direction only, e.g., in feelings of reverence for the divine presence. Finally, when involuntary distractions occur, they do not make the prayer worthless; such a prayer is not indeed a perfect interior prayer, but it is nevertheless an efficient "sacrifice of the lips."

3. Since the catechist should endeavor to instil into the children a spirit of prayer that will abide with them through life, he ought to remember that religious emotions once they have gripped the heart, utter themselves in words and expressions which remain with the children for ever. In this manner the petitions of the Our Father might be so impressed upon their hearts that they come to use them incontinently as fervent ejaculatory aspirations.

4. An especially efficient means to cultivate the spirit of prayer in the children is: thorough instruction

on the necessity of grace. We need divine grace for the performance of all supernatural good works, for the triumph over temptation, for perseverance in virtue. Man must be above all concerned about obtaining God's grace, and the ordinary means to this end is prayer. When the children become intimately convinced of this, — and it is not a difficult task since the child more than the adult realizes his helplessness, while, e.g., the Kyrie and the Confiteor at the beginning of Mass offer a ready opportunity to enforce this lesson — they will pray readily and fervently. Moreover, their helplessness extends to prayer itself. Only in the humble acknowledgment that prayer itself is a work of grace, a permanent foundation is found: the first prayer then is: Lord, teach me how to pray.

And here also we cannot expect permanent results from one exhortation. Children are forgetful, and hence they must be reminded frequently and insistently of the necessity of grace, and the only certain means of obtaining it: humble prayer.

213. When should the Children Pray? — We have said repeatedly that the children should be exhorted to pray often, whether for the sake of impressing certain formulas upon their mind, or to the end that the true spirit of prayer may be instilled in their hearts. They must also be shown what special opportunities they have for prayer: not only in the morning, evening and at meals; but how, by means of short ejaculations they may sanctify the whole day, e.g., by renewing their good intention every time the clock strikes: in union with the intention for which the Sacred Heart of Jesus prays and offers itself constantly on our altars,

I also today and every day will pray, work and suffer. They may do the same when some contrariety befalls, e.g., when they are the victims of some injustice: forgive us our trespasses as we forgive those who trespass against us. Or when confronted with difficult work: Jesus, all for love of Thee. Even times of relaxation may be made the occasion of prayer.

Prayer in time of temptation is not only advisable and profitable, but it is absolutely necessary: it must become as a second nature to children to turn spontaneously to God in earnest prayer whenever temptations, especially against purity, assail them. In innumerable cases a fall can be traced directly to the neglect of this precaution. In order however that the means may be at hand when danger threatens, prayer for God's help in time of temptation must also be resorted to as a preventive means. Hence teach the children to add an invocation in their morning and evening prayers to their Guardian Angel and the divine Mother. Most catechisms contain special short prayers for these purposes, and those prayers are very often indulgenced.

In places where congregational prayer is held in honor, and zealously practised, it is easy to accustom the children to participation in the usual devotions. Moreover, the catechist need not think it impossible to lead the children to practise some form of contemplative prayer with good results. (See No. 117, where we treated of meditative prayer: see the persons, listen to what they say, consider what they do.)

All devotions, even for the school child, should center around the sacrifice of the Mass. Let the catechist lay special stress on the explanation of all catechism lessons referring thereto. In choosing the Mass prayers to be recommended to the children, let him be guided by the principle that it is better to concentrate the attention on the essentials of the unbloody sacrifice itself, than to indulge in allegorical explanations of the individual actions at the altar. Details of minor importance should not obscure the main truth: on the altar the sacrifice of the Cross is renewed. A good prayer-book cannot but prove very helpful in facilitating attention at Mass.

214. Prayer-books for Children. — For some time theoricians and practical catechists alike have insisted, and rightly so, on the great importance of the prayer-book as a means of familiarizing the children with the devotional life.

Prof. Göttler asserts that the child's prayer-book should be used for its instruction even before the catechism, since the first effect of a good religious instruction is to lift up the heart to God: "Expressions of wonder at God's wisdom, power, greatness; feelings of thankfulness, of mutual love, of confidence; or good resolutions, prayers," all these go to make up a prayer-book. A good prayer-book affords the best means of familiarizing the children with the essentials of the devotional life (confession, communion, devotion at Mass, etc.). For surely mere instruction on contrition is insufficient; it needs also to be practised, and this is most easily done by explaining the act of contrition in clear terms and forceful examples, and by having it prayed with deep feeling.

Let the catechist see to it that as far as possible all the children use the same prayer-book. When he has at hand a diocesan manual of prayers, which is not too far above the intelligence of the average child, it is undoubtedly best, with a view to its permanent future use, to familiarize the child with it at an early date. In most cases however it becomes necessary to provide a special prayer-book for children. Many books of this kind published at present, are of little value. When making his selection, let the catechist choose one that has stood the test of time. Before introducing a new book, he should examine it carefully, and consult with men of experience. Conferences of priests will find here a fruitful topic for their deliberations. When the catechist, after mature deliberation, has settled upon a prayer-book, he can have recourse to various means to give it as wide a circulation as possible amongst the children: he may show it to them in school, make a present of it to poorer children; on the occasion of some festival call the attention of the parents to it, exhorting them to make a present of it to their little ones; make arrangements with the publishers or retailers as to price, exhibit some copies of it in attractive binding.

When the book is in the hands of a certain number of children, use it for prayer before and after school, for daily Mass, at special devotions: Communion, Stations of the Cross, Sodality Sundays. The necessary explanations should be given in catechetical instruction. In this way the prayer-book introduces the children almost unawares, yet to their great joy, to the spirit of the ecclesiastical year, and to the devotional life. At any rate, no child should leave school without a good prayer-book, preferably one that has become dear to him by long use.

§ 2. THE ACTS OF FAITH, HOPE, CHARITY, AND CONTRITION

215. The Importance of these virtues justifies us in insisting more at length on them, although what was said in the preceding paragraph on prayer also applies here, and we have treated of them extensively in the Third Part.

The three divine virtues surpass all the others in excellence, and perfect contrition includes them all. The preparation for the reception of the Sacraments consists essentially in making these acts; the prayers for the dying are but another form of them, especially of contrition. The latter, when perfect, wipes away all sin, even before the reception of the sacrament of Penance, i.e., it enables the soul once more to perform works meritorious for eternity. It secures also the soul in case of sudden death, prevents it from falling deeper into sin, helps it to practise virtue with greater facility.

From all this it is clear that the greatest care should be devoted to training our Christian people and our Christian youth in making the acts of love and contrition, so that none may remain ignorant of them. The fear that too much insistence on perfect contrition might deter people from the reception of Penance is groundless, when it is made perfectly plain in the instruction that justification through confession is far more certain. And if in some cases it should indeed occur that those fears were realized, the evil might readily be allowed in consideration of the great benefits derived from the frequent renewing of contrition proceeding from perfect love.

216. The Manner and Method of familiarizing the pupils with these acts is similar to those for prayer: good formulas should be deeply impressed upon the minds of children; the motives for faith, hope and love contained in these formulas should be developed in such a manner that they arouse the soul effectively to the practice of these virtues. When this result is obtained, definitions are easily understood by the children. On the other side, mere definitions and word explanations will never lead to a complete understanding, without the actual exercise of these virtues.

"The children should learn those formulas by heart, so as to recite them fluently and remember them through life. The priest should see that this is done; but even then his task is far from complete. For man's emotional activities are not aroused by mere words; to have faith or contrition is something totally different from saying the formulas which summarize the motives of faith and contrition as also the acts themselves. For any one can read or recite these formulas with attention and complete comprehension of their meaning without eliciting the act itself in his heart. The latter takes place only when the knowledge of the corresponding truths is vivid, thorough, clear; when they are earnestly meditated and taken to heart, and the grace of the Holy Ghost enlightens and moves the soul. One of the chief preoccupations of the catechist should be to explain to the children with warmth and thoroughness the motives for those acts and the truths contained therein, thus leading them to elicit in their own hearts the supernatural acts under consideration. For it is difficult for men in general to see a suprasensible and more especially a supernatural truth, since these are grasped only by faith. This would not prove so arduous a task by far, however, if they had been instructed from their early youth. And the best manner of training the children in them is for the catechist to explain them, not in a dry and uninteresting manner, but by giving the supernatural grounds for these virtues in clear, vivid, warm language, or, to use the technical expression, with such 'unction' and conviction that the children's souls are gripped, and led to elicit the acts in question. This is not a difficult task, provided the priest himself be animated by the same feelings, speaks from the heart, and not merely in hollow language. For children's hearts are impressionable, and since divine grace meets with but few obstacles, they form pious habits more easily than adults. When faith, hope, love, and contrition are living realities to them, it becomes easier to explain what they are. A mere definition and abstract explanation will fail to make these notions clear, just as from a mere description of them a blind man will fail to grasp the nature of colors."

217. Among the Means calculated to arouse supernatural emotions and virtues — and presupposing in the catechist a deep conviction and vivid realization of them — we may recommend in the first place the use of historical narratives. These should be drawn from pure sources, not evolved from the imagination. "Instead of this trifling of many catechists who explain the notion of hope by representing to the children what they may expect from their father, or from a rich man, or from a king, we should at once put before them what they may expect from God; and children especially are very susceptible to this language. Instead of spinning childish tales to make plain to them the gnawing of conscience, contrition, etc., have recourse to biblical scenes such as Adam and Eve, Cain, Joseph's Brethren, David, and the incomparable parable of the Prodigal Son in which all the constituent parts of penance — acknowledgment of sin, contrition, resolve, accusation, satisfaction — are delineated in such a masterly manner."

This is after all but another phase of the fight against the detestable intrusion of naturalism in the domain of religion, an intrusion which has altogether gained too much headway. In the same vein is the more or less familiar example adduced to explain contrition: A sheepherding boy has grievously offended his mother, and sits down under a tree weeping bitterly. A stranger passes by, and on his inquiring after the cause of such deep misery the child begins to philosophize about the reasons for its sorrow. . . . Such children may exist in the moon, but to transplant them to our planet, evidences a penible lack of truthfulness. No one need delude himself into thinking that children of eight years are not intelligent enough to feel this, and to find the whole performance flat and unconvincing. Why not retell the dramatic stories of Peter and Magdalen, or of the penitent thief, or some impressive passage from Church History? Why not the historical instead of ill-adapted fiction, the real instead of the imaginary, the supernatural instead of the natural, the word of God instead of human inventions?

In the second place, when treating of those supernatural activities, which are here under consideration, never lose sight of the necessity of divine grace. Children may be especially impressed with this truth if the catechist cultivates the habit of invoking the assistance of the Holy Ghost before reciting the acts of faith, hope, love, etc. Moreover (see No. 212, 3) the doctrine about the need of grace should be thoroughly explained to the children, and often recalled to their mind, with the exhortation to pray for this grace whenever they are called upon to practise these virtues.

In the third place, a correct notion of these acts of virtue is absolutely necessary; hence it is well to caution the children against a fallacy not infrequently met with. However desirable it may be that our emotions play their rôle in the supernatural activities of the soul, and that not only the spiritual but also the sensible appetite share in all acts of virtue, yet it remains true that in consequence of our fallen nature sensible emotions are not completely under the control of the free will. Hence it is well to instruct the children to invoke the Holy Ghost, and beg of Him to touch their hearts; and on the other side, to make them understand they need not fear their contrition is worthless because they are not provoked to tears. For not unfrequently we meet with people who weep for their sins, yet take no steps to avoid the same. Hence the one thing of supreme importance is to make a firm and sincere resolution to avoid all occasion of sin and to die rather than offend God again. When this is done, no doubt need be entertained about the validity of confession.

218. A Few Words must be Added about Perfect Contrition. — Preachers and catechists sometimes hold and teach incorrect if not false views on this subject.

1. It is erroneous that perfect contrition only forgives sin in case of necessity. The condemnation of the 71th proposition of Baius by Pius V, Gregory XIII and Urban VIII shows that the efficacy of perfect contrition is not limited to this case.

2. It is also erroneous that perfect contrition is something very difficult and almost impossible of attainment by the ordinary Christian. Under the Old Law the only means of justification was by perfect contrition; could conversion be so very difficult while God's mercy was so great? And in the New Testa-

ment at any rate contrition has not become more onerous. If hardship there be it should be found in this that perfect contrition goes hand in hand with perfect love. Now every Christian is bound frequently to make acts of perfect love. How often, is a question for theologians to solve, but practical considerations demand that those having the cure of souls exhort their charges to make these acts as frequently as possible. This practice, approved by general usage, supposes however that, in the present dispensation of grace, love of God and perfect contrition should not entail extraordinary effort. (See No. 173.)

On the other side all teaching that would tend to trifle with Christian dogmas is also to be sharply condemned. Let us hold to fundamental objective truths and avoid all subjective explanations which lead from one extreme to the other.

3. It is also inaccurate that in order to perfect contrition we must exclude all reference to our own salvation or to any eternal reward. As we have shown above (No. 173), gratefulness for divine blessings is a sure way to divine love; thus also fear of eternal punishment, or desire for everlasting happiness may become powerful incentives to the formulation of an act of perfect contrition. The truth then is that fear or hope alone are not adequate motives for perfect love and contrition. But they may not be excluded as if they were obstacles in the way of perfect contrition: on the contrary, they are an effective preparation for the latter.

4. There is no warrant for the view that perfect contrition must extend also to all venial sins.

Finally, the intention to confess our sins, required for perfect contrition, need not be explicitly formulated; nor is it necessary in order to perfect contrition — except under special circumstances — that a resolution be made to confess as soon as *at all* possible. However much such acts of virtue that go beyond essential requirements may be recommended, yet this must never be done to the hurt of objective truth.

§ 3. INSTRUCTION FOR CONFESSION

219. The Importance of a thorough preparation for confession follows clearly from the fact that wherever the Sacrament of Confession is seldom received, or is received in a careless manner, Christian morals decline. Nor could it be otherwise. For whoever knows his own heart, realizes that his greatest need is ceaseless watchfulness and constant cleansing from sin. Whenever this is not done by the reception of penance, obnoxious tares soon spring up in the soul in great abundance.

The words of the Holy Ghost: "A young man according to his way, even when he is old, he will not depart from it" (Prov. 22, 6) may also be truly applied to the use of the means of grace. The catechist needs to train the children with great care and in a thorough and practical manner for a frequent and worthy reception of the Sacrament of Penance, and guard them against all abuse of the same. In doing this he secures for them peace of heart and mind, happiness in this life and the next.

Gerson enumerates the following means as best calculated to lead the children back to Christ: public preaching, private admonitions, piety in the teacher, confession. And he adds: "Others may have their personal opinion on this subject; but as for myself I am convinced that confession, if rightly received, affords the surest way to Christ."

From these considerations on the importance of confession follow some general conclusions of practical value:

1. The children must be taught to esteem highly this Sacrament, so that they may always receive it worthily, never in a frivolous and superficial manner. In order to inculcate this spirit of reverence, the catechist himself must be filled with it, be able to explain to them the salutary effects of this Sacrament in convincing language, and to impress upon their minds that it is better not to confess than to make a bad confession.

A so-called "trial confession" does indeed decrease respect for this sacrament; the external actions: how to enter the confessional, how to kneel, what prayers to say and in what order, all these may indeed be practised so as to render the children familiar with them. But the actual accusation of sins should not be included; it is essentially a secret, important, sacred matter which would be profaned by a test practice. Practical preparation for confession can be accomplished in a different manner, and the catechist might go about it in this wise: suppose a child has told a lie to his mother in this way; how should he confess it? Experience testifies that the reverent treatment of this Sacrament leads the children to receive the same in holy earnest.

2. Over and again should the children be impressed

with the need for a sincere contrition and firm purpose to avoid sin; the instruction on this point must be exceedingly thorough. Otherwise there is danger that confession may do them more harm than good.

3. They must also be aroused to a firm resolution never under any circumstances to conceal a mortal sin sacrilegiously in confession. Hence explain the seal of Confession clearly and repeatedly; encourage the children by telling them that they have nothing to fear since the confessor will never exhibit any surprise or anger at the sins they reveal.

At times harm has been done by ill-arranged confessionals which allow the children neither to kneel nor to stand, and prevent them from making themselves understood. In this regard things should be made as easy as possible, especially for beginners. Moreover, children should be allowed a certain freedom in the choice of confessors. And the catechist must watch himself very closely lest in his external behavior, or in the meting out of punishment, any suspicion gain ground that he is influenced by ought he may have heard in confession.

Sincerity in confession must never be allowed to degenerate into scrupulosity: hence all exaggeration should be avoided in the instruction, e.g., concerning the necessity of confessing venial sins.

220. The More Important Points in the Instruction on Confession. — Besides keeping in mind the general rules given above, the catechist must also pay heed to various particular requirements, so as to obviate many mistakes often made by children.

Hence he should: 1. Not rest content with having

the children learn by heart the usual formulas used in confession. Explain them exhaustively; otherwise confession is turned into a mechanical recitation of meaningless stock phrases, which detract from the reverence due the Sacrament. As far as possible, use only short formulas.

2. The children should be thoroughly instructed on why the Holy Ghost is invoked before the examination of conscience: without the help of His grace we can neither know, nor confess aright, what sins and virtues have their abode in our soul. Hence it is advisable that, already during the instruction, the catechist pray together with the children to the Holy Ghost for the grace of a good confession, that he remind them often to pray all through life for this divine assistance before confession, and this not only immediately before, but also at some remoter time.

3. As regards the examination of conscience, accustom the children to a certain order: commandments of God and the Church, the capital sins, the duties of our state of life. It is not advisable to have them examine their conscience according to the places in which they have sinned, for this will lead to useless repetitions, and often leaves the confession incomplete. The examination of conscience according to the commandments is far more generally in use, and is also more satisfactory.

A much mooted question of late is whether the children should make their examination of conscience with the aid of some table of sins.

In his pastoral letter of August 26, 1882, Bishop v. Leonrod wrote as follows anent this subject: "We do not deny that a table of sins makes the catechist's task seemingly much easier, and that the child need not make any great effort to look up his faults and sins in such a table. But this very facility, which absolves the child from deep and earnest thinking, and renders the difficult task of self-knowledge easier, is sufficient in our eyes to raise a doubt concerning the real value of this means. There may be exceptions, as when dealing with very dull children, or when the lack of priests makes a regular, thorough preparation for confession impossible; but, generally speaking, the supposed benefits are illusory. For no one can deny that a thorough examination of conscience demands that we probe the very depths of our own hearts; and a uniform mechanical processus can never take the place of the self-scrutinizing of an individual soul whose life and activity are different from every other."

As a matter of fact, circumstances are mostly such that the children must be given a table of sins. But it should answer its purpose, and be in reality a help, — what cannot be said of all tables indiscriminately. And even when it answers all requirements, it must be carefully explained to the children. It should never be made to take the place entirely of oral instruction. Nor will the catechist be tempted to use it as such, (a) as long as he gives a practical turn to his lessons, applying the teachings of the catechism to daily life, especially that of the children; and (b) if he accustoms his pupils to examine their conscience daily. They should be familiarized with this practice not merely during the last years of school, but almost from the outset. Exhort them frequently to be faithful to it, but do not inquire of them directly in school whether they have practised it: for this inquisitive meddling in public with matters of such private concern might easily lead the child to conceal his neglect by a lie. Inquiries into this subject should be made privately, particularly in the confessional, while in public the teacher should limit himself to a mere rhetorical query which does not call for a direct answer from the children, e.g., I hope you have examined your conscience.

The following few rules may profitably be kept in mind:

1. The table of sins should follow the Decalog, throughout all the school grades.

2. The queries about the time of the last confession, the precepts of the Church, the capital sins, should be stated separately, and not indiscriminately included with the others. For the examination of the capital sins leads to a deeper self-knowledge, since it lays bare the roots of sins, and helps us, moreover, to discover sins which otherwise might be easily overlooked, e.g., sloth, gluttony.

3. The table should be limited to what is absolutely necessary.

4. The form, the contents, and the order it follows should correspond to those of the diocesan catechism. If it differs widely from the catechism used in the school, confusion results; while on the other side, a catechism whose explanation of the commandments is not given in terms suitable for a confession table is not adapted for practical use.

5. The table should be made up of direct questions in the first person of the perfect tense.

6. The questions should be short, uniform, and clear.

7. They need not contain anything about the number of sins (oral instruction should caution the child about giving the number and the circumstances). A remark at the end of the table must suffice: do not omit to indicate the number of mortal sins.

8. The table should not undergo any changes when it is to be used for older children, but the required additions should make an organic whole with the rest.

The table is intended primarily to be a help in catechetical instruction, and only secondarily as an aid in the immediate preparation for confession. Under no circumstances should the children be allowed to read it in the confessional.

4. With regard to that all-important requirement for a good confession, contrition, nothing further need be said. Although our previous treatment of the subject was primarily concerned with perfect contrition (No. 215, ff.), which is not absolutely required for a good confession, let the catechist accustom the children not to be satisfied, when receiving the Sacrament, with an imperfect contrition. If the instructor keeps in mind what we said above about making frequently an act of perfect contrition, the latter will all the more easily be elicited in the preparation for confession.

5. Although it must needs be general in scope, yet in order that the purpose of amendment may prove really effective, teach the children to dwell more strongly in their resolve on some particular fault, e.g., on the predominant passion (worldliness, anger, disrespect in prayer, sloth, untruthfulness), or on some particular virtue (zeal in prayer, diligence, obedience, patience, meekness). As an aid to translating the resolve into practice, exhort the children to call this particular point to mind in their morning prayer, to make an act of contrition whenever during the day they fail in it, praying meanwhile to God for renewed assistance; to examine themselves at night more especially on this particular point: in this manner even inveterate bad habits may in time be eradicated.

This is nothing else but a recommendation of the particular examen. Let no catechist imagine that the latter is intended only for priests and religious. It is meant for all who strive after perfection; and it is not beyond the grasp of children, provided some assistance be afforded them in the confessional: direct the attention of each young penitent to one particular failing or virtue, encouraging him to persevere in this practice until the next confession; inquire in this next confession about the progress made, and praise him for his fervor.

6. With regard to confession itself or the accusation of sins, attend to the following:

(*a*) The children should not make a list of their sins to be read in the confessional; at most may they be allowed to make some annotations for a general confession, and in that case warn them insistently to destroy the slip at once after confession.

(*b*) Do not oblige the children to give always the exact number of venial sins; it makes confession needlessly onerous, and moreover tends to blur the distinction between venial and mortal sin. The smaller penitents may be told: in the case of graver, bigger sins, always tell how often you committed them.

(*c*) Call the children's attention to the distinction between temptation and sin; then the fear of having sinned will not subject them to needless worry. Besides, when they accuse themselves of temptations, which is a laudable practice, they will learn to add that there was no full consent of the will.

7. Other points present no special difficulty. However, it is well to insist on good external behavior; a quiet and reverential attitude. Good results in this regard also are bound to follow when the instruction has been earnest and dignified.

Often disorder results because too many children come to confession at once, and are obliged to wait for a long time: thus recollection and devotion are jeopardized. Hence it is well for the catechist so to arrange matters with the teacher that only small groups of children shall come at one time.

221. When and How Often should Children Confess? — There is no solid warrant for postponing unduly the time of the first confession: as soon as children are able to distinguish good from evil, they are exposed to the danger of sinning; hence the remedy against sin, the Sacrament of Penance, should be made available to them. And the First Communion decree of Pius X has stopped all further caviling on this point.

Then only will the results of Penance become fully apparent when it is received frequently and with thorough preparation. The catechist should consider it a sacred duty on his part to make access to it as easy as possible. In many places it may become an onerous task, but he should shoulder it willingly, for it is one of his most important obligations. And as a rule he is amply rewarded for his pains in the joy he finds at the sight of the obvious and wonderful effects which divine grace works in the hearts of the children.

Gerson, whom we quoted above on this subject, gives some further advice well worth consideration. He does not demand that one should confess daily; yet, on the other side, once, or even four times a year is insufficient. And then, if the children could make a thorough confession once a year! But since there are so many, and the Easter time is short, and the confessor is not at leisure to make exhaustive inquiries, it is advisable that every child be at least given an opportunity at some other time to open his heart completely and freely to a good confessor, and be granted ample time therefor.

Gerson's requirements are undoubtedly necessary, and must

in some manner be met or supplied. How much more a zealous teacher of youth can accomplish, appears from what Canisius tells us about his instructors (No. 178).

§ 4. PREPARATION FOR FIRST COMMUNION

222. Need of Modifying the Old Discipline. — Whatever zeal for souls and deep reverence for the Holy Eucharist were manifest in our time-honored discipline, are not to be condemned, nor are they to be abated in any wise. But the prescriptions of Pius X have made it clear how unsound influences, which in the course of time had tainted Catholic practice, must now be done away with. The Pope Himself has plainly indicated the roots of the evil: Jansenistic rigorism and erroneous philosophical tenets of the time.

They were principally as follows: 1. The overemphasizing of purely mental training, thus reducing the devotional life to mere intellectualism; the consequence was that for the reception of Holy Communion an extensive religious knowledge was demanded, such as no child could acquire. 2. A certain fear of the supernatural. In the domain of the Sacraments this led to an undervaluation of the *opus operatum*, while great stress was laid on personal preparation, as if in the end all depended on the recipient of the sacraments. 3. Jansenistic errors came to the fore in making the Holy Eucharist appear primarily as a reward, and an act of honor and reverence, while it was designed to be the food of our soul.

The changes to be introduced must henceforth aim at reducing to their real value the exaggerated requirements formerly insisted upon for the reception of Holy Communion. Does this mean that this preparation is now of little importance? By no means. Pius X has only made clear wherein consists the right disposition of the child for the fruitful reception of the Holy Eucharist. Much of what hitherto had been considered as indispensable, especially the amount of knowledge acquired by systematic instruction, is indeed but of secondary importance. The indispensable requisites are: the state of sanctifying grace, and a right intention proceeding from love of God, and humble acknowledgment of our own weakness and defects.

The first condition, the state of grace, is generally present with average Catholic children, and more surely at seven than at twelve or fourteen years of age. Whenever a child, no matter how young, has wilfully committed a mortal sin, he must obtain forgiveness first by a good confession. And the second requirement also sets forth nothing that cannot be taught to a child coming to the age of reason, together with the knowledge of God and the Saviour.

It remains true however that as the child grows older, his religious knowledge must also grow; but it does not follow that Holy Communion should be postponed on that account. For, in the first place, without Holy Communion it will be almost impossible to keep the children pure. And moreover, early First Communion is the best preparation for subsequent worthier communions. Finally, and this is the decisive reason, the postponement of First Communion is contrary to the commandment of Christ and His Church: as soon as the child has reached the age of reason, it is bound by the explicit command of Christ to receive the Holy Eucharist. The doctrine of the Church has been so clearly stated by Pius X that no room is left for quibbling.

223. The First Communion Preparation in the Future. — We prefer the term "preparation" to the term "instruction" as being more appropriate under the new discipline.

The preparation should: 1. Begin already in the parental home. As good Catholic parents are accustomed to tell their children about God from the very dawn of reason, they may also from then on begin to acquaint them with the Holy Eucharist. The child will easily understand when it is told about the Child Jesus living in the little house of the tabernacle, and lovingly inviting the children to Him. This instruction by the parents must be corroborated by their own example: when the child accompanies his parents to church and sees them pray with reverence and devotion before the tabernacle, and watches them humbly approaching the Holy Table, it will soon have acquired all that is necessary for a fruitful reception of the Holy Eucharist.

Vogelsang recalls this agreeable experience of his youth: "My parents were simple, upright people and thorough straightforward Christians. Regular attendance at divine services in the morning and mostly also in the afternoon, and timely reception of the Sacraments, were to them self-evident duties. Even now I am moved at the thought of seeing father or mother return from church after partaking of the Sacraments, their face radiant with happiness, — and yet twenty years have elapsed since then."

Hence the duty of the priest to remind parents and educators in the pulpit, in the confessional, in the parish societies, in private, of the great influence for good which their frequent reception of the Sacraments will have on the younger generation. And moreover, the First Communion decree states explicitly: "The Holy Father orders all bishops to call the attention not only of pastors and the clergy in general to this decree, but also of the people. Therefore it is to be read to the people in the vernacular every year during Easter time." This reading of the decree will give ample opportunity for the necessary exhortations to parents and teachers.

2. The eucharistic education begun in the parental home, is continued by the catechist in the school. And it is well to notice here that we have in mind the continued eucharistic education, and not the immediate and final preparation for Holy Communion. In this treatise we have repeatedly pointed out that the all-important dogma, the central doctrine of all catechetical instruction, is the doctrine of the God-man, His love for us, and our duty to return this love. For the purposes of the eucharistic education we may combine this pivotal doctrine with the mystery of the Holy Eucharist.

It may be done in this wise: when speaking of God's Omnipresence, point to the presence of Christ on the altar. Teach the children to seek help, consolation, and strength from on high at the foot of the tabernacle. Various events in the Old Testament and many passages in the catechism afford a starting-point for eucharistic instruction. The indispensable prerequisite for success in this work is a true devotional spirit in the priest who seeks at the door of the tabernacle only strength and inspiration for his lifework.

3. After the explicit prescriptions of the Pope, the question of what should constitute the instruction

immediately preceding the reception of Holy Communion offers scarcely any difficulty. Much less instruction than was hitherto deemed necessary does now suffice. At any rate we need not go beyond the following: a knowledge of the four catechetical formulas: Creed, Decalog, Lord's Prayer, Sacraments; besides, some other prayers, especially the act of contrition. When explaining the more important commandments which are of practical value for the children, try to arouse in them a great hatred of sin, sorrow for past offenses, reverence and love for God and His commandments. The explanation of confession and the Holy Eucharist should aim at making the children realize that in confession the Savior cleanses the soul from all sins sorrowfully acknowledged to Him, in the person of the confessor; that in Holy Communion the Saviour feeds the soul with His own Body and Blood, thus nourishing and strengthening it, as material food does the body. — Naturally the catechist must instruct and train the children in the externals of confession and the reception of Holy Communion.

Let it be remarked here that the above is an attempt at giving a fairly complete instruction in the faith: it is rather a desirable ideal, which however should never be lost sight of altogether. But what is absolutely required, is of far less extent: the child need but know that the Eucharistic bread is not an ordinary food but something infinitely greater and holy; then, that the sorrowful confession of our sins to the priest cleanses the soul; and lastly, the three great mysteries of faith: God who punishes evil and rewards good, the

Trinity, the Incarnation of the Son of God. And even this indispensable knowledge need not reach a high degree of perfection, but it is sufficient that these truths be grasped by the children in their own limited way. Should it prove impossible to impart to the children all the knowledge which it is desirable for them to possess, they must not on that account be withheld from Holy Communion, as long as they are familiar with the most necessary truths.

When should this preparatory instruction for Holy Communion be given? It may be done during Lent, as was formerly the custom in many places, so that the children may receive Holy Communion at Easter.

It may happen, of course, that the catechist is put to extraordinary trouble in preparing some children, especially at the present day when the religious education in the parental home is so often neglected. When a child starts school without any previous religious training, as if it were descended from heathen parents, or perhaps already as a moral pervert, then it will have to be instructed, exhorted, trained by prayer and good example with more care and perseverance, until the soul has become purified, clad in grace and prepared for the feast of divine love.

4. Besides the remoter preparation in home and school, there is required moreover, for a good First Communion, a proximate preparation extending over a few days prior to its reception. The instruction already given should be deepened, and the heart well disposed by exhortations to prayer, acts of love and contrition. If circumstances permit, the catechist, during those days, might take the children to church for a heart-to-heart talk on the Holy Eucharist, fol-

lowed by Benediction of the Blessed Sacrament. (Decree, No. 10, V.)

224. First Communion Celebrations. — In the future First Communion may continue to be celebrated publicly and with special ceremonies, if however individual First Communion be not thereby excluded. In some dioceses definite rules have been laid down already in this regard.

When a public celebration takes place, its aim should be especially to increase the children's devotion. Hence let all the children, and as far as possible, the whole parish, take part in it; to the end at least that all may pray for the First Communicants, and be edified by their example. A special allocution may be held to them; they may renew their baptismal vows with lighted candle in hand; but prevent all display of expensive clothing or worldly music: these things do not contribute to the sanctity of that great day.[1]

225. The Duties of Educators after First Communion are thus described by the Holy Father: "Those who have the care of children should use all diligence so that after First Communion the children should often approach the Holy Table, even daily if possible, as Jesus Christ and Mother Church desire, and that they do it with a devotion becoming their age. . . . Moreover, educators are bound in conscience to look after the further religious education of the children. For after its First Communion the child will be obliged

---

[1] Well worth while reading in this regard is the Pastoral Letter published in 1911 by Cardinal Fisher, Archbishop of Cologne, on: First and Frequent Communion. English translation for sale by The Society of the Divine Word, Techny, Ill.

to learn gradually the whole catechism according to its ability." The duty of educators therefore is twofold: preserve the life of grace in the soul especially by frequent Communion, and further religious instruction.

1. That the preservation and cultivation of the life of grace is a grave duty, is evident, since eternal salvation depends upon it. And the most important, though not the only means towards this end, is the heavenly food of which Christ said: He who eateth this bread shall live forever. And he who in conformity with the will of Christ eats this heavenly manna daily is in no danger of neglecting other spiritual helps, such as prayer and self-denial, so that the child of Adam may die, and the child of God may live. Undoubtedly, the practical carrying out of frequent Communion for children is bound to meet with many obstacles. No catechist is expected to thrust these aside rudely. Let him introduce the practice gradually, in a quiet but consistent manner. For it must be remarked that the frequency of Holy Communion does not bind in the same manner as its reception in general: the latter is commanded by Christ to every one who has attained the use of reason; its frequent reception is a fond wish and an urgent invitation on our Saviour's part. Yet to oppose frequent Communion of children on principle, is not to be condoned. Our norm in this matter is the explicit wish of Christ and His Church: subjective views and time-worn prejudices must give way to it.

2. The other duty devolving upon the religious teacher, viz., to continue the religious education of the child, needs no further explanation. We have

emphasized it all through this treatise. Let it be called to mind however that the catechist and pastor should not lose sight of those youths who have left school to take up their lifework, but should continue to take a deep interest in their spiritual welfare. The frequent reception of Holy Communion should keep pace with religious instruction, and the latter in turn benefits by the former: those children who receive Holy Communion often will prove more tractable, attentive, zealous; they will drink in the truths of faith with greater discernment and greater joy, since the Saviour dwells in their hearts, filling them with His spirit and grace.

226. Overberg and His First Communicants. — In the beginning of this paragraph we noted that, although changes are bound to take place in the First Communion of children, zeal for their preparation and reverence for the Holy Eucharist which were always so conspicuous in former catechists, should in no wise be abated. We conclude therefore with a few words about one of the best catechists of the past, B. H. Overberg, whose tireless efforts in preparing First Communicants are well worthy of imitation.

Overberg's zeal and fervor increased as the time for First Communion drew nearer. With redoubled application he devoted himself to each child in particular, and he strove to know his character, thus the better to influence and guide his heart and will. The whole instruction, as it were, rose to sublimer heights, and although generally he was not averse to the presence of others (adults of all classes, rich and poor, learned and unlearned, flocked to his lessons) yet he reserved a few hours especially for his children. And not only during the appointed hours, but at all times did he instruct and guide them, entering into closer contact with their parents to give them valuable hints concerning their children during this preparatory period for First Communion. The children went more frequently to confession, and were often exhorted to prayer and self-denial. So great and continuous were his exertions during those days, that several times his health broke down under the strain.

Once, thinking himself on the point of dying (1812) — although fortunately his fears were not realized, and he labored at his task for fourteen years more — he wrote to his children as follows: "Dear Children: Wishing to be united with you in love on this great day, to which you have looked forward with so much joy, I have received Holy Communion at the same time you did. I hope that, when in good health, I may see you all once more. If however God decrees otherwise, whose will is not only good but best, I thank you all, my good, studious, obedient children, whom, for twenty-seven years, I have prepared for First Communion in this parish. I thank you for your application and especially for the great satisfaction you have given me after your First Communion. You are my joy, my crown, and you will fill my cup of happiness when I see you all back at the right hand of the Saviour."

§ 5. A WORD ABOUT CONFIRMATION

227. The Purpose of Confirmation. — The Roman Catechism begins the chapter on Confirmation thus:

"If the diligence of pastors was ever required in explaining the Sacrament of Confirmation, it is certainly necessary to elucidate it in a special manner at present, when this sacrament is altogether omitted by many in the Holy Church of God, whilst there are very few who study to derive therefrom the fruit of grace which they ought."

At the present day there are fortunately not very many Catholics who could be reproached with omitting altogether to receive this sacrament; but that there are many who do not derive therefrom the fruit of divine grace which they ought, is altogether too apparent.

Since the publication of the decree on early First Communion numerous discussions have arisen which, it is hoped, may lead to a greater appreciation of this sacrament. The question has repeatedly been asked: at what age should Confirmation be received? That, irrespective even of its relation to the question of early First Communion, this is an important topic, is quite plain. The nature and the purpose of this sacrament offer the best grounds for a solution.

The Roman Catechism describes at length the nature and effects of this sacrament. When comparing it with Baptism, it says: by the grace of Baptism we are begotten to a newness of life, whereas by that of Confirmation we grow to full maturity. Hence it is sufficiently understood that the same difference which exists in the natural life between birth and growth, exists also in the supernatural between Baptism which has the power of regenerating, and Confirmation by virtue of which the faithful increase, and acquire perfect spiritual strength. Besides, as a new and distinct kind of sacrament is to be constituted when the soul has to encounter any new difficulty, it may easily be perceived that, as we require the grace of Baptism to imbue the mind with faith, so it is also of the utmost advantage that the minds of the faithful be strengthened by a different grace, that they be deterred by no danger or fear of pains, tortures, death, from the confession of the true faith. This is accomplished by the sacred chrism of Confirmation.

Already Pope Melchiades thus distinguishes Baptism and Confirmation: "In Baptism man is enlisted into the service, and in Confirmation he is equipped for battle. At the baptismal font the Holy Ghost imparts plenitude to accomplish innocence; in Confirmation he ministers perfection to augment grace. In Baptism we are regenerated to life; after Baptism we are fortified for the combat. In Baptism we are cleansed; after Baptism we are strengthened; regeneration of itself saves those receiving Baptism in peace; Confirmation arms and prepares for conflicts." These are truths not only recorded already by other councils, but specially defined by the Holy Council of Trent, so that we are no longer at liberty not only to think otherwise, but even at all to entertain a doubt regarding them.

This clear teaching concerning the aim of Confirmation leads to the solution of the question:

228. At what Age should Confirmation be Received? — Confirmation is intended to give to those who have already been baptized the strength they need courageously to profess their faith. When, as a general rule, are men thus openly obliged to profess their faith? Not altogether at the dawn of reason, but during that period of development which no longer submits to being led altogether by authority, but wishes to gain an insight into the foundation of doctrines and commandments; the period when self-consciousness awakens and renders men sensitive to ridicule and attacks upon their holiest convictions. And this is the case of every child somewhat advanced in age.

Moreover the Roman Catechism directs at what age Christians are to be admitted to this sacrament. "Confirmation may indeed be administered to all; but until children have attained the use of reason, its administration is inexpedient. Wherefore, if not to be postponed to the age of twelve, it is most proper to defer this sacrament at least to that of seven; for Confirmation has not been instituted as necessary to salvation, but that by virtue thereof we might be found very well armed and prepared, when called upon to fight for the faith of Christ; and for this kind of conflict assuredly no one will consider children, who still want the use of reason, to be qualified."

When we go back to the distinction of various ages (No. 96) which we have made the foundation of the plan of studies and of the whole catechetical processus, we notice that the above age for Confirmation fits in with it very well. The highest grade, composed of those common school children who are soon to enter upon their lifework, will be all the better prepared against the dangers they are soon to face, if at that time the sacrament of Confirmation comes to strengthen them with its supernatural help. And perhaps, Confirmation looked at from this viewpoint, may also help to bring about the triumph of the right view of First Communion. In places where thus far First Communion has been deferred until a late age, until graduation time, and celebrated with great ceremony, the celebration of Confirmation might now take its place.

229. In Conclusion we may be allowed to quote the words of Jungmann: "'It is a beautiful task,' thus wrote Clemens Brentano in 1828, 'to spin from the heart of every child an unbroken thread, which, originating in the Sacred Heart of Jesus and guiding the child at its entrance into the labyrinth of life, leads back to It at the end of all our wanderings. And perhaps also we can offer the sick and poor no more abiding comfort than a good Christian education.' — In these words the genial poet has vividly pointed out the crucial point in religious education. Catechization develops the supernatural powers; it fructifies, through the word of God, the germs of supernatural knowledge and Christian endeavor which the Holy Ghost in Baptism has deposited in the hearts of children; in this wise it spins the eternal thread of religious conviction, the thread of lively faith and strong love which never end. But this faith must be founded on the living cornerstone elected by God (I Petri, 2, 4–6). Charity becomes viable only by striking root into the one vine, deriving therefrom strength and nourishment. Only then does this thread of religious principles and Christian morality possess strength and endurance, only then is it a dependable guide on the devious roads of earthly existence, when the Heart of the Son of God constitutes the immovable rock to which early education and instruction have fastened it."

And they that instruct many to justice shall shine as stars for all eternity. — Dan. 12, 3.

SUMMARY REVIEW OF THE FUNDAMENTAL PROPOSITIONS

Part I. Catechetical Instruction

I. Its Aim

1. The primary purpose of catechetical instruction is not to develop the natural faculties, but the supernatural virtue of faith (No. 45).

2. In catechetical instruction the priest should stand before the children as the messenger of God and His Church, and keep in mind that the faith of the children, and the divine truths he teaches must be founded on the authority of God and the testimony of the Church (No. 47).

3. Hence the catechist must nurture in the children, and train to the highest degree a feeling of complete dependence upon God and submission to the authority of the Church (No. 52).

4. The child must be deeply convinced that the only true, divinely ordained and perfect faith is that which manifests itself in works, in a Christian life, i.e., a living faith (No. 56).

II. The Object of Catechetical Instruction

5. The diocesan catechism is (1) The chief object and center of all catechetical instruction, and (2) The foundation and guide for the oral teaching of the catechist (No. 72).

6. Bible History is the second object of catechetical instruction; it is the most appropriate and at the same

time the necessary adjunct of the catechism. Therefore Bible History should be closely interwoven with the catechism. Besides, Bible History is also of great educational value in catechization (No. 79).

7. Besides the catechism and Bible History, catechetical instruction should also embrace, as far as possible, Liturgy, Church History and Church Music (No. 81).

III. THE METHOD OF CATECHETICAL INSTRUCTION

1. *Plan of Studies*

8. The three branches of catechetical instruction should not be treated successively, but simultaneously, i.e., catechism, Bible History, and complementary instruction do not come one after the other, but interpenetrate one another (No. 97).

9. Elementary catechization, i.e., in the lower grades, should principally be imparted by means of biblical illustrations. In the selection of matter the catechist should limit himself to what is necessary for these pupils (No. 98).

10. (Applies equally to instruction in the catechism.) In the higher grades the catechist should not treat a different part each successive year but endeavor to go through the whole catechism every two years, at least through the essentials of it. The fundamental catechism however, i.e., those doctrines that constitute the essential parts of Christianity, should be treated or reviewed every year (No. 101).

11. No important point of Christian Doctrine should be overlooked in catechetical instruction, even

if it be not thoroughly understood by the children, or be of less practical value for them (No. 106).

12. In order better to attain the end of catechetical instruction, the catechist should carefully plan his matter, arranging it according to months and weeks, and also draw up a practical schedule of the lessons (No. 109).

2. *Means of Teaching*

13. (A) No Mechanical Uniformity. — The catechist should devote the greatest care to those doctrines which are of greatest importance for the Christian life, and should see to it in the first place that all children are thoroughly familiar with them.

14. (B) Stage of Apprehension or Notice of the Subject. — In order that the children may get a correct notion of the Christian doctrines, the catechist should: (1) Strive to make his teaching perspicuous; (2) Use language within the grasp of the children, yet; (3) However much he may accommodate himself to their mental capacity, he must present the Christian truths to them in their entirety and scrupulously avoid all half-truths (No. 117).

15. The catechist should combine acromatic and erotematic teaching; the purpose of the latter is twofold: 1. To arouse the children's attention and personal mental exertion; and 2. To find out whether the children thoroughly understand and remember what they have been told.

16. (C) The Explanation. — The explanation is of paramount importance in catechetical instruction: hence the catechist should devote great care to it, being mindful of the correct rules, so that the children may grasp the religious truths (No. 130).

17. **(D) Catechetical Proofs.** — In order to plant the Christian faith on a firm foundation, the catechist should: 1. Give appropriate proofs of the religious truths he teaches; and 2. Train the children to make acts of faith, with the help of divine grace, especially after the explanation of every doctrine (No. 137).

18. **(E) Stage of Assimilation.** — The end of catechetical instruction is not attained unless the children remember at least the chief truths of the Christian religion. Hence the catechist should take care: 1. That they study the catechism by heart; and 2. He should have frequent reviews (No. 141).

19. In order to train the Christian conscience of the children, the catechist should: 1. Continually apply individual doctrines to the concrete cases of real life, i.e., draw from those doctrines consequences of practical value for the age of his pupils; moreover, 2. They must be brought to practise of themselves what they have been taught (No. 150).

Part II. Catechetical Training

20. Of greater need, and of greater importance even than religious instruction, is the duty of the catechist to train the will of the children and to fashion their hearts for a Christian life (No. 155).

I. GENERAL AIDS FOR TRAINING THE HEART

1. *Unction in Catechization*

21. All catechetical teaching should be characterized by unction, i.e., it should arouse vivid religious emo-

tions in the heart, thus leading them effectively to definite practices (No. 157).

2. *Use of Right Means*

22. The right motives by means of which the catechist should influence the heart are not natural but supernatural motives. They are especially: the goodness and love of God for us (Incarnation), His infinite majesty, His justice. All motivation however should tend to awaken and nourish the love of God in the hearts of the children (No. 162).

3. *Practices of Virtue in General*

23. The catechist should take care that the children become grounded in the Christian life by the constant practice of virtue. Temptations offer an especially frequent opportunity for the practice of virtue: let the catechist train the children to resist the visible and invisible enemies of the Christian life (No. 174).

II. THE PRIMORDIAL VIRTUES

24. The catechist should endeavor to train the children more especially in earnest piety and Christian self-denial, in serious and orderly work (No. 179).

25. He should devote special care to cultivating in their hearts the virtues of obedience, truthfulness and chastity (No. 187).

III. NECESSARY CONDITIONS

26. Three conditions make for success in catechetical instruction:

1. The catechist must know how to maintain discipline;

2. As far as possible he should make catechization light and agreeable;

3. Above all he must gain the hearts of the children (No. 194).

Part III. Special Catechetics

27. Every lesson should constitute a methodical unit, i.e., it should revolve around one theme which the children apprehend clearly and distinctly. Moreover, at the beginning of each lesson the children should be put in the right disposition, i.e., filled with a desire to know the truths about to be explained (No. 205).

Table of Contents

	PAGE
TRANSLATOR'S NOTE	5

INTRODUCTION (1–23)

I. DEFINITION AND OBJECT OF CATECHIZATION AND CATECHETICS 7
   1. The Word "Catechesis." 2. Object of Catechization and Means to be Used. 3. Relation of Catechization to Education in General. 4. Catechetics.

II. IMPORTANCE AND OBLIGATION OF CATECHIZATION 14
   5. Beware of Underestimating Its Importance. 6. The Importance of Catechization in the Light of Faith. 7. The Obligation of Catechization. 8. Requisites for the Catechetical Office.

III. DIVISION OF THE TREATISE 20
   9. The First Principle of Division and its Application. 10. A Second Principle of Division. 11. About the Terminology. 12. Our Position with Regard to the History of Catechization.

PART I. HISTORICAL OUTLINE OF CATECHIZATION AND CATECHETICS (24–77)

I. CATECHIZATION IN THE PRIMITIVE CHURCH 24
   13. From the Beginning till the Organization of the Catechumenate. 14. The History of the Catechumenate. 15. The Existence of Classes of Catechumens. 16. Preliminary Preparation for Admission to the Catechumenate. 17. Admission to the Catechumenate. 18. Instruction of Catechumens and their Rights. 19. Duration of the Catechumenate. 20. The Competents. 21. The Neophytes. 22. Slow Disintegration of the Catechumenate. 23. Retrospect.

II. Catechesis in the Middle Ages 40
  24. The Parental Home. 25. The Clergy. 26. Instruction for Confession. 27. Means of Instruction. 28. Catechetical Instruction held in High Esteem. 29. Retrospect.

III. The Sixteenth Century 49
  30. The Reformers. 31. Revival of Catholic Catechization. 32. The Most Important Catechisms. 33. The Roman Catechism. 34. Catechetics.

IV. Decline of Catechization during the Rationalistic Period 61
  35. New Catechisms. 36. The Theory of Catechization Influenced by Illuminism.

V. Restoration of Catechization in the 19th Century . . 66
  37. Overberg, Hirscher, Gruber. 38. Catechisms. 39. The Vatican Council and a Uniform Catechism.

VI. The Latest Catechetical Movement 72
  40. Leaders of the Movement. 41. Negative Factors. 42. Positive Factors. 43. Conclusion: The Conditions of Success in Catechization.

PART II. CATECHETICAL INSTRUCTION (78–250)

44. Summary.

Chapter I. The End of Catechetical Instruction (79–102)

I. The End in Itself 79
First Principle: The Direct Aim is the Upbuilding of Faith 79
  45. Explanation. 46. Proof of Our Principle.

II. Conclusions 83
  47. First Conclusion. Catechetical Instruction indirectly also Develops the Child's Natural Reason. 48. Second Conclusion: Catechization is not a Branch Co-ordinated with Others, but is Superior to All.

TABLE OF CONTENTS

SECOND PRINCIPLE: THE PRIEST IS THE MESSENGER OF GOD AND THE CHURCH 86

49. The First Part of the Thesis. 50. The Messenger of God Before the Children. 51. The Second Part of the Second Thesis.

THIRD PRINCIPLE: DEPENDENCE UPON GOD AND THE CHURCH . 92

52. Explanation. 53. First Mistake: Overemphasizing the Proofs from Reason. 54. Second Mistake: Excessive and Inappropriate Questioning. 55. Third Mistake: Separating Natural from Revealed Religion.

FOURTH PRINCIPLE: UPBUILDING A LIVING FAITH 100

56. Explanation of the Principle.

CHAPTER II. OBJECT OR CONTENT OF CATECHETICAL INSTRUCTION (103–152)

57. Synopsis.

I. THE CATECHISM 103

58. The Catechism Question.

PRELIMINARY REMARKS

A. HISTORY OF THE CATECHISM 104

59. Did the Primitive Church Possess a Catechism? 60. A General Proof. 61. Closer Investigation confirms the General Proof. 62. Evolution of the Fundamental Formulas of the Catechism. 63. Characteristics Common to All Catechisms. 64. Conclusion.

B. PURPOSE OF A DIOCESAN CATECHISM 111

65. The Diocesan Catechism is Primarily the Official Manual of the Christian Religion. 66. Proof. 67. The Diocesan Catechism Must besides Serve a Double Purpose. 68. The Diocesan Catechism as a Book for The People.

C. QUALITIES OF THE CATECHISM 116

69. The Most Necessary Qualities: Accuracy, and Definiteness of Expression. 70. Completeness. 71. Other Qualities: Brevity, Easy Style, Edification, Dignified Appearance.

THE PLACE OF THE CATECHISM IN CATECHIZATION

FIFTH PRINCIPLE: THE DIOCESAN CATECHISM CENTER AND CHIEF OBJECT OF ALL CATECHETICAL INSTRUCTION   119

    72. Explanation. 73. Opponents of Our Theory. 74. Proofs of Our Principle. 75. Internal Grounds in Favor of Our Thesis. 76. Refutation of Objections. 77. Practical Conclusions.

II. BIBLE HISTORY   130

    79. Historical Notions.

SIXTH PRINCIPLE: BIBLE HISTORY IS THE SECOND OBJECT OF CATECHIZATION; ITS GREAT USEFULNESS   131

    79. Necessity of Bible History. 80. Relations between Bible History and the Catechism. 81. Importance of Bible History for Catechization in General. 82. Conclusions. 83. Two Questions: Extent of Biblical Instruction, and Its Relation to Liberal Exegesis.

III. COMPLEMENTARY INSTRUCTION   140

SEVENTH PRINCIPLE. BESIDES, THE CATECHISM AND BIBLE HISTORY, CATECHIZATION SHOULD INCLUDE LITURGY, CHURCH HISTORY AND CHURCH HYMNS.   140

A. LITURGY   140

    84. Participation of the Faithful in the Liturgy. 85. The Ecclesiastical Year. 86. Holy Places and Objects. 87. Most Important Liturgical Actions. 88. Most Important Sacramentals. 89. When to Give Liturgical Instruction.

B. CHURCH HISTORY   146

    90. Why should It be Taught. 91. How is It to be Taught.

C. CHURCH HYMNS.   148

    92. Why should they Be Taught. 93. How to Proceed.

CHAPTER III. THE CATECHETICAL METHOD (153–250)

    94. Preliminary Notions. 95. The Catechetical Method.

I. THE PROGRAM OF STUDIES   155

    96. Necessity of a Program.

TABLE OF CONTENTS

EIGHTH PRINCIPLE: THE THREE BRANCHES OF THE CATECHETICAL SUBJECT-MATTER SHOULD BE TREATED SIMULTANEOUSLY . 157

    97. General Notions.

NINTH PRINCIPLE: ELEMENTARY CATECHIZATION SHOULD BE IMPARTED BY MEANS OF BIBLE HISTORY, AND LIMITED TO ESSENTIALS 158

    98. Proof of the First Part. 99. More Detailed Description of the Matter for the Lower Grades. 100. Concluding Remarks anent the Youngest Children.

TENTH PRINCIPLE. THE CATECHIST SHOULD NOT TREAT A SPECIAL PART OF THE CATECHISM EACH YEAR, BUT SHOULD ENDEAVOR TO GO THROUGH THE WHOLE CATECHISM AT LEAST EVERY TWO YEARS; THE FUNDAMENTAL CATECHISM SHOULD BE REVIEWED EVERY YEAR 165

    101. Explanation. 102. Proof of the First Part of the Thesis. 103. Proof of the Second Part of the Thesis. 104. Concentration. 105. Objections.

ELEVENTH THESIS. NO IMPORTANT PART OF CHRISTIAN DOCTRINE SHOULD BE OMITTED FROM CATECHIZATION 174

    106. Meaning of the Thesis. 107. Proof. 108. Where to Find a Good Program of Studies.

TWELFTH THESIS. NECESSITY OF A MORE DETAILED PLAN FOR EFFICIENT WORK 182

    109. A Detailed Plan of the Matter. 110. The Time Schedule. 111. How to Proceed in One-class Schools.

II. THE TEACHING METHOD 186

    112. Synopsis.

A. NO MECHANICAL UNIFORMITY 191

THIRTEENTH PRINCIPLE. DOCTRINES OF IMPORTANT PRACTICAL BEARING ARE TO BE TREATED WITH SPECIAL CARE 191

    113. Explanation. 114. Proof. 115. What are the Indispensable Doctrines. 116. The Doctrine of Jesus Christ.

B. STAGE OF PRESENTATION. 197

TABLE OF CONTENTS

FOURTEENTH PRINCIPLE. MAKE YOUR TEACHING PERSPICUOUS, BUT PRESENT NO HALF-TRUTHS 197

    117. Perspicuity. 118. Aids for Perspicuous Teaching. 119. The Blackboard. 120. Perspicuity of Language. 121. The Catechetical Language. 122. How to Master an Appropriate Catechetical Language. 123. A Danger to be Avoided. 124. Practical Consequences.

FIFTEENTH PRINCIPLE. COMBINE THE LECTURE FORM AND THE QUESTION FORM 209

    125. Relation Between Lecturing and Questioning. 126. The Aim of Questioning in Catechization. 127. Some Practical Rules. 128. The Form of the Questions. 129. The Answers of the Children.

C. THE EXPLANATION 215

SIXTEENTH PRINCIPLE. THE EXPLANATION IS THE MOST IMPORTANT PART OF CATECHIZATION 215

    130. The Importance of Catechetical Explanation. 131. Follow the Catechism strictly. 132. Two More Rules, concerning the Explanation of the Object and the Word. 133. Complementary Remarks. 134. Synthesis or Analysis. 135. Hold to the Right Course in Your Explanation. 136. A Means often Overlooked: Practice of Acts of Faith.

D. CATECHETICAL PROOFS 225

SEVENTHTEEN PRINCIPLE. FAITH IS FIRMLY GROUNDED IN THE CHILDREN'S SOULS BY APPROPRIATE PROOFS, AND THE MAKING OF ACTS OF FAITH 225

    137. Preliminary Remarks. 138. What is a Proof. 139. Proofs for Children. 140. Making Frequent Acts of Faith.

E. STAGE OF UTILIZATION 233

EIGHTEENTH PRINCIPLE. ATTEND TO CAREFUL MEMORIZING AND TO RECAPITULATION 233

141. Explanation of the Thesis. 142. First Rule for Memorizing. 143. Other Rules. 144. Practical Training of the Children in Memorizing. 145. What is to be Learned by Heart. 146. The Value of Frequent Reviewing. 147. Further Rules for Recapitulation. 148. Tests in Religious Instruction. 149. Immanent Recapitulation.

NINETEENTH PRINCIPLE. THE TRAINING OF A CHRISTIAN CONSCIENCE DEMANDS FREQUENT APPLICATION OF THE DOCTRINES EXPLAINED AND PRACTICE OF THE DUTIES FOLLOWING THEREFROM 244

150. The Expression "Application." 151. The Importance of the Application. 152. Practice of Duties. 153. Rules to be Observed.

PART III. CATECHETICAL EDUCATION OR TRAINING OF THE HEART (251–336)

154. Preliminary Remarks.

TWENTIETH PRINCIPLE. THE TRAINING OF THE HEART IS MORE IMPORTANT THAN INSTRUCTION 252

155. Explanation and Proof. 156. Authoritative Testimonies.

CHAPTER I. GENERAL MEANS FOR TRAINING THE HEART (257–291)

I. UNCTION IN CATECHIZATION 257

TWENTY-FIRST PRINCIPLE. CATECHIZATION SHOULD BE FULL OF UNCTION 257

157. Explanation. 158. (A) First Means: Prayer. 159. (B) Second Means: Enthusiasm of the Catechist. 160. (C) Third Means: Presentation of Motives. 161. What Religious Emotions to Cultivate.

II. USE OF THE RIGHT MOTIVES 265

TWENTY-SECOND PRINCIPLE. THE RIGHT MOTIVES ARE DRAWN FROM REVELATION. ALL MOTIVATION SHOULD TEND TO INCREASE THE LOVE OF GOD 265

162. Importance of this Thesis. 163. The Right Motives. 164. Two Fallacies. 165. An Example from Gruber. 166. Another Mistake. 167. In how far May the Motive of Temporal Benefit be invoked. 168. The Chief Motives. 169. Love of God the Ultimate Aim of all Motivation. 170. How to Proceed in Order to Arouse Love of God. 171. The Greatest Obstacle to Divine Love. 172. Two False Conceptions of Divine Love. 173. Continuation.

III. THE PRACTICE OF VIRTUE IN GENERAL 283

TWENTY-THIRD PRINCIPLE. NECESSITY OF PRACTICING VIRTUE. TEMPTATIONS 283

174. What does the Practice Consist in. 175. What should the Practice Bear on. 176. Ways and Means. 177. Temptations. 178. Arming the Children against Spiritual Dangers.

CHAPTER II. THE MOST IMPORTANT VIRTUES (292–313)

TWENTY-FOURTH PRINCIPLE. TRAIN THE CHILDREN TO WORK AND TO PRAY 292

179. Meaning of the Thesis. 180. Piety. 181. Obstacles to Piety. 182. Work. 183. Some Rules: Love of Work. 184. Familiarization with Work. 185. Orderly Work. 186. Recreation.

TWENTY-FIFTH PRINCIPLE. TRAIN THE CHILDREN IN OBEDIENCE, TRUTHFULNESS, AND CHASTITY 303

1. *Obedience* 303
   187. Its Importance. 188. Means of Training in Obedience. 189. Mistakes of the Teacher.

2. *Truthfulness.*
   190. Nature and Importance of Truthfulness. 191. Dangers to Truthfulness. 192. Sources of Untruthfulness. 193. Helpful Means.

CHAPTER III. NECESSARY REQUIREMENTS FOR SUCCESS IN CATECHIZATION (314–336)

TWENTY-SIXTH PRINCIPLE. LET THE CATECHIST MAINTAIN DISCIPLINE, MAKE CATECHIZATION AGREEABLE AND EASY, AND GAIN THE HEARTS OF THE CHILDREN 314

1. *Discipline* 314
   194. What is Discipline, and What does it Aim at. 195. Means to Preserve Discipline. 196. Reward and Punishment. 197. The Spirit of Emulation in Catechization.

2. *Ease and Charm of Catechization* 325
   198. Negative Precautions. 199. Positive Means.

3. *Winsomeness of the Catechist* 328
   200. First Requirement: Piety. 201. Second Requirement: Love of Children. 202. Cheerfulness of the Catechist. 203. Obstacles and Aids to Cheerfulness.

PART IV. SPECIAL CATECHETICS (337–388)

204. Summary.

CHAPTER I. HOW TO PROCEED IN INDIVIDUAL LESSONS (238–348)

I. CATECHIZATION IN GENERAL 338

TWENTY-SEVENTH PRINCIPLE. EACH LESSON SHOULD CONSTITUTE A METHODICAL UNIT, AND BE MADE TO APPEAL TO THE CHILDREN FROM THE OUTSET 338
   205. Explanation and Proof.

II. THE CATECHISM LESSON. 342
   206. Arrangement of the Lesson. 207. Abridgments and Complements.

III. BIBLICAL CATECHIZATION 345
   208. Its Arrangement.

CHAPTER II. PIOUS PRACTICES (349–388)

I. PRAYER 349
   209. Formulas of Prayer. 210. Prayer in Common. 211. The External Part of Devotion. 212. Interior Devotion. 213. When should the Children Pray. 214. Prayer-books for Children.

II. The Acts of Faith, Hope, Charity and Contrition . . 360
   215. Importance of Making these Acts. 216. The Manner and Method of Making Them. 217. Means to be Used in Training the Children. 218. Perfect Contrition.

III. Instruction for Confession. 366
   219. Its Importance. 220. The More Important Points in the Instruction on Confession. 221. When and How Often should Children Confess.

IV. Preparation for First Communion 375
   222. Need of Modifying the Old Discipline. 223. The First Communion Preparation in the Future. 224. First Communion Celebrations. 225. Duties of Educators after First Communion. 226. Overberg and His First Communicants.

V. A Word About Confirmation 384
   227. The End of Confirmation. 228. Age at which it should be Received.
   229. Conclusion.

Summary Review of the Fundamental Propositions 389

Table of Contents 395

Index 405

INDEX

NUMBER REFERS TO PAGE

Aachen, synod of, 41
Acts of Faith, Hope, Charity and Contrition, 360
Albi, synod of, 41
Alcibiades, 273
Alcuin, 42, 47
Aloysius, St., 147
Altergarten, 68
Ambrose, St., 302
America, North, 70
Analysis and synthesis, 221
Analytical method, 73, 189
Anne Boleyn, 274
Anointing with oil, 31
Answers of children in catechism, 213
Apologetical arguments, 230
Application in catechization, 244
—— rules for, 248
Aquinas, St. Thomas, 47, 97, 325
Arcadius, 16
Aristides, 273
Aristotelian philosophy, 72, 188
Arsenius, 16
Audientes, 28, 29
Auger, Edmund, 56
Augsburg: Diet of, 52
—— Catechism of, 52, 109
Augustine, St., 9, 30, 33, 34, 35, 37, 39, 67, 69, 86, 176, 214, 219, 277, 326, 332, 334

Baden, 68
Baeumer, Father Suitbert, 105, 107
Barnabas, Epistle of, 27
Bavaria, 70
Bellarmine, Cardinal, 55, 56, 71, 87
Bellord, Bishop, 72
Bernard, St., 47, 253
Bible Commission, 138, 140
Bible History, 120
—— or catechism, 123
—— teaching of, 130
—— necessity of, 131
—— relation between, and catechism, 133
—— importance of, 134
—— and liberal exegesis, 137
—— and elementary catechization, 158
Bible stories or children's tales, 203
Bibles of the Poor, 46
Blackboard, use of, in catechization, 200
Boniface, St., 42
Borromeo, St. Charles, 57
Bossuet, 110, 134, 176, 196, 239, 282
Boudon, 60
Braunsberger, Otto, 55
Brennan, Rev. R., 148
Brentano, Clemens, 388
Bruno of Würzburg, 47

Busaeus, Peter, 53
Busing, L. C., 148

Canisius, Peter, 53, 56, 109, 112, 117, 124, 290
Canonical mission of catechist, 19
Catecheses, mystagogical, 34, 37
Catechesis theotisca, 50
Catechetical, societies, 72, 75
—— instruction, 23, 78
—— education, 23, 256
Catechetics, 13, 59
Catechism, meaning of, 10
—— Roman, 56, 70, 71, 76, 124, 384
—— of St. Thomas, 47
—— of Luther, 49–50
—— after the Reformation, 52
—— Canisian, 54, 61, 108, 109
—— new, 61
—— of Overberg and Hirscher, 69
—— of Schuster, 70
—— uniform catechism of Vatican Council, 71
—— in primitive Church, 104
—— formulas of the, 105
—— of Augsburg, 52, 109
—— scientific, 111
—— diocesan, 111, 114, 115
—— qualities of, 116
—— place of, in catechization, 119
—— historical, 125
—— as official textbook of the Church, 129
—— fundamental, 166
Catechization, end of, 10
—— obligation of, 18
—— history of, 22, 24
—— conditions of success in, 75
Catechumen, meaning of, 9
—— classes of, 28

—— preparation of, for baptism, 29
—— rights of, 31
Catechumenate, history of, 14
—— admission to, 30
—— duration of, 32
—— disintegration of, 37
Celsus, 92
Charlemagne, 42
Chateaubriand, 255
Cheerfulness, in catechetical office, 67, 332
—— obstacles and aids to, 333
Chrysostom, St. John, 14, 336
Church history and catechization, 120
—— why and how to teach it, 146
Church music, its importance, 150
—— how to teach it, 151
Clement, Pope VII, 55
—— Pope XIII, 58
—— St., of Rome, 107
Comenius, Amos, 198
Competents, 29, 33, 39
Concentration in teaching, 169, 243
Concentric circles, teaching in, 166
Confirmation, when to be given, 384
Confraternities of Christian Doctrine, 51
Confession, 35
—— in Middle Ages, 43
—— formulas of, 45
—— books, 45
—— tables, 45, 369, 370
—— instruction for, 366, 368
—— accusation of sins in, 373
Coran, 59
Council, of Nice, 33
—— of Trent, 51, 101

INDEX 407

Council of the Vatican, 56, 71, 92, 94, 112, 147
—— provincial, of Melbourne, 180
—— provincial, of Vienna, 113
—— provincial, of Prague, 113
Cyril, St., of Jerusalem, 33, 34, 37, 39

Decius, 28
Deharbe, Father, 55, 70, 112
De Ledesma, Jacobus, 59
Deogratias, Deacon, 40, 332
De Sales, St. Francis, 60
Descuret, 254
De Soto, Peter, 52
Didache, 27
Dietenberger, John, 52
Discipline in catechism class, 314
—— means to preserve, 316

Ecclesiastical persons, 144
Education, catechetical, 251
Elect, 29
Eliseus, 135
Emotions, appeal to, in catechization, 258, 263
Emulation in catechization, 323
Ephpheta, 39
Eschius, Nicholas, 290
Exegesis, liberal, in catechization, 137
Exorcism, 30, 35, 38, 40
Explanation, in catechization, 215
—— rules for, 216

Falk, 44, 49
Felbiger, Ign. von, 64, 67
Ferdinand II, 149, 151
Ferrandus, Deacon of Carthage, 38

First Communion, preparation for, 375
—— celebration of, 381
Fisher, Cardinal, 381
Fleury, Claude, 60, 110
Formulas, of catechism, 105
Förster, 88, 254, 286, 305, 310, 312, 317, 322
Francis Xavier, St., 231
Fulgentius, Bishop, 38
Fürstenberg, Vic. general, 67

Galitzin, Princess, 67
Geiler, of Keisersberg, 44, 45
Genuflectentes, 29
Gerson, John, 15, 44, 47, 366, 374
Godparents, their duty, 40
Goethe, 198
Graser, 66
Graz, synod of, 112
Gregory, St., 354
Gruber, Archbishop Aug., 69, 74, 95, 96, 162, 174, 196, 205, 206, 207, 262, 268, 270, 324, 333, 334, 340

Harnack, A., 107
Hasak, 49
Helding, Michael, 52
Henry VIII, 273
Hesshus, 58
Hirscher, 15, 68, 70, 174, 231, 254, 261, 263, 265, 303, 318, 320
Hoffaeus, Paulus, 57
Holzhauser, Bartholomew, 60
Honorius, 16
Hrabanus Maurus, 47
Hymns, church, importance of, 148
—— how to teach them, 151

Ignatius, St., 278
Ildephonse, St., 30

Illuminism, 62, 64, 68
Imposition of hands on catechumens, 30, 31
Inerrancy of Bible, 139
Isidore, St., 30

Jansenism, 375
Janssen, 44, 49
John Nepomucene, St., 147
John the Deacon, 31
Jungmann, 74, 76, 77, 99, 194, 205, 255, 276, 280, 283, 328, 340, 388
Justin, St., Martyr, 27

Kant, 63
Kellner, Lorenz, 67
Kero, monk of St. Gall, 51
Knecht, Auxiliary Bishop, 66, 347
Kremers, Mathias, 52

Lavour, synod of, 50
Lecturing, relation between, and questioning, 209
Leo XIII, 140, 179, 301
Liturgy, teaching of, 120, 140, 145
Lohner, Tobias, 60
Lourdes, 147
Love of God, the supreme motive in catechization, 276
—— obstacles to, 278
—— false conceptions of, 279
Luther, catechism of, 49, 50

MacCaffrey, Father, 148
Mainz, catechism of, 55, 61, 70, 105
Maltiz, Bishop John, 52
Manuzio, Paolo, 57
Martin, St., 147
Melanchthon, 62
Melbourne, provincial council of, 180

Melchiades, Pope, 386
Memorizing, rules for, 235
—— what to give for, in catechism, 238
Messchler, Father, 25
Messmer, Archbishop, 61, 131, 231
Method, socratic, 65
—— analytical, 73, 189, 221
—— synthetic, 73, 189
—— exegetical, 73
—— catechetical, 153, 186
Mey, 159, 161, 162, 202, 205, 353
Middle Ages, catechesis in, 40, 48
More, Thomas, 274
Motives, importance of, in catechization, 262
—— use of right, 265
—— natural, in catechization, 270, 272, 274
—— supernatural, 275
—— love of God the supreme motive, 276
Münch, Dr., 305
Munich, society of catechists of, 72, 73, 75
Münzenberger, 49

Natural religion, 98
Neophytes, 36
Nicholas, St., 147

Obedience, training children in, 303, 305
—— mistakes in training children in, 307
Objections, against catechism as center of religious instruction, 126
—— against concentric method, 174
Origenes, 92
Original sin, 62

Ottfried von Weissenburg, 51
Overberg, B. H., 66, 70, 177, 383

Pelagianism, 208
Perspicuity, in catechization, 197
—— of language, 201
Pestalozzi, 65, 67
Picture Bibles, 46
Piety, training children in, 294
—— obstacles to, 296
Pius, St., V, 51, 57
—— Pope, IV, 57
—— Pope, X, on liberal exegesis, 138, 140
—— on Church music, 140, 141, 150
—— on early First Communion, 156, 163, 165
Poggiano, Gulio, 57
Possevinus, 47, 59
Practice, its importance in catechization, 247
—— of virtue, 283, 349
Prague, provincial council of, 113
Prayer, in catechism lessons, 49, 259, 349
Prayer-books for children, 358
Preambles of faith, 99
Program of studies, necessity of, 155
—— where to find good, 180
—— arrangement of, in one class schools, 184
Proofs in catechization, 225
Punishment, and reward, 321

Questioning, and lecturing, 209
—— aim of, 210
—— rules for, 211
Questions, form of, 212
Quietism, 283

Rationalism, 61
Recreation and work, 302
Reddition, of Creed and Our Father, 35
Reviewing, of fundamental catechism, 165
—— in general, 239
—— rules for, 241
—— immanent reviewing, 243
Rewards and punishments in catechism class, 321
Ringseis, 100
Rituale Salisburgense, 259
Rochow, 67
Rostock, 107
Roth, L., 330
Rousseau, J. J., 174, 304

Sacchini, 16
Sacramentals, 144
Sacramentary, Gelasian, 36
Sailer, 326
Salt, blessed, given to catechumens, 30, 31, 38
Schmid, Dr. Ulrich, 143
Schurer, E., 107
Schuster's catechism, 70
Schwarzel, 66
Scrutinies, 36, 38
Secret, discipline of the, 35
Seeberg, Prof. A., 107, 108
Seipel, Ign., 143
Senarius, 31
Serlet, Cardinal, 57
Sisters of Notre Dame, 148
Socialism, 118, 194
Socrates, 65, 69
Solon, 273
Spirago, 61, 119, 131
Stages of Learning, 187
Stieglitz method, 74

Stolz, Alban, 69, 176, 205, 256, 329
Swoboda, H., 143
Synthesis and analysis, 221
Synthetic method, 73

Table of sins for confession, 370
Talmud, 59
Tarterius, Ivo, 59
Temptations, rôle of, in Christian life, 286
Tertullian, 35, 36
Theodoret, Bishop of Cyprus, 91
Thomas, St., Aquinas, 47, 97, 325
Time schedule in catechetical instruction, 183
Titelman, Francis, 52
Tobias, 32, 108, 135
Training of the heart in catechization, 251
Trent, Council of, 51, 101
Truthfulness, training in, 308, 310
—— dangers to, 309

Unction in catechization, 257

Untruthfulness, sources of, 310
Utilization of knowledge, 233

Vaughan, Father, 220
Vienna, 69, 72, 75
—— Provincial council of, 113
Virtues, most important, for training the heart, 292
Vogelsang, 377
Von Falk, 49
Von Ketteler, Bishop, 113, 116, 117
Von Leonrod, Bishop, 114, 127, 129, 208, 369
Von Stolberg, Count, 206

Weber, Beda, 176
Weideman, 50
Wiese, L., 319, 322
Willmann, 187, 273
Winsomeness of catechist, 328
Winter, Vitus A., 63, 65, 66
Works of Mercy, 108
Work, training children to, 297
—— and recreation, 302